OUR
TRIUNE
GOD

OUR TRIUNE GOD

A Biblical Portrayal of the Trinity

PETER TOON

REGENT COLLEGE PUBLISHING
• Vancouver, British Columbia •

Copyedting: Robert N. Hosack
Cover photo: Bruce Jeffrey

Unless otherwise noted, Scripture quotations are from
the *Revised Standard Version of the Bible*, ©1946, 1952, 1971, 1973.
Other quotations are from the *Authorized (King James) Version* (KJV).

National Library of Canada Cataloguing in Publication Data

Toon, Peter, 1939–
Our triune God

Includes bibliographical references and index.

ISBN 1-55361-052-0 (Canada)
ISBN 1-57383-226-X (International)

1. Trinity. I. Title.

BT111.2.T66 2002   231'.044   C2002-910491-2

DEDICATION

For Charles Caldwell

who believes, teaches, and confesses

THE HOLY TRINITY.

CONTENTS

PREFACE

What greater joy can a theologian have than to contemplate the glory of God the Father in the face of Jesus Christ, his Son, by the illumination and inspiration of the Holy Spirit! What greater privilege can a theologian have than to seek to expound the doctrine of the Mystery of the Blessed, Holy, and Undivided Trinity — God blessed forever and unto the ages of ages. Is not the chief end of man to enjoy and glorify God forever?

In the summer of 1994, it was my pleasure to go to Grand Rapids, Michigan at the invitation of the Institute of Theological Studies. In its studio I recorded twenty-four lectures on the origins and development of the church doctrine (dogma) of the Holy Trinity. Together with the printed booklets I also wrote, these tapes are now being used in thirty or so seminaries for extramural credit in their Master of Divinity programs. The idea of writing the book followed the making of the tapes.

This study is intended to set forth the biblical doctrine of the Holy Trinity. I may express this purpose more accurately by stating that I seek to discover and present the implicit trinitarianism of the New Testament — the apostolic vision of the Trinity.

The book, however, is not written in the way that I would

normally expect a modern biblical scholar to write such a book. The truth of the matter is that (from a technical point of view) I am not a biblical scholar. If I am anything — rather than "a jack of all trades and master of none" — I am a theologian, who is committed to the Faith expressed in the Nicene Creed from the fourth century. I approach and expound the Scriptures within this credal and doctrinal framework. Yet in doing this I do not reject the modern historical-critical method of studying the Bible, but make use of it in all kinds of ways.

Having taught college and seminary courses in theology and doctrine for many years, I have tried to maintain an academic and intellectual level which is neither too easy nor too demanding for the average student. Further, I have written in such a way that Christians who are used to serious reading, but who do not have seminary training in divinity, can follow the presentation. Also, I have provided a helpful list of books for further reading at the end of each chapter.

There is another matter on which I must make a brief comment. I have deliberately made no concessions in this book to modern feminist ideology and political correctness in terms of either the naming and addressing God or the naming and addressing of human beings, who are created by God in his image and after his likeness. My refusal to accommodate inclusive language is not because I am an obdurate hard-liner and right-winger, who lives in the "androcentric" terminology and ideas of the past. It is because (as I hope will become clear to my reader by chapter 12) the biblical and credal portrayal of the Holy Trinity requires that we do not use inclusive language of Yahweh-Elohim, who is the Father, the Son, and the Holy Spirit. For this reason I have used the older RSV as my primary translation.

In the history of the church the most famous book on the doctrine of the Trinity is *De Trinitate* by St. Augustine of Hippo. I shall refer to this book at various points in the chapters which follow. Here I would like to identify myself with Augustine in the request he made to his readers.

Let me ask of my reader, wherever, alike with myself, he is certain, there to go with me; wherever, alike with me, he hesitates, there to join with me in inquiring; wherever he recognizes himself to be in error, there to return to me; wherever he recognizes me to be so, there to call me back; so that we may enter together upon the path of charity, and advance towards Him of whom it is said, "Seek His face evermore." And I would make this pious and safe agreement, in the presence of our Lord God, with all who read my writings . . . which inquire into the unity of the Trinity of the Father and the Son and the Holy Spirit; because in no other subject is error more dangerous, or inquiry more laborious, or the discovery of truth more profitable.[1]

I ask my readers to reflect upon the last three points made by Augustine — the danger of error, the heavy intellectual demands, and the profit of knowing the truth.

In gratitude for his friendship and kindness to my family, I dedicate this book to the Rev. Dr. Charles Caldwell, who has just retired as a professor of pastoral theology at Nashotah House Episcopal Seminary in Wisconsin. In a variety of ways and in our own minimal way, the two of us have sought to keep alive a joyful Trinitarian Orthodoxy in Anglicanism. May he, with his family, always experience and faithfully proclaim "the grace of our Lord Jesus Christ, the love of God our Father, and the fellowship of the Holy Spirit."

In the providence of God I actually completed the writing of this book on the Blessed, Holy, and Undivided Trinity on the day when the Western Church calls the faithful to celebrate their Trinitarian Faith — Trinity Sunday, June 11, 1995. On this day it was my privilege to preach twice on the Holy Trinity at St. Edmund's Episcopal Church, Elm Grove, outside of Milwaukee; then, in the afternoon I attended the graduation of my daughter, Deborah, from Oconomowoc High School, Wisconsin.

Blessed by YHWH (Yahweh-Elohim)! And thus: "Glory be to the Father, and to the Son, and to the Holy Spirit, now and always even unto ages of ages. Amen."

Peter Toon
The Feast of the Holy Trinity,
June 1995

PART ONE

BACKGROUND

AND

CONTEXT

1

WHO IS GOD?

Apparently most people who attend church services today have never heard a sermon expounding the doctrine of the Blessed, Holy, and Undivided Trinity—the transcendent, living God, Yahweh-Elohim, worshiped by Christians through the centuries. Further, they have had either little or no instruction in the importance, or the actual content, of this doctrine of the Father, the Son, and the Holy Spirit—the Trinity in Unity and Unity in Trinity. In fact, many seem to think that the Holy Trinity is a mathematical problem belonging to the realm "above" and therefore has little or no practical importance.

GOD OF HUMAN EXPERIENCE

From the perspective of orthodox Christianity, the hearing of no sermon could *perhaps* be said to be good, in the sense that the doctrine of the Blessed, Holy, and Undivided Trinity is so basic to all hymnody, prayer, and preaching that a sermon on the Trinity is not necessary. It is assumed the Trinity is proclaimed implicitly and explicitly in all that is said and sung. We can imagine that this situation could exist in a church which has a learned and godly pastor and keeps close to Protestant orthodoxy, or a parish which uses an ancient or classic liturgy—for example, the essentially patristic Greek liturgy of St. Chrysostom or the English liturgy of the Anglican *Book of Common Prayer* (1662). A study of these written forms of worship shows that structurally they relate the church to the Holy and Transcendent Father, through the Incarnate Son and in/by the Holy Spirit in worship and for salvation. Of course, the presence of carefully expressed Trinitarianism in a liturgy does not automatically guarantee living faith in the Blessed, Holy, and Undivided Trinity in the hearts of those who use the liturgy. What it does, however, is to ensure always the possibility of the church being genuinely orthodox in mind and heart.

On the other hand, where there is no formal, orthodox liturgy, the absence of teaching on the living God as a Unity in Trinity and a Trinity in Unity could *perhaps* be said to be bad, in the sense that the absence of the doctrine means exactly what it appears to mean. The pastor and congregation seem to get on quite well without any regular, explicit reference in song or sermon to the Blessed, Holy, and Undivided Trinity. While they obviously believe in one, personal God, they do not appear to believe in, or to place any obvious importance upon, the eternal Trinity of Persons, the Holy Triad. Possibly they believe in one personal God, who has three names ("Father, Son, and Holy Spirit" or "Creator, Redeemer, and Sanctifier"), with whom all are encouraged to have a "personal relationship." Or possibly they believe that the Father is God and that Jesus Christ is also God (in some lesser way), but the Spirit is simply and only God active in the world in an invisible way.

In fact, what seems to be widely held in the West in both conservative and liberal Christianity concerning the "Godness of God" is that God as God, or God in his Godhead, is unreachable, unknowable, and beyond all appropriate description. God is Mystery. Therefore, to speak to, or describe, such a God we must use the best names, images, phrases, and metaphors available to us. If we are conservative, we take our forms of address and description from Scripture and holy tradition—the experience of yesterday; and, if we are liberal, we take them from contemporary human experience and such experience of the past as resonates with our present needs. In the former case, we find it natural to speak of God as "the Father, Son, and Holy Spirit," as well as of "the Lord" and "the King"; in the latter case, we see it as a duty — in being politically correct — to speak of God[dess] as "Father-Mother," "Friend," and "Parent," as well as "Creator, Redeemer, and Sanctifier."

If we take a look back over what Western thought has intended by the word "God" (which is normally masculine in grammatical gender in Western European languages), we find that the prominent meaning is that of monotheism — there is one and one only true and living God, Creator of the universe. However, there have been other meanings, some of which are becoming prominent today. Various Europeans have been intellectually committed, for example, to pantheism (the world is God and God is the world), panentheism (the world is contained within God), and deism (God is wholly beyond the world and takes no interest in it). Further, for those (the majority) who do not feel the need for, or are incapable of arriving at, any intellectual clarity, and who do not follow Christian orthodoxy, the word "God" has stood for "something" or "someone," which/who is supernatural and invisible, and which/who is known through feelings, in religious experience or by intuition. This undeveloped sense, conviction, or idea of God is probably nearer to pantheism today than to classical monotheism.

Further, when it is said today from many parts of the major Christian denominations that God is Mystery and unknowable and that we are to choose the most appropriate names and images from our experience by which to speak of "him/her," it is not to be assumed that we are into monotheism — let alone Trinitarian monotheism! More likely we are into panentheism or pantheism.

The late C.S. Lewis' *Miracles* devotes chapter 11 to pantheism as popular religion. "So far from being the final religious refinement," he wrote, "Pantheism is in fact the permanent natural bent of the human mind; the permanent, ordinary level below which man sometimes sinks, under the influence of priest-craft and superstition, but above which his own unaided efforts can never raise him for very long."[1] Lewis also wrote:

We who defend Christianity find ourselves constantly opposed not by the irreligion of our hearers but by their *real* religion. Speak about beauty, truth and goodness, or about a God who is simply the indwelling principles of these three, speak about a great spiritual force pervading all things, a common mind of which we are all parts, a pool of generalized spirituality to which we can all flow, and you will command friendly interest. But the temperature drops as soon as you mention a God who has purposes and performs particular actions, who does one thing and not another, a concrete, choosing, commanding, prohibiting God with a determinate character. People become embarrassed or angry.[2]

Not a few committed Christians who are self-consciously Trinitarian have experienced what Lewis describes, even in supposedly "orthodox" congregations and denominations.

A century or so before Lewis began to write his books, a Frenchman, Alexis de Tocqueville, visited and studied American society. Then he wrote what has become a famous book, *Democracy in America*. It is still much read in America—especially in college courses. One of the chapters concerns religion in a democracy, and it is of importance to us because of the ties which de Tocqueville saw between the grand experiment of democracy in the new world and the seductive power of pantheism within the American nation.

In his brief chapter 7, "What Causes Democratic Nations to Incline toward Pantheism," de Tocqueville comments on the increase of pantheism in Europe—within philosophy in Germany and within literature in France. Then, with America in mind he wrote:

When the conditions of society are becoming more equal and each individual man becomes more like all the rest, more weak and insignificant, a habit grows up of ceasing to notice the citizens and considering only the people, of overlooking individuals to think only of their kind. At such times the human mind seeks to embrace a multitude of different objects at once, and it constantly strives to connect a variety of consequences with a single cause. The idea of unity so possesses man and is sought by him so generally that if he thinks he has found it, he readily yields himself to repose in that belief. Not content with

18

the discovery that there is nothing in the world but a creation and a Creator, he is still embarrassed by this primary division of things and seeks to expand and simplify his conception by including God and the universe in one great whole.[3]

When people were seen as belonging to tribes and families and when their personhood was defined in relation to others, they were not seen atomistically and not regarded as "individuals." Rather, they were seen as persons in relations as part of a grand ordered universe. But democracy ultimately rests upon seeing human beings not in tribes and families but as "individuals" — and this creates the problem for the human mind. So de Tocqueville continues:

If there is a philosophical system which teaches that all things material and immaterial, visible and invisible, which the world contains are to be considered only as the several parts of an immense Being, who alone remains eternal amidst the continual change and ceaseless transformation of all that constitutes him, we may readily infer that such a system, although it destroy the individuality of man, or rather because it destroys that individuality, will have secret charms for men living in democracies. All their habits of thought prepare them to conceive it and predispose them to adopt it. It naturally attracts and fixes their imagination; it fosters the pride while it soothes the indolence of their minds.

Among the different systems by whose aid philosophy endeavors to explain the universe, I believe pantheism to be one of those most fitted to seduce the human mind in democratic times. Against it all who abide in their attachment to the true greatness of man should combine and struggle.[4]

Since the publication of this book, others have observed that the tendency of the American soul, raised in the excessive culture of individual rights, is toward pantheism. A recent study of rock music, *The Triumph of Vulgarity*[5] by Robert Pattison, traces this music to nineteenth-century British pantheism. The beat in the music is the heartbeat of mother earth!

The insights of Lewis and de Tocqueville raise the possibility that the external rite (i.e., the words, symbolism, music, dramatic action, and ceremonial of the worship service) can be objectively orthodox (in terms of holy tradition), while the mind-set of some, if not all, participants can be pantheistic. Further, it is also entirely possible that even where there is a vocal commitment to the inerrancy, inspiration, and authority of Holy Scripture, pantheism and natural religion can be present in hearts and attitudes. This is because in this case the attitude to the Bible can be at the level of commitment to an ideology rather than as an expression of living, personal faith in the Father, the Son, and the Holy Spirit — the Blessed, Holy, and Undivided Trinity.

Perhaps it is appropriate to add that pantheism or panentheism is the belief we would expect and indeed find in modern people, who feel the need to believe in "God" and who live in a culture where the general belief in development, progress, and evolution is taken for granted. Here God is the *Zeitgeist* or the animating Spirit or the Mind or the Life-Force of the evolving culture and universe. In this kind of general environment it is possible to speak quite sincerely in the manner of a trinitarian theist and really be a pantheist.

This can best be illustrated by referring to the presence today of "Modalism," which is an ancient but ever-present heresy. What Modalism teaches is very simple. It asserts that there is one and only one God; at different times in human history God is known in different ways and by different names. His chief names for Christians have been "the Father, Son, and Holy Spirit." The use of these prominent names does not mean he is truly a Trinity; it means only that he is like a triangle with three "sides" — sometimes God is fatherly, sometimes he is universal Spirit, and sometimes he is best looked for in Jesus. Where Modalism is accompanied by an emphasis on the majesty and transcendence of God then it is really a form of Unitarianism. But where it is held in the context of experiencing the nearness, availability, and immanence of God, it is often nothing more than a form of pantheism — pantheism using Christian vocabulary. I fear that the union of modalism and pantheism is more common in North American religion than most of us would care to admit.

UNDER ATTACK

So we see that the received doctrine of the Holy Trinity, passed down in ecumenical creeds and local confessions of faith, is under silent attack from within. It is being eroded by the inbred and incipient pantheism within the individualized soul of Western man, particularly in North America. Further, the teaching that God is Three in One is under attack from without. It is being set aside or revised by feminist theologians (who, in terms of their sex, are both female and male).

Feminist theologians are supported by people within the leadership of denominations as well as in seminaries and colleges — people who often have not thought through what they are being asked to believe. This attack upon "the Name of the Father, the Son, and the Holy Spirit" is a crucial part of the larger attempt to dismantle the received linguistic structure of Christianity. Of the latter, Robert W. Jenson has offered this intriguing observation.

> One may fear that the current crisis, where it is in progress, is equaled in the previous history of the Faith only by the gnostic crisis of the second and third centuries, and by the crisis of vulgar Enlightenment at the hinge of the eighteenth and nineteenth centuries. If one historical event could fully repeat another, one might even say that the "inclusivist" crisis is a simultaneous rerun of the two, joined into one by recapitulation also of the causal relation between them.[6]

Further, this current crisis generates great energy. This is because those who wage the war for the new ways are able not only to appeal to the mind and ethos of modern culture for support, but are also able to use in battle weapons forged in earlier times both by orthodox and liberal theologians.

What is the nature of the attack upon the linguistic structure of classic, dynamic, biblical, orthodox trinitarian theism? As far as I can see, the strategy involves creating an ethos and mind-set in which new ways of describing and addressing God are deemed both appropriate and necessary. This is achieved through a combination of the following: (1) by making use of what is known as apophatic theology; (2) by emphasizing the importance of modern secular and religious experience for the knowledge and naming of God; (3) by the use of "metaphorical" theology; (4) by accepting feminist teaching on the wickedness of patriarchy, androcentricism, and sexism; (5) by following the more extreme form of the historical-critical method in the reading and interpretation of the Christian Bible; and (6) by adopting a concept of God from the insights and principles of process theology and/or panentheism.

Underlying all these is the deliberate confusion of sexuality with gender. That is, the word *gender* is used where *sexuality* is required. For example, "The church is to be free of racial and *gender* [i.e., sexual] bias." In the study of a language we refer to the gender of nouns and pronouns. Grammatical gender has nothing whatsoever in principle to do with sexuality, which is the reality of being physically a male or a female. Yet, by constantly speaking of gender instead of sexuality, femininist theologians give the impression that sexuality in human beings is only as important as gender in grammar. The French say "La table" (feminine gender) because that is how they have always spoken. Yet the gender could have been masculine or neuter and then they would now say "Le table"; but they don't because the gender for unknown reasons is female.

We now turn to the sixfold strategy of the feminist theologians:

(1) Apophatic theology. There is a long tradition both within certain forms of Platonic philosophy and in Greek Orthodox theology of assuming and claiming that God as God, or God in his essential deity, is unknowable, inexpressible, incomprehensible, and ineffable. In Orthodoxy this apophaticism consists in negating that which God is not — for example, he is not any part of the visible or invisible created order, not goodness, love, and wisdom, and not even being itself. "He has made darkness his abode" (Ps. 18:11). Yet this negative way is balanced by the positive way. The claim of cataphatic theology (which always accompanies apophatic theology) is that God has revealed himself definitively in Jesus Christ. This self-revealing God is the God to whom the believer says "Thou." Thus God in his ineffa-

ble essence is beyond all knowledge—he is supra-essential and supra-celestial. However, God in his energies is knowable for he actually unveils himself and reveals himself. He tells us his name(s). Examples of the apophatic and cataphatic style abound in the Divine Liturgy of St. Chrysostom and that of St. Basil.

Feminist theology makes much of the apophatic dimension and divorces it from the cataphatic. So God is said to be Mystery, which we are to name. That is, if God is beyond knowledge and description, and if this God who is Mystery has not given any definitive self-revelation, then human beings are left to search for God and to name, to address, and to describe God according to their own lights and experiences. Thus God has had and will have many names. Feminists name God out of their own feminine experience.

(2) *Religious experience.* Ever since the Enlightenment and the influential writings of Friedrich Schleiermacher at the beginning of the nineteenth century, theologians in the liberal tradition have seen the raw material of theology as the religious experience of Jews and Christians. Thus they have used the Bible not as an account of divine revelation to be received by the church as authoritative, but as a collection of accounts of a variety of religious experiences to be received critically by the church for reflection and guidance. Then to this recorded experience of Jews and Christians theologians have added the further experience of the church through space and time, including their own space and time.

Feminists now also insist that the general and religious experience of women as women must be taken fully into account within the "raw material" upon which the theologian reflects. This major dimension (involving the experience of half of "humankind") has been absent from theological reflection until the present, they say, and therefore the theology of the past cannot be wholly trusted for it has been biased in favor of men.

(3) *Metaphorical theology.* If ultimate Mystery (that is God or God[dess]) has not revealed his/her true name and nature, then human beings will do (and have done) their best or their worst to describe and address God[dess] from within their specific experi-

ence of the divine and from within their own cultural horizons. As there can be no literal descriptions of the ineffable God[dess], all forms of address must be either in simile (e.g., "God is like a mother hen") or metaphor (e.g., God is a "Rock," "Father/ Mother," and "Divine Friend,"). And these similes and metaphors (sometimes called "models") will change from place to place, culture to culture, and time to time. Those used by the Israelites, Jews, and early Christians belong to their own context and times and do not necessarily have any value or worth for today.

Feminists call for the development of metaphors and models for deity which reflect the experience of God[dess] by women. These will include, but will not necessarily be only, feminine images such as "Mother." Such expressions as "Great Lover" and "God of many names" will also have a place, as also will "Life-creating Wisdom" and "Name Unnamed."

(4) Feminist ideology. Here the key words and concepts are "patriarchalism," "androcentricism," and "sexism." It is assumed that the culture and society presumed in both the Old and New Testaments as well as throughout European Christian history expressed in greater or lesser degree these evils. Men were in charge and everything existed primarily for the good of men. So it is not surprising, say feminists, that in Scripture, as well as in synagogue and church, God was always "He" and conceived via male images such as Lord, King, and Master. And the Trinity was "the Father, the Son, and the Spirit." Thus androcentric religion has buttressed male domination (and vice versa) since, in the oft-quoted words of Mary Daly, "If God is male then the male is God."[7]

Living now in times of liberation, the church has a solemn duty to elevate the status of women, claim feminists, and as a sign of this duty to begin to name and address God with non-masculine or feminine metaphors. Obviously many metaphors and models can be used and God as a Trinity (if God[dess] is experienced in the world as Threefold) could be "Creator, Redeemer, Sanctifier," or "God, Christ, Spirit" or "Mother, Lover, and Friend," or any other set of three names.

(5) Historical-critical method. It is obvious that to use the Scriptures as they do, the feminist theologians have drunk deeply of

the modern historical-critical method in its more agnostic forms. That is, they treat the books of the Bible as ordinary, ancient, religious books and seek to explain them in terms of the times and contexts and concerns in which they were originally written. In this explanation they do not allow for any unique or even special "inspiration and illumination of the Holy Spirit." They treat the Scriptures as unique simply because they are the first in line, belonging to the foundational period of Christianity, not because they are authoritative in any stronger sense.

(6) *Pantheism/panentheism.* Because they reject classical, trinitarian theism with all its supposed masculine features, because they wish to emphasize the immanence rather than the transcendence of God, and because they desire to name God[dess] in feminine ways, feminist theologians find themselves by design or default embracing views of God which link God's being intimately with the cosmos. Many have been influenced by process theology and speak of the world as "God's body." They claim that while God is not strictly identical with the world, the world is nevertheless within God. Some feminists, however, do claim to experience God in a threefold way and so from within their panentheism there is still talk of God as some kind of Trinity (as there is also in non-feminist panentheism, particularly in the philosophy of Hegel and those who follow him). However, the purpose of this Trinity is usually stated as being that of providing a model of community for humanity — a model which does not foster patriarchalism!

STUDYING THE BIBLE

In response to this feminist campaign and teaching, which has deeply influenced Western Christianity in both its conservative and liberal expressions, there are two basic ways of doing a study of the biblical teaching on the Trinity. One is to ignore the underlying pantheism, the linguistic crisis, and the feminist attack and allow the Bible to speak for itself on its own terms, believing that the Holy Spirit will convince people of the truth of the biblical doctrine, if the evidence is fairly stated. Such a work would conceivably look like Lockyer's *All the Divine Names and*

Titles in the Bible: A Unique Classification of All Scripture Designations of the Three Persons of the Trinity. [8]

The other is to set forth the biblical evidence for belief in the Holy Trinity and, in doing this, face some of the challenges and questions raised not only by the latest feminist theology but also by pantheism and liberal theology. Some of the writers in the symposium *Speaking the Christian God: The Holy Trinity and the Challenge of Feminism* have attempted to do this in short essays.[9]

What I shall attempt to do in this book fits somewhere between these two approaches, but is certainly more of the latter than the former. We are all affected by the call to become "politically correct" in our use of language; thus, in some way or another, we all face this modern, feminist challenge when we think theologically or address God in prayer. Regrettably, in my opinion, modern translations of the Bible (e.g., the NRSVB, NEB, and NJB) have moved toward the general use of inclusive language, and the tendency in biblical translation and in the editing of Christian books for publication seems to be toward the way of accommodation with politically correct language.

Since this is primarily an exercise in biblical doctrine (i.e., what is specifically assumed and taught by the writers of the sacred books of the Bible), it is necessary for me briefly to state how I view the canon of Scripture. The New Testament is an *authoritative collection of inspired, authoritative books.* The author (and editor where there was one) of each book was/were inspired by the Holy Spirit in what he/they wrote so that the content of what is written reflects the will of God, the Father. So each book is *authoritative,* pointing to Christ, the Lord. However, the early Christian church during the first four centuries decided which books were actually to be within the canon or collection called the New Testament. Now certainly the pastors of the church in the first four centuries were led by the Holy Spirit in this process of sifting and choosing which books to include, but we must allow that the church (through pastors and synods) was actually an authority (under Jesus Christ the Lord by the Holy Spirit) in the creation of the canon of the New and in the accepting of the canon of the Old Testaments.

And if we allow that the early church was an *authority* under Jesus Christ in terms of the creation of the canon, then it is reasonable to grant that the doctrinal understanding of the same church in terms of such great themes as the identity of God the Father, of Jesus Christ his Son, and the Holy Spirit ought to be received by us with the utmost respect. In other words, along with the New Testament we received from the same church and at the same time as the agreed canon of the New Testament a creed, or rather, two creeds. First, the Creed of the Council of Nicea (325) and then, secondly, the longer Niceno-Constantino-politan Creed approved by the Council of Constantinople (381) with their teaching on the Persons and the work of the Father, the Son, and the Holy Spirit. The latter creed is normally called "the Nicene Creed" today (and we shall have more to say about it in the next chapter).

Over the centuries Christian teachers have held that they are to hear and read the Bible with minds which have accepted and appropriated this authoritative statement of the identity of the Persons and work of the Holy Trinity. In fact, once the church had clarified and put into careful statement the central themes of the sacred Scriptures, then the Bible was read from this particular point of view within worship. Thus, the very teaching which the Bible had yielded (and continued to yield) to patient and prayerful study, then became the doctrinal basis upon which the church actually read the Scriptures in its Liturgy and Daily Offices over the centuries.

Thus it seems that all a Christian is doing when he writes a book on the biblical basis for the doctrine of the Holy Trinity is looking in Scripture for that which as an orthodox Christian he already believes. Actually it is probably true to say that in his own study and experience he is doing personally and quickly what the church did corporately in the first four centuries. Of course, he knows what the church decided and that is his faith. So he is looking at the Scriptures while facing the challenges raised and the questions asked in his own time (e.g., through the use of the historical-critical method and by the critical estimate of the Bible in feminist theology). He studies to see whether in the light of such criticisms the Scriptures still yield to the prayerful student the doctrine of the Holy Trinity. And because of the experience of the church in twenty centuries, he will be very surprised not to be encountered by the Holy Trinity.

THE HOLY TRINITY AND
BIBLICAL INSPIRATION

Since we are considering the testimony of the Scriptures, perhaps the best way to introduce the "biblical" doctrine of the Holy Trinity is to consider briefly the implications of what is said of the Scriptures by the Scriptures in terms of their relation to God.

It is well known that Jesus himself, as well as his apostles and disciples, believed that the authors of the books of what we now call the Old Testament were inspired by the Holy Spirit. Zechariah, the father of John the Baptist, declared that "the Lord God of Israel" is the God who "spoke by the mouth of his holy prophets from of old" (Luke 1:68, 70). The Apostle Peter insisted that "no prophecy ever came by the impulse of man, but men moved by the Holy Spirit spoke from God" (2 Peter 1:21). Paul, Apostle to the Gentiles, explained that "all Scripture is inspired by God and profitable for teaching, for reproof, for correction, and for training in righteousness, that the man of God may be complete, equipped for every good work" (2 Tim. 3:16-17). Further, in several places, Paul speaks of the Old Testament as a whole and in terms of being like a thinking, rational, omniscient subject and person: thus the Jewish Bible is "God's oracles [utterances]," in and from which God is heard to speak (Rom. 3:2; 9:17; 10:11).

When asked, "What is the primary message spoken by the divine oracles?" the answer of Jesus and his apostles was "the Messiah." On the road to Emmaus, the resurrected Jesus spoke of his own suffering and crucifixion to the two disciples. "O foolish men, and slow of heart to believe all that the prophets have spoken! Was it not necessary that the Christ should suffer these things and enter into his glory?" Then, "beginning with Moses [i.e., the Five Books of Moses] and all the prophets, he interpreted to them in all the Scriptures the things concerning himself" (Luke 24:25-27).

Peter told the churches in Pontus, Galatia, Cappadocia, Asia, and Bithynia the following:

> The prophets who prophesied of the grace that was to be
> yours searched and inquired about this salvation; they

inquired what person or time was indicated by the Spirit of Christ within them when predicting the sufferings of Christ and the subsequent glory. It was revealed to them that they were serving not themselves but you, in the things which have now been announced to you by those who preached the good news to you through the Holy Spirit sent from heaven, things into which angels long to look (1 Peter 1:10-12).

The prophets not only spoke the word of the Lord to their contemporaries but they also spoke of the future Messiah, even though they did not understand all of the word they proclaimed.

As we reflect upon what the writers of the New Testament have to say about the inspiration of the Old Testament, we get an insight into the way in which Yahweh-Elohim, the Lord God of Israel, related to and acted toward his covenant people. Obviously Moses and the later prophets are prophets of Yahweh-Elohim, the God of Abraham, Moses, and David. At the same time they are inspired, even indwelt, by the Spirit of the Lord God (also "the Spirit of Christ"), who actually speaks God's words through them; further as they speak and write they point to Jesus, the suffering and glorified Messiah, who is in himself as a Person the Word of God, and who as such speaks God's words. Thus we see (even if "in a mirror dimly," 1 Cor. 13:12) the Three, whom the resurrected Lord Jesus named "the Father . . . the Son, and . . . the Holy Spirit" (Matt. 28:19), revealed in the origin, content, and purpose of the Holy Scriptures.

Our task in the rest of this book is to look for both the "raw material" and the implicit and explicit statements of the doctrine of the Holy Trinity in the Bible. This work will cause us not only to look at the Bible itself, but also at what various writers have said about the doctrinal themes and contents of the Bible.

FOR FURTHER READING

Baker, D.L. *Two Testaments: One Bible*. Downers Grove, Ill.: InterVarsity, 1976.

Bruce, F.F. *The Canon of Scripture*. Downers Grove, Ill.: InterVarsity, 1988.

Lewis, C.S. *Miracles*. London: Collins, 1965.

Lockyer, Herbert. *All the Divine Names and Titles in the Bible: A Unique Classification of All Scripture Designations of the Three Persons of the Trinity.* Grand Rapids: Zondervan, 1975.

Metzger, Bruce. *The Canon of the New Testament.* New York: Oxford Univ. Press, 1987.

Tocqueville, Alexis de. *Democracy in America,* trans. George Lawrence, ed. J.P. Mayer. New York: Doubleday, 1969.

Specifically on feminist theology:

Hitchcock, Helen Hull, ed. *The Politics of Prayer: Feminist Language and the Worship of God.* San Francisco: Ignatius, 1992.

Hook, Donald D., and Alvin F. Kimel. "The Pronouns of Deity." *The Scottish Journal of Theology* 46 (1993): 297–323.

Kimel, Alvin F., ed. *Speaking the Christian God: The Holy Trinity and the Challenge of Feminism.* Grand Rapids: Eerdmans, 1992.

Martin, Francis. *The Feminist Question: Feminist Theology in the Light of the Christian Tradition.* Grand Rapids: Eerdmans, 1994.

Toon, Peter. *The End of Liberal Theology: Contemporary Challenges to Evangelical Orthodoxy.* Wheaton, Ill.: Crossway, 1995.

2

GOD IN RELATION TO US

In this chapter we shall first examine briefly three simple yet profound descriptions of God — a task which will introduce us to the biblical vision of the Holy Trinity and prepare us for the biblical study in chapters 4 to 11. Then, so that we shall not be reading and studying the Bible in a vacuum, we shall turn to examine the origins of the ecclesial doctrine/ dogma of the Holy Trinity as this was developed in the early and medieval church and recorded later in the confessions of faith of the Protestant churches of the Reformation. To know the ecclesial dogma will help us both to appreciate the biblical vision of the Holy Trinity and the concept of the development of doctrine.

The three simple yet profound statements concerning God all appear in the Johannine writings of the New Testament and, upon examination, yield a lively conception of God as the Father, the Son, and the Holy Spirit.

GOD IS SPIRIT

John, the evangelist, reports that in his conversation with the Samaritan woman at the well Jesus said, "God is Spirit" (John 4:24). Too often this has been taken out of context and made to mean such things as "God is a Spirit—one among several" or "God is invisibly present everywhere and can be approached anywhere at any time howsoever we will." It has also been seen as a slogan for pantheism. Yet, it appears in a context where we read that "those who worship him must worship in spirit and truth" (4:24).

If we inquire concerning the identity of the God who is Spirit, then the answer provided by the text of the same conversation is, "the Father," whose "only Son" is Jesus. "The hour is coming, and now is," said Jesus, "when the true worshipers will worship the Father in spirit and truth, for such the Father seeks to worship him" (4:23).

Some people of a philosophical disposition have supposed that the statement "God is Spirit" is a metaphysical and ontological definition of the eternal nature of the invisible deity. Though God (according to philosophical theism) is eternal, uncreated Spirit, the meaning here has less to do with eternity and more to do with space and time. "God is Spirit" is the same general kind of statement as two others found in 1 John, which we shall examine below. They are "God is light" (1:5) and "God is love" (4:8). In all three statements it is God in relation to us, God acting with respect to us, which is being affirmed. John is telling us how the Father really is, or truly acts, toward us in history and on a Person-to-person basis.

Jesus is not attempting to speak of God-as-God-is-in-himself in his eternity. His message is of God as God-is-toward-and-for-us; the Father is the One who gives the Spirit (John 14:16), and it is in and by the Spirit that the Father relates to human beings as his creatures. Therefore, "God [the Father] is Spirit" in the sense that, as the invisible God, he makes himself known through the medium of the Spirit, whom he actually sends into the world.

True worship also is in the sphere of "Spirit." Human beings who worship their Creator and Lord must worship "in spirit [Spirit]," as those who are reborn by water and the Spirit (John 3:5) and who have been baptized with that baptism in the Spirit of which John the Baptist spoke (John 1:33). It is necessary that they worship in this way, for no other approach is acceptable to the Father. Genuine worship must be prompted, energized, and brought to fulfillment by the presence and sanctifying power of the Holy Spirit. Without the Holy Spirit worship by human beings remains merely a human activity which has no guarantee of reaching the Father.

And there is a further necessary component! True worship is also "in truth." John's Gospel makes it very clear that the Spirit and the Word (the Son) exist and work in perfect harmony in God's economy of grace. Jesus as the Word (1:1) is also the Truth (14:6), who reveals the very reality of God (8:45; 18:37). In fact, the Spirit is "the Spirit of truth" (14:17; 15:26; 16:13) in his relation to the Word made flesh, Jesus, the Son. And Jesus is the Truth, who reveals the Father, who does the will of the Father, and who makes access to the Father possible for sinners by his sacrificial death as the Lamb of God. He is the Son of the Father who becomes the man of flesh and blood. Further, as Jesus told the Samaritan woman (4:26), he is the "I am" without any predicate — the "I am," *Ego eimi* = Yahweh of Exodus 3:14ff, and of Isaiah 41:4 and 43:10 (see further John 6:20; 8, particularly vv. 24, 28, 58; 13:19; 18:5-8). Thus true worship must be offered to the Father through (i.e., according to the Truth which is) Jesus and by/in the Spirit, who is given by the Father and who rests upon and takes from the Son.

It would be false to conclude from John 4:23-24 that worship must only be spiritual, confined to the heart, and without any outward expression of form or ceremony. The apostolic church worshiped through the ministry of Word and Sacrament; and it is highly probable that John 6:53-58 refers to the Eucharist as a primary means of worship. To worship in Spirit and in Truth is to worship the Trinity by the Trinity. Those who believe on the name of the Son, and who are born from above by the Spirit, worship the Father through the Son and in the Spirit. And they do so because the Father, through the Son and by the Spirit, has not only created them but also revealed himself to them, as the God who gives eternal life because of his Son's perfect obedience unto death.

GOD IS LIGHT

The contrast of light and darkness is found in many religions. This is entirely what we would expect for they are such obviously contrasting symbols of the good and the evil. In terms of Christianity, the advent of the Logos, the only Son of the Father, was the coming of light into the world (John 1:4-9; cf. Matt. 4:16; Luke 2:32) — the light shining in darkness. Jesus is *the* light of the world" while God, the Father, is "light."

> This is the message we have heard from him [Jesus Christ] and proclaim to you, that *God is light and in him is no darkness at all.* If we say we have fellowship with him while we walk in darkness, we lie and do not live according to the truth; but if we walk in the light, as he is in the light, we have fellowship with one another, and the blood of Jesus his Son cleanses us from all sin (1 John 1:5-7).

Obviously the Lord our God as the true and only God is of necessity and always light both in himself as the transcendent God and in his relations with the world as its Creator and Redeemer. It is the latter which is in view here. The whole context of 1 John makes it clear that "God as Light" is not a philosophical, speculative statement about the being and nature of deity but is a declaration of God's relation to the world as Revealer and Savior.

In the Old Testament light is used to symbolize truth in contrast to error, and righteousness in contrast to wickedness (see Ps. 36:9; 119:130; Isa. 5:20; Micah 7:8). Thus in Hebrew terms to say that "God is light" is to confess that he is absolute in his glory, in his truth, and in his holiness.

The Father is light, the incarnate Son is *the* light, and believers are called to live and walk in the light and have fellowship one with another and with the Father through his only Son. But, we ask, how is this walking and fellowship possible? John answers, "You have been anointed by the Holy One" (1 John 2:20; cf. v. 27); that is, you have received the gift of the Holy Spirit. For one to see the light, to have the light shine in his heart, and to walk in the light, he needs the illumination of the Holy Spirit of light. In other words, light shines upon and within him from the Father, through the Son, and by the Spirit. Therefore, what the psalmist prayed (36:9) — "In thy light do we see light" — is wonderfully fulfilled.

GOD IS LOVE

The word love is often on the lips of modern people. Yet rarely does it have that meaning communicated by the Greek word *agapē*, or even the word *philia* (the loving feeling of friendship). When we read that "God is love" (1 John 4:8) it is the word *agapē* which describes God. God is love in that he wills that which is the best for his creatures and he commits himself wholly to achieving this end. Further, it is not only that God is the source of love but that all of his intentions and activity are loving. We read in 1 John 4:7-12:

> Beloved, let us love one another; for love is of God, and he who loves is born of God and knows God. He who does not love does not know God; for *God is love.* In this the love of God was made manifest among us, that God sent his only Son into the world, so that we might live through him. In this is love, not that we loved God but that he loved us and sent his Son to be the expiation for our sins. Beloved, if God so loved us, we also ought to love one another. No man has ever seen God; if we love one another, God abides in us and his love is perfected in us.

In this paragraph the verb *(agapeo)* and the noun *(agapē)* occur fifteen times. The logic of love is very obvious. God, who is the Father, is love in that he sent his only Son into the world to be the propitiation/expiation for human sins. "For God so loved the world that he gave his only Son, that whoever believes in him should not perish but have eternal life" (John 3:16). Yet, God's love is not merely a past determination to do good which was completed by the resurrection of Jesus Christ. God is still love in that his Son, Jesus Christ, was raised from the dead and is alive forevermore willing the good of mankind, believers in particular. Further, God is still love in that he abides in those who believe. "By this we know that he abides in us, by the Spirit which he has given us" (1 John 3:24). The Holy Spirit dwells in the souls of the faithful, and it is by his inspiration and power that love is perfected in them and believers are enabled to love one another, thus fulfilling the command of Christ.

The Father loves the Son; the Son loves the Father; and the Spirit is the presence and expression of the love of the Father and the love of the Son. The Father loves the world and sent his only Son into the world; the Son also loves the world and gave himself as a propitiatory and expiatory sacrifice for the sins of the world; the Spirit brings the love of the Father and the Son into the hearts of those who believe, so that they may love God and one another.

Reflecting upon this theme of "God is love," Paul K. Jewett writes:

> Beyond the love of John 3:16 is the eternal love that God is in himself. Before all worlds [ages] he is the Father who loves the Son (John 3:35) and the Son who loves the Father—in the Spirit. God, then, from all eternity, is the One-who-is-for-Others in himself; that is, he is a Trinity of holy love. And as such he reveals himself. In creation he becomes the One-who-is-for-others-outside-himself, namely, his creatures. In redemption he becomes the One-who-is-for-sinful-others, namely, his people whom he restores to fellowship with himself. Thus the eternal fellowship of the divine, trinitarian life grounds God's fellowship with us to whom he gives himself in love as our Maker and Redeemer.[1]

So it is that the church has never been able to divorce what is called the ontological or immanent Trinity from the economic Trinity for God in himself is holy love and God turned outward from himself toward us is also holy love.

CONSIDERATION AND REFLECTION

From the evidence provided by the examination of these Johannine texts, we can make certain preliminary judgments concerning the identity of God, who is known, worshiped, and served by Christians.

First of all, God (theos) has a name and that name is "the Father." In the Gospel and letters of John, it can be claimed that "God" means "the Father" on virtually every occasion where it occurs in the text. One exception is perhaps the exclamation of

Thomas the Twin addressed to the resurrected Jesus: "My Lord and my God!" (John 20:28)

If God is "the Father" then the question arises, "Of whom is he the Father?" The answer is clear. The Father has an "only Son," who has been with him "from the beginning" as the Word, who became man, Jesus of Nazareth. The Son reveals the Father and his will. To see the Son is to see the Father. In order to know the Father and to receive his gift of eternal life, one must believe in the Son. The Son is both the Revealer of the Father and the Way to the Father. He comes from the Father, and he returns to the Father for "us and for our salvation" (Nicene Creed).

In John's Gospel (chaps. 14–16), the Holy Spirit, who is sent into the world by the Father for the sake of the Son, is described in personal terms (as he who dwells within the disciples, teaches them, and bears witness to and glorifies Jesus). In these chapters, together with chapter 17 wherein is the high priestly prayer of Jesus, we are given a wondrous revelation of the identities and relations of the Father, the Son, and the Holy Spirit.

In summary we may say that to speak of God is to speak of "the Father." To speak of God is also to speak of "the Father and his only Son." Further, to speak of God is to speak of "the Father, his only Son, and his Spirit, who is also the Spirit of his Son."

There is a movement of grace (creation, revelation, salvation) from God toward the world—from the Father through the Son and in/by the Spirit; and there is a movement of grace (faith, love, obedience) from the world to God—to the Father through the Son and in/by the Holy Spirit.

What, of course, is not decided, by the inspired presentation of God in relation to us as the Father through the Son and in the Holy Spirit in the Johannine texts, is whether the Son and the Holy Spirit just as equally possess divinity as does the Father. Obviously in what we may call the divine economies of creation, revelation, and redemption the Father is first in order and the Son and the Holy Spirit are subordinate—that is they are second and third in order. Since the Father sends the Son and also sends the Holy Spirit there is a natural and logical priority of the Father. The authoritative answering of the question as to the precise, metaphysical or ontological relation of the Father and the Son and the Holy Spirit to each other had to wait several centuries for the deliberations of the ecumenical councils of Nicea (325) and Constantinople (381).

THE DOGMA OF THE TRINITY

The full exposition of the ecclesial, ontological doctrine of the Trinity did not occur overnight. It took a long time and developed in contrasting but essentially complementary ways in the East and West after the production of the creeds of the councils of Nicea and Constantinople. The major difference between East and West is the addition to the commonly held Niceno-Constantinopolitan Creed (381) of the *filioque* in the West in the early Middle Ages. This is the teaching that the Holy Spirit proceeds both from the Father *and from the Son,* as from one principle. In contrast, the East insisted that the Holy Spirit proceeded not merely from the Father, but from the Father alone. However, the East allowed the explanation that the Holy Spirit proceeds "from the Father through the Son" both within the eternal, essential, and immanent Trinity (God as God is in himself) and in the divine work of creation, revelation, redemption, and deification (God as God is toward us — the economic Trinity).

Let us begin our reflections on the development of the ecclesial doctrine of the Holy Trinity with the notion of God as the *Pantokrator.* This is the word which appears in the first sentence of the Nicene Creed and which we translate as "the Almighty." It is a dynamic word meaning "God the Pantokrator does everything": that is, the one Lord God is the supreme, universal actively ruling Power over all things. The reference is to an actuality of power and to the fact that the divine action is universal in its scope, extending over the whole world of nature, and including under its dominion all processes whatsoever, cosmic or historical. So God, the Father, is for Christians the Pantokrator as he is also the Creator of heaven and earth.

In the pre-Nicene period of the early church it was customary to refer to God as the Pantokrator in terms of "the Monarchy." This was because in the hellenistic religions to teach the divine Monarchy amounted to defending the logically unimpeachable proposition that only One can be the Almighty. So the early Christians saw an opportunity in the language of their time to proclaim important truths concerning both the identity of God and the relation of God to the cosmos. Yet, in so doing, they raised a major question. Is the Monarch the Godhead (the divine nature) or the Father, or the One (Jesus the Christ) who is called "the Lord"?

Following the lead of the New Testament, the answer given in the second and third centuries was that the Monarch is truly "the Father" and, more specifically, "the Father within the Trinity." Certainly the Father has absolute, divine authority over creation (as the Nicene Creed was to declare), but logically prior to this rule and within eternity the Father is the Monarch in relation to the Word and the Holy Spirit. The eternal Son and the eternal Spirit, distinct from each other and distinct from the Father, are nevertheless both within the divine eternity and also in their external missions into the cosmos "subjects" of the Monarch, the Father. However, the early fathers also insisted that this doctrine does not imply the inferiority of the Son and the Holy Spirit. Rather it points to "holy order" within the eternal Godhead.

Such talk, however, could easily lose its way and thus run the risk of encouraging the idea that the Son and the Holy Spirit were in some sense less divine than is the Father. In fact, as is well known, Arius propagated such an idea in Alexandria and this eventually led to the calling of the Council of Nicea (325) by Constantine the Great. The major concern of this first ecumenical council of the church was to make it as plain as possible that Jesus of Nazareth, while being personally distinct from the Father, possesses the Godhead (is truly God) in the fullest sense. That is, he is fully God by derivation and in the possession of communicated deity, but truly divine and equal to the Father with a derived equality. Or, put another way, God because he is *homoousios* (of identical essence or substance) with the Father and God because he is eternally begotten of the Father.

The council rejected the attractive possibility offered by Arianism of a simple monotheism with the doctrine that Jesus was the highest of creatures and the uniquely adopted Son of the God, the Father. The bishops present at Nicea knew that the testimony of the Gospels and the experience of the presence of the Lord Jesus Christ in his church led them to one conclusion only—Jesus is "God from God, Light from Light, true God from true God, and consubstantial with the Father."

It is important for us to note that the *homoousion* was neither a new truth nor a new revelation from God. What this teaching did and does is to reduce the multiplicity of scriptural truths concerning who Jesus is into the unity of a single affirmation: that the Son is *consubstantial* with the Father is the sense of everything that the Scriptures declare concerning the Son. However, to use such language is to state the truth of the Scriptures in a new mode of understanding. There has been a transition from a mode of understanding that is primarily descriptive, relational, historical-existential, and interpersonal (i.e., what Christ is to us) to a mode that is definitive, explanatory, absolute, and ontological (i.e., what Christ is in himself).

The full, ontological doctrine of the consubstantiality of the Holy Spirit with the Father and with the Son had to wait until the Nicene teaching of Jesus Christ had been appropriated by the church during the fourth century, and for the theological clarity of the teaching of the Cappadocian Fathers (Basil the Great, Gregory of Nazianzus, and Gregory of Nyssa) concerning the Person of the Holy Spirit to be received. So the Creed of the Council of Constantinople (381) declares that the Holy Spirit is to be worshiped and glorified with both the Father and with the Son.

We recall that what the early church had to avoid at all costs were two deviations from the doctrine of the consubstantiality of the Father and the Son and the Holy Spirit. One was *modalism* which maintained the unity of God at the cost of denying the reality of the Three Persons in the One Godhead. That is, the Father, the Son, and the Holy Spirit were/are merely three modes of the one God's self-revelation. The other deviation was *tritheism*, the teaching that the Three Persons do not share one Godhead but are Three related but different Gods. The Father is the superior divinity and the Son and the Holy Spirit are lesser divinities. Certain forms of Arianism were in essence forms of tritheism. Authentic trinitarianism may be seen as a delicate balancing act between modalism and tritheism.

THE CHRISTIAN EAST

In the East the formula which most clearly conveyed the doctrine of the Trinity was "three divine *hypostaseis* in one *ousia.*" The origins of this go back to the use of the word *homoousios* (of identical substance) in the Nicene Creed (325). The *ousia* in this Nicene formula is the substance (deity, godhead) of the Father and the Son. It is what philosophers call the *deutera ousia,* the specific essence, not different but identical in two individuals of the same species. After the Council of Nicea, it was a relatively straightforward move (though complicated by historical circumstances) to confess that the Holy Spirit is also *homoousios* with the Father and with the Son. Thus the Trinity is Three Persons each of whom possesses in entirety the one Godhead, the identical *ousia.*

In its literal sense the word *hypostasis* is "understanding"; in its active sense it means "that which gives support" and in its passive sense it means "that which lies beneath." As used in both Christology (see the definition of the Council of Chalcedon of 451 on the Person of Christ) and in Trinitarianism, the active sense is the one being used. So there are three *hypostaseis* but only one *ousia* (where *ousia* is being used in the passive sense as the one essence shared by the Three).

In order to clarify the distinctions between the Three Persons and at the same time affirm that there is one God, the Cappadocian Fathers of the fourth century spoke of the internal relations within God as God-is-in-and-unto-himself. What differentiates the Three is their mutual interordination, expressed by the three particularities of *agennēsia, gennēsis,* and *ekpempis* (ingeneration, generation, and promission). Further, they applied to each of the Three the phrase *tropos hyparxeos,* meaning "mode of existence." Thus the whole Godhead is in its concrete totality instantiated in each of the Persons, paternally in the Father, filially in the Son, and pneumatically in the Holy Spirit.

"Mode of existence" was applied to the particularities that distinguish the Three Persons, in order to express the conviction that in the three *hypostaseis* one and the same divine being/essence is presented in objective and permanent expressions, though with no variation in divine content. Therefore, the emphasis from the Cappadocians is on the triplicity of objective presentation rather than on the unity of essential being, even though the latter is never denied. (In modern times Karl Barth has used the expression *tropos hyparxeos* [usually translated in his works as "mode of being"] to speak of each of the Three because he believed that the modern meaning of the word "Person" had moved too far from its original meaning. It is, however, difficult in prayer to address a "mode of being"! Further, Barth speaks of God as being "One Person" in Three "Modes of Being."[2])

To clarify what the Cappadocians had taught concerning the relations of the Persons within the Trinity, an anonymous theologian made use of the word *perichoresis* (coinherence). It served to describe the mutual interpenetration and embracement of the Three Persons through the possession by each, in his own proper way, of the totality of the one, divine *ousia*. Soon it became part of the language of orthodoxy.

The developed Eastern doctrine of the Trinity, making use of these technical terms, is found in the eighth-century book, *On the Orthodox Faith* by John of Damascus (d. 749) and has passed into the divine worship of the Orthodox Churches. Anyone who wishes to seek to understand the Orthodox doctrine of the Blessed, Holy, and Undivided Trinity is advised to go to the latter source and carefully read the Liturgies of St. Chyrsostom and St. Basil.

THE CHRISTIAN WEST

In the West the significant expositions are associated with the names of Augustine of Hippo and St. Thomas Aquinas, and the statement of orthodoxy is "three divine *personae* in one *substantia.*" Here *substantia* (philosophically *substantia secunda*) is the equivalent of *ousia*, for it is substance considered in abstraction from its determination to the individual: this is, strictly speaking, what is also called *natura* and *essentia*. Then, also, *persona* (meaning the concrete presentation of an individual) is the equivalent of *hypostasis*.

A further key word, whose meaning was developed by Augustine, is *relatio* (relation). In Aristotelian logic *relatio* is "accidental," but Augustine lifted it out of the subclass of accidents to make *relatio* to occupy the same level as *substantia*.

So Augustine taught that the Three Persons are identical in terms of their substance and distinct from each other through the different relations in which they stand to their substance. Everything that belongs to one Person belongs to the other Two (wisdom, truth, goodness, etc.), but what differentiates them is their relations — paternity in the Father, filiality in the Son, and procession in the Holy Spirit.

The relations of the Three Persons to the one divine *ousia* are themselves expressed in terms of their relations to one another — paternity, filiation, spiration; and the different ways in which each of the Persons is actually God arise solely from the processions within God — from the generation of the Son and from the spiration of the Holy Spirit. Put another way, Godhead can exist only paternally, filially, or by spiration; Godhead is to be found nowhere but in the Father, the Son, and the Holy Spirit.

St. Thomas Aquinas in his *Summa Theologiae* supplied further clarification of God-as-God-is-in-himself. He showed that there are in God two processions — the generation of the Son and the double procession of the Spirit (from the Father and the Son). Then there are four relations — paternity, of the Father to the Son; filiation, of the Son to the Father; spiration, of the Father and the Son, as one principle, to the Holy Spirit; and procession, of the Holy Spirit to the Father and the Son. Further there are five notions ("proper ideas for knowing a divine Person") — unbegottenness *(innascibilitas)* and paternity for the Father; common spiration for the Father and for the Son; and procession for the Spirit.

TRINITY IN UNITY: UNITY IN TRINITY

In both the East and West there is the clear statement of Unity in Trinity and Trinity in Unity within the Godhead. In the East the Unity is expressed by the coinherence of the Three Persons in each other, while in the West it is expressed through the real identity of the divine nature with the Three Persons.

In terms of God-as-God-is-toward-us, the Father is made known through the Son, and the Son is made known by the Holy

Spirit. However, there is no fourth divine Person to make the Holy Spirit known. This is because he is the *locus*, as the Son is the *agent* (not the object), of revelation. The divine movement is *from* the Father *through* the Son and *in* the Spirit and the creatures' response is *to* the Father *through* the Son and *in* the Spirit. The Holy Spirit is experienced by creatures like the air they breathe, that is by his effects, rather than like a visible external object.

So the traditional Western structure of liturgical prayer is offered to the Pantokrator, the transcendent Father "through Jesus Christ our Lord, thy Son, who livest and reigneth with thee in the unity of the Holy Spirit, God for ever and ever, Amen." In contrast, but not in disagreement, the classic Eastern liturgical prayer ends with the words: "For unto thee are due all glory, honor and worship, to the Father, and to the Son and to the Holy Spirit, now, and ever, and unto ages of ages. Amen."

Obviously the words *hypostasis* and *persona* are technical terms and do not carry modern notions of either an individual morally responsible decision-maker or such a person viewed as having a personality. So when it is said today that God is personal or when a claim such as "God may be more than personal, as we know personality, but he cannot be less" is made, the reference is not to the technical word "person" and thus to the Persons of the Father, of the Son, and of the Holy Spirit; rather it is to a divine attribute, which is an aspect of the one, divine nature and is therefore common to all Three Persons. The use of the word Person (*hypostasis, persona*) in the technical sense within classical theology is not to characterize what the Three Persons have in common; it is to establish and to emphasize their different modes of possessing the common, divine *ousia/substantia*.

One of my teachers during the early 1960s, the distinguished theologian, the late Dr. Eric Mascall, delighted to teach the classic, orthodox doctrine of the Trinity and wrote:

> The Trinity is not primarily a doctrine, any more than the Incarnation is primarily a doctrine. There is a doctrine *about* the Trinity, as there are doctrines about many other facts of existence, but, if Christianity is true, the Trinity is not a doctrine; the Trinity is God. And the fact

that God *is* Trinity—that in a profound and mysterious way there are three divine Persons eternally united in one life of complete perfection and beatitude—is not a piece of gratuitous mystification, thrust by dictatorial clergymen down the throats of an unwilling but helpless laity, and therefore to be accepted, if at all, with reluctance and discontent. It is the secret of God's most intimate life and being, into which, in his infinite love and generosity, he has admitted us; and it is therefore to be accepted with amazed and exultant gratitude.[3]

So the church has looked to the Trinity, saying, "Glory be to the Father and to the Son and to the Holy Spirit, as it was in the beginning, is now and ever shall be, world without end. Amen."

Regrettably, however, there have been long periods in the history of the church when the doctrine of the Trinity has been taught in the universities and seminaries in such a way as to divorce it from worship, piety, and practical theology. Especially was this so within the Roman Catholic Church during the period when theology followed the Scholastic method of the Middle Ages and seminarians were apparently taught that the doctrine of the Trinity is only the doctrine of the ontological or immanent Trinity. It seemed to be merely speculation concerning God-as-God-is-in-himself with little reference to God-as-God-is-toward-us!

Further, as Karl Rahner has pointed out in his influential book, *The Trinity* (1970), the decision made by Thomas Aquinas and those who followed him (e.g., Roman Catholic as well as Protestant scholastics from the seventeenth century) to discuss first the Unity of God *(De Deo uno)* and then, having established this to deal with God as Trinity *(De Deo triuno)*, had a big impact upon the way the doctrine of the Trinity was received within the church. It came generally to be held that the numerical unity of God was the primary assertion concerning God and thus the doctrine of the Holy Trinity took second place. Thus a "unitarian" mind-set was developed by the way the doctrine of God was studied in the universities and seminaries in the West. Further, theologians tended to discuss the unity of God, next the attributes of God, and only then God as Trinity. So even the attributes came to be thought of as attributes of the divine nature rather than of the Three Persons.

If we ask what role the doctrine of the Trinity had in theological systems in modern times (i.e., from 1800 when the Enlightenment began to affect Protestant theology to 1930 when neo-orthodoxy became a vital force), we find that there were three fundamental possibilities. In traditional theological circles, both Protestant and Roman Catholic, the traditional doctrine was seen and presented in textbooks on systematic theology as the direct deliverance of an authoritative Bible (or an authoritative Bible and holy Tradition). It was taken for granted that the doctrine was there in sacred Scripture in a full yet (philosophically) imprecise form and thus there was need for a clarification of it by the Fathers at the Council of Nicea and Constantinople, in later medieval councils, and by scholastic theologians.

In liberal theology, beginning with Friedrich Schleiermacher and Albrecht Ritschl, the traditional, scholastic doctrine was regarded as not essential to the expression of the Christian Faith, although it might perhaps be useful. So it was not often mentioned; alternatively the doctrine in some form was treated in an appendix to systematic theology, as in Schleiermacher's famous book on theology, *The Christian Faith.*

Finally, in the refined atmosphere of philosophical theology, influenced by Hegel, the doctrine of threefold Reality was released from its biblical roots and expounded as a metaphysical truth, more or less independently of the Christian revelation.

However, since the great Swiss theologian, Karl Barth, gave great prominence to the doctrine of the Trinity in his monumental *Church Dogmatics* (published in German at Zurich as *Kirchliche Dogmatik* from 1932 to 1967), study of this subject by theologians has much increased, but not usually by the methods used in the nineteenth century. Within the renewal of interest in this doctrine as central to Christian Faith, two types of approach may be discerned from the 1930s through to the 1960s.

The first treats the doctrine as a necessary "synthesis" of several fundamental elements of the record of Revelation in the Bible and of Christian experience of God. These include the received monotheism of the Old Testament, the belief in Jesus as Incarnate God, the worship of Jesus Christ in the churches, and the indwelling of the Holy Spirit in human souls. Here the doctrine of the Trinity is the completion of the doctrinal system, the ultimate doctrine of faith, and the necessary safeguard of the truth of Christianity. An example of this approach is Leonard Hodgson, *The Doctrine of the Trinity* (1944).

The second (and here we place Barth himself) treats the doctrine not as the completion but as the first item of Christian theology. That is, the concept of God as Trinity is an immediate implication of the Revelation to which Scripture witnesses and points. It is, therefore, the first principle of all Christian faith and thought and life. In God's self-revelation (and here is intended God as Creator, Revealer, Redeemer, and Judge) there is made known to the eyes of faith the Three — God, the Revealer; God, the Revelation; and God, the Revealedness. God, who is the Lord, makes himself known as the One who is the Father (Revealer), the Son (Revelation), and the Holy Spirit (Revealedness). So Barth expounds this doctrine of the Trinity in the Prolegomena to his *Church Dogmatics.*

When we examine books published since the second World War, in the wake of Barth's decisive description of God as Holy Trinity in Self-Revelation, we notice that the vast majority belong, as we would expect, to what is usually called historical, dogmatic, and systematic theology. These studies certainly usually notice the biblical evidence and often reflect upon it, but they are not primarily exercises in what in academia is normally called biblical theology. Rather, their aim is to formulate or investigate the way the church has believed, taught, and confessed the Blessed, Holy, and Undivided Trinity, or to propose new or revised ways of so doing. For example, a recent book, entitled *God in Three Persons* (1995), written by the evangelical Baptist theologian, Millard J. Erickson, fits into this general category. So also does another recent book, *The Triune God: A Biblical, Historical and Theological Study* (1994), by an Irish Roman Catholic theologian, Thomas Marsh.

For Roman Catholic writers such as Marsh it is not Barth as such but Barth via Rahner, with Rahner's own particular questions and insights, which determine the treatment of the doctrine of the Trinity. The thesis which Rahner proposed, and which has been much discussed as a protest against the scholastic tendency of the textbooks for Catholic seminarians to equate the doctrine of the Trinity with only the immanent or ontological Trinity (thereby neglecting the economic Trinity), is: *the "economic" Trinity is the "immanent" Trinity and the "immanent" Trinity is the "economic" Trinity.* If this means that we can say nothing of "God-as-God-is-in-himself-as-Holy Trinity" then, as we shall see, the thesis is overstated. Further, if it means that God as the One God became in eternity a Trinity of Persons for the purpose of becoming the Creator of the world, then it is false. However, if it means that the Lord God, whom we know through his self-revelation as the Father, the Son, and the Holy Spirit, is identical with the God who is eternally in himself the Holy Trinity, then it is an acceptable thesis.

When we inquire as to books on this topic, which are strictly within the area of biblical studies, we find that there are very few books dealing specifically with the doctrine of the Trinity as this is actually presented in, or implied and suggested by, sacred Scripture. Perhaps the best known of these is Arthur W. Wainwright, *The Trinity in the New Testament* (1962), which we shall examine, along with several other approaches, in the next chapter.

FOR FURTHER READING

Erickson, Millard J., *God in Three Persons*. Grand Rapids: Baker, 1995.

Fortman, Edmund J., *The Triune God: A Historical Study of the Doctrine of the Trinity*. Philadelphia: Westminster, 1972.

Hapgood, Isabel F., comp. and trans. *Service Book of the Holy Orthodox-Catholic Apostolic Church*. Englewood, N.J.: Antiochian Orthodox Archdiocese, 1983.

Jewett, Paul K. *God, Creation & Revelation*. Grand Rapids: Eerdmans, 1991.

Kelly, J.N.D. *The Athanasian Creed*. London: Adam and Charles Black, 1964.

_____. *Early Christian Creeds*. 3rd ed. London: Adam and Charles Black, 1972.

_____. *Early Christian Doctrine*. 5th ed. San Francisco: Harper & Row, 1978.

Marsh, Thomas. *The Triune God: A Biblical, Historical and Theological Study.* Mystic, Conn.: Twenty-Third, 1994.

De Margerie, Bertrand. *The Christian Trinity in History.* Still River, Mass.: St. Bede's, 1982.

Pelikan, Jaroslav. *The Christian Tradition: A History of the Development of Doctrine,* Vols. 1–3. Chicago: Univ. of Chicago Press, 1972–1978.

Prestige, G.L. *God in Patristic Thought.* London: William Heinemann, 1936.

Rahner, Karl. *The Trinity.* New York: Herder & Herder, 1970.

Toon, Peter. *Yesterday, Today and Forever: Jesus Christ and the Holy Trinity in the Teaching of the Seven Eucmenical Councils.* Swedesboro, N.J.: Preservation, 1995.

3

THEOLOGY—

METHODS AND APPROACHES

A variety of influences since the 1950s has led to the investigation of the New Testament documents to discover in what sense, if at all, their content may be described implicitly or explicitly as "Trinitarian." The claims of Karl Barth concerning the Holy Trinity as the immediate implication of revelation initially fueled this search. Other factors such as the charismatic movement, which raised the question of the precise identity of the Holy Spirit, the biblical theology movement (allied to the historical-critical method) within the Roman Catholic Church, and the modern emphasis upon supposed "community" within the Godhead (to foster and justify community action on earth and to counter "individualism") have added further momentum.

In this chapter we shall notice five approaches to the question of the relation of the church doctrine/dogma of the Trinity, which was explained in the last chapter, to the content of the New Testament.

A.W. WAINWRIGHT

Perhaps the most-used textbook in the 1960s and 1970s on the biblical basis of the doctrine of the Holy Trinity was *The Trinity in the New Testament* (1962) by the Englishman, Arthur W. Wainwright. Its purpose was to trace "the emergence of the problem of the Trinity" in New Testament times. So chapter 1 is devoted to explaining "the problem of the Trinity." The problem concerns (1) how the Father and Son could both be God and yet God still be truly one, and (2) whether or not the Spirit is a Person and, if so, then whether God is in some sense threefold rather than twofold. "It is our task," he wrote, "to investigate whether the New Testament writers themselves were aware of the problem, either in the form of the relationship between Father and Son, or in that of the relationship between Father, Son and Spirit."[1]

Wainwright argues that the problem of the Trinity was in the minds of certain writers of the New Testament and that they made an attempt to answer it. However, none of their writings was written specifically to deal with it, and the evidence or signs that a writer has faced it are incidental. Since, in Wainwright's judgment, there is no systematic answer to the problem aimed at producing a distinct doctrine, he preferred the word "problem" to "doctrine" when speaking of the theological content of the New Testament. He fully acknowledges that in the second, and even more so in the third, centuries the problem was fully faced and a doctrine was created (e.g., by Tertullian)—a doctrine which was itself subject to development as further thought was given to it.

So Wainwright makes the comment: "Naturally a problem must be clarified before it can be answered. In the New Testament it is easier to see the first attempts to clarify the problem than the first attempts to answer it. But an answer begins to emerge and it would be misleading to say that trinitarian theology is entirely post-biblical."[2]

This beginnings of an answer or doctrine within the New Testament to the "problem" of the relations of the Father, the Son, and the Holy Spirit is found, however, not in philosophical, metaphysical discussions of the nature of God, but in declarations and expositions of the creating, saving, and sanctifying work of the Father, the Son, and the Holy Spirit. Wainwright insists that the biblical authors were more interested in the activity than the nature of God. Thus, for example, since they held that Christ shared in the divine activities of creator, savior, and judge, they could not wholly avoid thinking about his relation to the Father.

Further, "the problem of the Trinity" cannot be faced without noting the way and content of worship in the apostolic churches. Clearly all the evidence points to the Father being worshiped through the Son and in the Holy Spirit, or, the Son being worshiped in and by the Holy Spirit. Wainwright is well aware of the mutual influence of worship upon the development of doctrine and of doctrine upon (and thus influencing the content of) worship both in the period of the New Testament and afterward.

The book is divided into four parts. In the first part Wainwright briefly looks at the Old Testament and of "plurality in unity" with respect to God. The second part is the longest and deals with the evidence for the divinity of Christ. In the third brief part the evidence for the divinity of the Holy Spirit is collected. Finally, in part four the rise of the trinitarian problem is presented.

At the end of the book, Wainwright summarizes his conclusions.

> The problem of the Trinity was being raised and answered in the New Testament. It arose because of the development of Christian experience, worship, and thought. It was rooted in experience, for men were conscious of the power of the Spirit and the presence and Lordship of the risen Christ. It was rooted in worship, because men worshipped in the Spirit, offered their prayers to God the Father through Christ, and sometimes worshipped Christ himself. It was rooted in thought, because the writers tackled first the Christological problem, and then, at any rate in the Fourth Gospel, the threefold problem. The whole matter was based on the life and resurrection of Jesus himself, who received the Spirit during his earthly life and imparted the Spirit to others after his resurrection.[3]

He believes that his investigations show that a biblical doctrine of God can begin with an account of the names and titles of the Father, the Son, and the Holy Spirit along with their divine functions and mutual relations. However, he recognizes that such an account of the Three in One or the Three as One cannot be summarized in any pithy formula. Thus, whatever doctrine of the Trinity there is in the Scripture, it is neither complete nor definitive but it is nevertheless present and real. This means that the later, developed church doctrine of the Holy Trinity can be seen as a continuation of that search for precision in the doctrine of God, which began in the New Testament.

So for Wainwright, the ecclesiastical doctrine of the Trinity is more the completion of rather than the first principle of the theological system.

G.W.H. LAMPE

Dr. Lampe, once Regius Professor of Divinity at Cambridge University, and the final editor of the *Patristic Greek Lexicon,* concludes his book *God as Spirit* (1977) with these words:

> I believe in the Divinity of our Lord and Savior Jesus Christ, in the sense that the one God, the Creator and Savior Spirit, revealed himself and acted decisively for us in Jesus. I believe in the Divinity of the Holy Ghost, in the sense that the same one God, the Creator and Savior Spirit, is here and now not far from every one of us; for in him we live and move, in him we have our being, in us, if we consent to know and trust him, he will create the Christlike harvest: love, joy, peace, patience, kindness, goodness, fidelity, gentleness, and self control.[4]

This sounds attractive. However, in terms of the classic orthodoxy of the patristic period, Lampe must be judged as a unitarian and an adoptionist. First of all, he believes that God is one Person, not three, and that the Spirit is simply the unipersonal God. That is, the Father is the Spirit and the Spirit is the Father in his activity toward, and within, the world. In the second place, he believes that Jesus is simply a man in whom God as Spirit was uniquely and incomparably active. Thus he denies that Jesus was preexistent before his human birth and insists that talk of incarnation is just mythology.

Lampe is able to come to this conclusion because of the way he interprets the New Testament. He does not deny that there is evidence within the documents that the early Christians believed in the personal preexistence of Jesus as well as in his continued "post-existence" as the resurrected and ascended Lord, who will come again. However, he follows the extreme wing of form criticism in modern biblical scholarship and attributes this belief and related ones to mistaken judgments made within the early church concerning the real identity of Jesus of Nazareth. In fact, Lampe uses his great scholarship to show the part that the concepts of preexistence and post-existence played in the attempts by the church in its earliest days to give expression to its memories and experience of Jesus Christ. Nevertheless, he concludes that these attempts were all based on a colossal, initial error!

What the early church ought to have realized and taught, he suggests, was that God is Spirit and that everything that is vital and good in Christianity can be adequately understood and experienced within this belief. "I believe," writes Lampe, "that the Trinitarian model is in the end less satisfactory for the articulation of our basic Christian experience than the unifying concept of God as Spirit."[5]

So for Lampe the doctrine of the Trinity is not essential to the Christian Faith, and what he attractively presents is a modern expression of the old liberal theology of the nineteenth century.

C.F.D. MOULE

Dr. C.F.D. Moule was the Lady Margaret's Professor of Divinity at Cambridge University and a colleague of Dr. Lampe. His views on whether or not the New Testament contains a doctrine of plurality within the unity of God are found in his book, *The Holy Spirit* (1978), and in an article, "The New Testament and the Doctrine of the Trinity," published in *The Expository Times*.

As is clear in his important study, *The Origin of Christology* (1977), Moule has a very high estimate of Jesus Christ. In fact, as the two studies mentioned above demonstrate, he holds that the New Testament points to a relation between God (the Father) and Christ such as suggests that (in later Nicene terms) the *homoousios* rightly reflects the implications of New Testament experience.

Moule brings our attention to what he considers to be the two primary and impressive "pointers" to the deity of Jesus Christ. "The first is the fact that, in the greetings of the Pauline epistles, God and Christ are brought into a single formula," and he adds that, "It requires an effort of imagination to grasp the enormity that this must have seemed to a non-Christian Jew."[6] In these greetings formulae, God and Christ together are actually the origin of divine blessings to Christians.

The second is "the fact that Paul seems to experience Christ as any theist reckons to understand God — that is, as personal but as more than an individual: as more than *a* person."[7] Moule has in mind the incorporative formulae — "in Christ" and "in the Lord" — which point to this "more than a person" and "more than an individual" dimension, and thus to preexistence and to the deity of the Son before space and time.

Because of these "pointers" and other evidence, Moule is ready to state that there is "a conception of God as differentiated unity, as unity in plurality — unity in at least duality." He has no doubt that as a minimum there is a binitarian conception of God in the New Testament. However, he is unable to take the further step and claim that there is a trinitarian conception of God in the New Testament. "What is not clear," he writes, "is that the Spirit is distinguishable from God [the Father] in the way in which Christ is distinguishable from both God and the Spirit."[8] He accepts that the New Testament furnishes evidence that Christians described their experience of God in "triple terms," but he doubts whether these statements actually point to "an eternal threefold differentiation within the Deity" in the same way as the experience of Christ points to an eternal, binitarian dialogue therein.

At the end of chapter 4 of *The Holy Spirit*, Moule writes: "When Spirit is the mode of God's presence in the hearts and minds of his people, then there is a good case for personal language [with respect to the Spirit]. But this still does not force upon us a third eternal 'Person' (in the technical sense) within the Unity [of God]." Then in the final lines of the same chapter he wrote:

Christian experience led to the recognition of at least two distinguishable "modes" of God's presence with men: the "mode," namely, in which Christ was experienced as Mediator, and Christians incorporated in him; and the "mode" in which the Holy Spirit was found in and among Christians, interpreting Christ and creating his likeness in them. It is thus intelligible that the Church came to speak of God as eternally Father, Son and Spirit. But threefoldness is, perhaps, less vital to a Christian conception of God than the eternal twofoldness of Father and Son.[9]

For Moule, it is sufficient to say that the Spirit is the presence of the personal God. And like Lampe, he is somewhat impatient of the later ecclesiastical distinctions in the formulation of the dogma of the Holy Trinity.

So Moule does not see the doctrine of the Trinity as either the first principle of, or the completion of the Christian theological system. He belongs to that movement of "modern" biblical theology which interprets the New Testament without reference to the way it was understood in the second, third, and fourth centuries of the Christian era.[10]

ROYCE G. GRUENLER AND CORNELIUS PLANTINGA, JR.

Royce G. Gruenler (Gordon-Conwell Theological Seminary) is an evangelical biblical scholar and the author of *The Trinity in the Gospel of John* (1986). One of his aims is to present what he has discovered in John's Gospel concerning the living God. He calls this the "social nature" of God, "the divine Community," "the divine Household," "the Triune Community," and the "Triune Society." However, he admits that, before studying this Gospel afresh, he has been impressed by the emphasis upon the social nature of reality in process philosophy and theology, as well as by the exposition of the social nature of God by Leonard Hodgson in *The Doctrine of the Trinity*.

With respect to methodology, he admits the influence of Michael Polanyi (see his *Personal Knowledge*, 1964) and writes:

I have used an exegetical approach that owes a consider-
able debt to the critical analysis intention of persons,
particularly in regard to the disclosures of their intention
in speech and action. What I have tried to do is to look
and see and listen and try to understand what Jesus is
doing and saying in the Gospel of John, and what he is
intending to convey to his audience in regard to his relationship with the Father and the Holy Spirit, and with the
new community comprised of his followers. This exegetical
approach aims to be primarily descriptive of the speech,
actions, and intentions of Jesus in the fourth Gospel, with a
view to understanding what he is saying about the divine
Community and the new community of believers.[11]

Though he uses the word "community" in virtually every
page of his book, Gruenler never defends the choice of this word
to describe the Holy Trinity. He simply assumes (along with a
growing chorus of modern writers) that it is appropriate and
meaningful. Therefore, he proceeds with this explanation:

As a historian and exegete with Christian convictions, I
find that noteworthy and distinguishing characteristics of
the Triune Community emerge in Jesus' dialogues, and
that an exegesis of the dialogues brings a new understanding of the social nature of God and the way in
which New Testament life and ethics are grounded in
the nature of the divine Triunity. Reflecting the divine
Household, the household of the church is to demonstrate God's social nature and hospitality and being there
at the disposal of others.

And he continues by claiming:

Perhaps most impressive is the discovery that Jesus described how Father, Son and Spirit defer to one another
and are at each other's disposal, and how they are
redemptively at the disposal of the new community of
disciples. Accordingly, the ultimate grounding of Christian life and behavior is seen to be in the social life and
behavior of the persons of the divine Family who are
there for one another in essential Triunity.[12]

In his exegesis of specific passages, Gruenler notes how mutual loving, generosity, glorification, equality, availability, disposability, and deference "characterize the divine Family in the Gospel as a whole."

Perhaps the most appropriate judgment on this book is to say that it claims too much and is not sufficiently careful in the use of social analogies for God. While the German word, *gemeinschaft* (meaning either corporate fellowship or community or both) is a word which perhaps may be used of the Holy Trinity, the American word "community" does not have the richness of meaning of the German word. In order not to cause confusion, it is better to use "communion of Persons" when speaking of the Holy Trinity.

Cornelius Plantinga, Jr. (Calvin Theological Seminary) is an evangelical systematic theologian, whose doctoral thesis at Princeton in 1982 was on the "social analogy of the Trinity." An important essay by him, "Social Trinity and Tritheism," appears in a collection of essays entitled, *Trinity, Incarnation and Atonement* (1989). As the title suggests, it is a defense of the social analogy of the Trinity against the charge of tritheism.

After considering the New Testament evidence, claims Plantinga, "a person who extrapolated theologically from Hebrews, Paul and John would naturally develop a social theory of the Trinity." Therefore, he proposes such a theory.

> The Holy Trinity is a divine, transcendent society or community of three fully personal and fully divine entities: the Father, the Son and the Holy Spirit or Paraclete. These three are wonderfully unified by their common divinity, that is, by the possession by each [one of them] of the whole generic divine essence – including, for instance, the properties of everlastingness and of sublimely great knowledge, love and glory. The persons are also unified by their joint redemptive purpose, revelation, and work. Their knowledge and love are directed not only to their creatures, but also primordially and archetypally to each other. The Father loves the Son and the Son [loves] the Father.

And to this he adds the following comment:

Extrapolating beyond explicit New Testament teaching, let us say that the Father and Son love the Spirit and the Spirit [loves] the Father and Son. The Trinity is thus a zestful, wondrous community of divine light, love, joy, mutuality and verve.[13]

We may also note that Dr. Plantinga uses the word *person* of each of the Three and tells us that he uses it "in a rich sense," by which he means that each of the Three is "a distinct center of consciousness." Yet he vigorously denies that this means belief in three "autonomous persons" or in three "independent persons."

Though Plantinga is more careful in his use of words and analogies concerning the living God than is Gruenler, he also allows his imagination to be overactive when he speaks of God as "a zestful, wondrous community." However, both writers are aware of the differences between the Barthian approach and the "Social Analogy" school of such recent writers as Leonard Hodgson and, while adopting the general approach of the latter, are also influenced by the former.

ANTHONY KELLY

Anthony Kelly is a Roman Catholic who has written *The Trinity of Love: A Theology of the Christian God* (1989). His method of reading the New Testament for Trinitarian doctrine is found in his chapter, "The Scriptural Foundations," where he presents four ways in which the books of the New Testament actually provide data for a doctrine of the Trinity, which he recognizes to be (in a full sense) an achievement of the post-apostolic church. We shall notice each of these ways.

The Rhetoric of Trinitarian Expression
By rhetoric Kelly means the creative effort of the writers of the New Testament (and of their fellow Christians in the church) to express in words their experience of God in Christ. "The awareness of momentous events provokes a search for the right words in a kind of verbal celebration of the transformation that has occurred, and to give it enduring public meaning. The wording

of the 'New' reality that has taken place in Christ is a complex linguistic event."[14]

The early Christians were aware not only of believing in Jesus Christ as the Lord but also of being "in Christ" as they "walked in the Spirit." They looked to him as the resurrected Lord and they experienced life and fellowship in "his Body." They learned to read the Hebrew Scriptures in terms of this Lord Jesus Christ, who had fulfilled the Law and the Prophets and the Psalms. So they spoke of Jesus in the terms available to them from the Scriptures — he is the Word of God, the Wisdom of God, the Son of God, the Messiah, and so on. Further, they knew that Jesus as Lord is intimately related to Yahweh, the God of Israel, and to the Spirit of Yahweh, who dwells in the church.

The vocabulary of the Hebrew Scriptures was not sufficient to do justice to the full reality of the New Covenant. So the early Christians began to express what we may call a trinitarian consciousness through the use of triadic formulations. In coming into words within the New Testament in a variety of places and forms of the triad of the Father, the Son, and the Holy Spirit was the natural expression of a Faith which could not remain within the terms of the Shema — "the Lord our God is one Lord and you shall love the Lord your God" (Deut. 6:4-5). The most familiar of these triadic expressions is "the grace of the Lord Jesus Christ [the Son], and the love of God [the Father] and the fellowship of the Holy Spirit" (2 Cor. 13:14), but this is only one amongst many.

The rhetoric is also to be seen in what Kelly calls "iconic" and "schematic" forms. By "iconic" he means such pictorial incidents as the baptism of Jesus (where the Father speaks, the Holy Spirit descends, and the Son hears and receives — Mark 1:9ff), and the conception of Jesus (where the Father sends the archangel and the Holy Spirit and where the eternal Son descends and unites to himself human nature in the womb of Mary by the Holy Spirit — Luke 1:32-35).

By "schematic" he means the general construction of major sections of Pauline letters (e.g., Rom. and Eph.), where there is the movement of salvation from the Father through the Son and in the Holy Spirit, and where there is the movement of response to the Father, through the Son, and in the Spirit. More particularly, he means the content of the Gospel of John, where we read so often of the Father and the Son and of the communion between them; further, we read in the same text of the Holy Spirit who proceeds from the Father at the request of the Son as the second Paraclete (see particularly John 16:12-16).

The Trinitarian Narrative

Learning from the modern school of theology called "narrative theology," Kelly asserts that the biblical narrative contains three stories or three versions of one story. Obviously, it is the story of the people of God, the old and new Israel, and of their history and experiences through space and time. It is the story of Abraham and Sarah, Isaac, Moses, Joshua, Deborah, David, Solomon, Isaiah, Jeremiah, John the Baptist, Jesus, Mary, Peter, Paul, and many others.

Yet the "inner criterion for the meaningfulness of this narrative, the whole reason for its telling, is that it deals with the activity and character of the one, true God."[15] The history of God's people lives from the "biography of God." And this God is the God who creates the world and then he elects, loves, and cares for his people. To them he sent his only Son, who lived, died, and rose from the dead and ascended into heaven for them. To them he sent his Spirit, who indwells them and guides them and leads them into all truth.

Apart from being a good story, the narrative becomes to those who read it as believers (united in the Holy Spirit to the Lord Jesus) a personal communication. In fact, Christians are wholly involved in this story because they are brought into union with the Father, through the Son, and in the Holy Spirit. The story, which is ultimately the story of the Holy Trinity, becomes their story. They are involved in the divine autobiography.

Trinitarian Symbolism

Kelly refers to the name of "the Father, Son and Holy Spirit" as being three biblical symbols, which are correlated in a dramatic interplay in the New Testament. He writes:

> They exist in a unified symbol-system meant to disclose the identity and saving presence of the One God. The

Father/Son symbolism is most clearly correlated. It discloses a communion of life, mutual knowledge, common will and reciprocal revelation as the Son reveals the Father and as the Father acclaims the Son and draws all to him. The Father and the Son, in different but related ways, give the Spirit. And the Spirit inspires new relationships to each of them. In this dynamic interplay of the symbols of God, the one relational and communitarian divine mystery is evoked.[16]

And he makes the point that this interplay of symbols occurs in the proclamation and embodiment of the reign of God by Jesus Christ. "The God of Jesus, the God who works in him, is intent on the healing and liberation of human beings."[17] So the religious imagination is challenged by the symbolism of a non-patriarchalist Father, by a Son who calls him "Abba," and by a Holy Spirit who destroys Satan's power.

Trinitarian Experience

Kelly believes that there are three interrelated levels of experience brought to expression in the New Testament — that of the early church, that of the disciples who were the primary witnesses to the Resurrection and, most mysteriously, the experience of Jesus himself.

(1) To expound the experience of the early church, Kelly makes use of the much quoted definition from Clifford Geertz of religious existence, which is:

A system of symbols which acts to establish powerful, pervasive and long-lasting moods and motivations in men, by formulating conceptions of a general order of existence and clothing these conceptions with such an aura of factuality that the moods and motivations seem uniquely realistic.[18]

So (a) the system of symbols is "Father, Son, and Holy Spirit"; (b) the moods and motivations are the cumulative sense of the "new" — the Incarnation, the Gift of the Spirit; (c) the conceptions of existence are the revealed plans of the Father whose will it is to bring all things to their fulfillment in Christ

Jesus; and (d) the aura of factuality is the conviction that the Father has been truly revealed by the Son and made known in the Spirit.

The experience of the church within this sense of religious existence is first of all in terms of "Spirit." There is a profound consciousness of new life and of new relationships — to the Father, to Jesus Christ, to the fellowship of Christians, and so on. Then there is a vital sense of mission inspired and guided by the Spirit — as portrayed in the Book of Acts.

In the second place the experience of the church is being addressed and spoken to "through the Son" (Heb. 1:2). In many various ways Yahweh-Elohim spoke in time past but now, they knew, he spoke in a vitally new way through his Son.

Thirdly, there is the experience of knowing God intimately, yet in reverence, as the Father of Jesus Christ and praying, "Abba."

Therefore, says Kelly, the early church had the vivid impression of God being with us in the Son, within us in the Spirit, and all-embracingly around and above us as the Father.

(2) To expound the experience of God in Jesus of the first disciples, who were with Jesus before and after his death and resurrection, Kelly makes use of a psychological reconstruction by Sebastian Moore in his book, *The Fire and the Rose Are One.* Kelly approves Moore's attempt to indicate an approach "to a grassroots derivation of the Trinity," and quotes these lines:

> For the understanding, the meaning of "God" is shaped by a person's psychological state. Thus while a person is still in guilt, "God" is to him the jealous, all-dominating one, the threat to man's fragile existence. For the disciples of Jesus, this "God" dies with the collapse of the Jesus movement. The "God" they next encounter, the next divine affective focus, is Jesus as a power stronger than death. As the meaning of this sinks in, they are able to experience the original God not as jealous or domineering, but as loving, as bringing us into immortal life. Finally, the sense of the sheer vitality of God can burst upon the soul and be named "Holy Spirit." Thus the matrix of the images of the divine persons in the "infinite

connection" as it undergoes the transformation of the encounter with the risen Jesus.[19]

Kelly holds that though such an interpretation is evocative rather than textually analytical, it does seem a reasonable account of what was going on in and with the disciples.

(3) The experience of Jesus himself is the most difficult of all to identify. However, it seems reasonably clear from the Gospel records that he was conscious of a unique and exclusive communion with the Father, whom he called "my Father." Further, it also seems clear that he was conscious of being possessed and indwelt, also in an unique and exclusive way, by the Spirit of the Lord. Kelly quotes with approval the words of James D.G. Dunn.

> Jesus thought of himself as God's Son and as anointed by the eschatological Spirit, because in prayer he experienced God as Father, and in ministry, he experienced the power to heal which he could only understand as the power of the end-time and as inspiration to proclaim a message which he could only understand as the gospel of the end-time.[20]

So the doctrine of the Trinity is "the conceptual unfolding of Jesus' conscious identity and of the mystery enacted through him."

It is of interest to compare the way Kelly proceeds with the way Roman Catholic theologians proceeded before the Second Vatican Council (1962–1965). For example, books on the doctrine of the Trinity by Joseph Pohle (1919) and Felix Klein (1940) see the doctrine delivered in propositional form within the New Testament books. In fact, the doctrine is seen as a part of the immediate deposit of faith. Between Klein and Pohle on the one hand, and Kelly (and modern Catholics) on the other, is the adoption of the historical-critical method by Roman Catholic scholars. Therefore, the New Testament is now most usually interpreted as supplying data for the development of the doctrine by the church after the apostolic period.

SUMMARY AND COMMENT

Each of the positions summarized above is found today in a similar or related form either in the teaching or in the liturgies of the various denominations. The basically conservative position represented by Wainwright, that the New Testament contains the recognition, if not the developed doctrine, of God as Holy Trinity, continues to be held by those who have a high regard for the authority of the New Testament. For example, the Baptist scholar, Ralph P. Martin, writes that "the doctrine of the Trinity is only embryonic in the New Testament literature" and that the New Testament "reflecting Christian experience gained in worship, provides the raw materials for the later dogma."[21] In contrast, Lampe's presentation of the unitarian doctrine that God is Spirit, together with the rejection of the full authority of the New Testament and the preexistence of Christ, is becoming increasingly common in the large liberal denominations, sometimes expressing itself as modalism or deism or even pantheism/panentheism.

Moule's view that binitarianism is clearly taught but that trinitarianism is not clearly (if at all) presented in the New Testament, probably is the view of not a few scholarly as well as pious folk. Certainly it is easy to appreciate such a position (which is essentially conservative) if the New Testament is interpreted without reference to the development of doctrine in the early church. In chapter 6 we shall make use of an important study of the origins of binitarianism in the New Testament by Larry W. Hurtado — *One God, One Lord: Early Christian Devotion and Ancient Christian Monotheism* (1988).

The doctrine of the social Trinity seems to be gaining acceptance in the liberal Protestant denominations as well as in the Roman Catholic Church. However, it is usually in a less traditional form than presented by Gruenler and Plantinga. Its growing popularity has to do with its usefulness in providing a model for community on earth. Therefore, it can be adapted by feminist, liberationist, political, as well as conservative activists to commend one or another version of human community as based on the way God actually exists as God (or the threefold way God is experienced by people on earth). One attractive presentation of this from a feminist perspective is Catherine M. LaCugna, *God for Us* (1992).

The position developed by Kelly represents the view of many Roman Catholics who hold to the development of doctrine in the church. In the New Testament are the various seeds and themes which, it is held, will develop under the guidance of the Lord of the church into fully developed doctrines/dogmas. With reference to the doctrine of the Holy Trinity, the seeds and themes of the New Testament reached their dogmatic expression in the Creeds of the Councils of Nicea and Constantinople and in later conciliar statements.

So we see that among scholars who are prepared to state that they are Trinitarians and that the confession of God as the Unity in Trinity/Trinity in Unity is fundamental to the Christian religion there is no clear agreement as to whether or not there is a formal doctrine of God as the Holy Trinity, that is, a threefold plurality in unity, anywhere in the New Testament. Some claim that there is such a doctrine therein, even though it is undeveloped and embryonic, lacking the intellectual clarity of the later church doctrine of *three hypostaseis in one ousia* (three persons in one substance). Others are ready to admit that there is an awareness by the apostolic writers of the problem that God is a plurality in unity—be it a binitarian or a trinitarian unity—and that this problem surfaces at specific points (e.g., the baptism of Jesus) and in various ways (e.g., in liturgical formulae). Yet others see no plurality in the unity of God at all: they see only a fuller revelation of the identity and character of the one, true God given through Jesus Christ and in/by the Holy Spirit.

In the light of this situation, it is necessary for me to be clear concerning my use of terminology when I am presenting my own interpretation rather than citing those of others. When I write of *the doctrine* or *the dogma* of the Trinity I am thinking specifically of the formal statements by the church of the Fathers: in particular, I am thinking of the teaching within the Creeds—the Niceno-Constantinopolitan Creed (381) and the later Athanasian Creed *(Quicunque Vult)*. In these cases there is formal doctrine, which is precise and which is stated so as to exclude alternative but erroneous possibilities (e.g., that of Arianism).

I do not believe that there is a precise or formal doctrine of the Trinity in the New Testament materials. At the same time, I do think that the whole of the New Testament bears witness— mostly implicitly but sometimes explicitly—to the plurality within unity of the one true God, Yahweh-Elohim. So I can say with Arthur Wainwright that the writers of the New Testament were aware of the problem of the Trinity and were moving toward a doctrine of the same; but, the word "problem" does not seem an appropriate term to describe this gracious and uplifting theme in the minds of the writers. I can also comfortably join George Tavard and speak of the "vision of the Trinity" (the title of his book): at least the word "vision" indicates that the writers were aware of more than they were able, ready, or desirous of expressing in words.

My own preference is to speak of the writers of the New Testament as having a "sense" or "conviction" or "conscious-ness" of a wonderful and mysterious plurality within the unity of God. This spiritual knowledge of God, the Father, through his Son, and in/by his Spirit, surfaces and is expressed in a variety of ways in their writings. This is because it is embedded in their Christian experience and is expressed in their corporate worship and personal piety. However, they did not explore or develop their convictions concerning the plurality within unity in a full, intellectual sense. Their concentration and emphasis were to de-clare and to explain the Gospel of God (the Father) concerning his Son (Jesus Christ) as they were guided and empowered by the Holy Spirit. So they provide much information about the eternal God, Yahweh-Elohim, as he is turned toward the world in the work of creation, redemption, and sanctification. In partic-ular they speak much of Jesus of Nazareth as the One in whom God is revealed and active. That is, within the statement of this divine activity and energy, they speak of the relations of the Father and the Son, the Son and the Father, the Father and the Spirit, the Son and the Spirit. Yet, while experience of God is the experience of the Father, the Son, and the Holy Spirit, there is no formal doctrine of Yahweh-Elohim as a Trinity in Unity and Unity in Trinity.

The Hebrew Bible (thus also the Septuagint and the Old Testament) bears witness to Yahweh-Elohim, Creator, Redeem-er, and Judge. In Part Two it will be our task to pay attention to this witness and to see how the mysterious plurality within the unique unity of this living God is made known to Christian readers. We shall experience the results of believing that "the New is in the Old concealed, the Old is by the New revealed."

FOR FURTHER READING

Berkhof, Hendrikus. *The Doctrine of the Holy Spirit*. Atlanta: John Knox, 1964.

Gruenler, Royce G. *The Trinity in the Gospel of John: A Thematic Commentary on the Fourth Gospel*. Grand Rapids: Eerdmans, 1986.

Hodgson, Leonard. *The Doctrine of the Trinity*. New York: Scribner's, 1944.

Hurtado, Larry W. *One God, One Lord: Early Christian Devotion and Ancient Jewish Monotheism*. Philadelphia: Fortress, 1988.

Kelly, Anthony. *The Trinity of Love: A Theology of the Christian God*. Wilmington, Del.: Michael Glazier, 1989.

Klein, Felix. *The Doctrine of the Trinity*. New York: Kenedy, 1940.

Lampe, G.W.H. *God as Spirit: The Bampton Lectures, 1976*. Oxford: Clarendon, 1977.

Moule, C.F.D. "The New Testament and the Doctrine of the Trinity," *The Expository Times* 78/1 (October 1976): 16-21.

_____. *The Holy Spirit*. Grand Rapids: Eerdmans, 1978.

Plantinga, Cornelius, Jr. "Social Trinity and Tritheism," in *Trinity, Incarnation and Atonement: Philosophical and Theological Essays*. Edited by Ronald J. Feenstra and Cornelius Plantinga, Jr. Notre Dame, Ind.: Univ. of Notre Dame Press, 1989.

Pohle, Joseph. *The Divine Trinity*, St. Louis: Herder, 1919.

Tavard, George H. *The Vision of the Trinity*. Washington, D.C.: Univ. Press of America, 1981.

Wainwright, A.W. *The Trinity in the New Testament*. London: S.P.C.K., 1962.

Welch, Claude. *In This Name: The Doctrine of the Trinity in Contemporary Theology*. New York: Scribner's, 1952.

PART TWO

THE WITNESS

OF THE

OLD TESTAMENT

4

YHWH—

THE ONE AND ONLY GOD

In this and the next chapter it will be our task to look at the Old Testament and Judaism to see both the clear statement of the unity of God and the hints at the plurality within God. Here we shall begin with a general description of the Jewish monotheism which Jesus and his first disciples received from their parents. This will prepare us to look at the Jewish Scriptures.

MONOTHEISM

Central to the consciousness of Judaism at the time of Jesus was the *Shema,* the most famous of Jewish prayers and taken from the Torah, "Hear, O Israel: YHWH our God is one YHWH; and you shall love YHWH your God with all your heart, and with all your soul, and with all your might" (Deut. 6:4). Although any general definition of first-century Jewish monotheism must begin from this text/prayer, it will not end with it for it will include reference to YHWH and the cosmos, YHWH and history/providence, and YHWH and the election of Israel.

Jewish monotheism was not henotheism—the belief that there are other gods, but the Jews worship only their own God.

For Jews the gods of the nations and of the heathen pantheons were idols. YHWH is not merely above them, but he is the one and only God, who is the Creator of the heavens and the earth. Further, he is active in his world. Such dynamic monotheism contrasts with pantheism for YHWH is not the impersonal universal deity which permeates and characterizes all that is (i.e., not the pantheism taught by the Stoics). He has created and upholds all that is, but he is entirely separate from the cosmos. Likewise Jewish monotheism also is not to be confused with any form of Gnosticism which teaches that the physical world was made by a supernatural being (a "god") distinct from the "supreme God." In the words of the psalmist: "For great is YHWH, and greatly to be praised; he is to be feared above all gods. For all the gods of the peoples are idols, but YHWH made the heavens" (Ps. 96:4-5).

YHWH is supremely alone outside space and time in his transcendence and wonderfully present within space and time in his immanence.

As the Creator of the heavens and the earth, YHWH is the One who works in and through both natural and supernatural events. He is not remote, far removed from his people in a distant heavenly abode. Further, the Jewish belief in angels, which apparently intensified in the intertestamental period, points not (as some mistakenly suppose) to an absent or detached God, who sends mediators. Rather, it points to the actual involvement of YHWH through heavenly messengers both in his creation and with his people. As the prophet declared: "I form light and create darkness, I make weal and create woe, I am YHWH, who do all these things" (Isa. 45:7).

YHWH is the God who is wholly involved in history as the God of providence.

Jewish monotheism is not only creational and providential, but also covenantal. That is, not only is YHWH the Creator and Preserver of the world who will cleanse and restore his creation, but he will do so through his elect people, Israel. Thus the prayer to YHWH: "Look down from thy holy habitation, from heaven, and bless thy people Israel and the ground which thou hast given us, as thou didst swear to our fathers" (Deut. 26:15). And thus the statement: "YHWH has declared . . . that you are a people for his own possession, as he has promised you . . . that he will set you high above all nations that he has made, in praise and in fame and in honor, and that you shall be a people holy to YHWH your God, as he has spoken" (Deut. 26:18-19).

This form of monotheism was strengthened in the heathen world by the stories in the Jewish Scriptures of pagans actually coming to acknowledge YHWH as the one, true God (see 2 Kings 5:15-18 [Naaman]; Zech. 8:22-23; Dan. 2:47; 3:28; 4:2-3, 34-37 [Nebuchadnezzar]) and of YHWH doing battle with pagan gods and defeating them (see 1 Sam. 5:1-5; 17:26, 36, 45-46; Isa. 37:23; 1 Macc. 4:30-33). From the watchtowers of Israel, it was announced, "YHWH has bared his holy arm before the eyes of all the nations; and all the ends of the earth shall see the salvation of our God" (Isa. 52:10). The defeat of Babylon is here the cause for rejoicing!

The Jews claimed to be the covenant people of YHWH, the Creator, Sustainer, and Director of the heavens and earth. They held that their God, precisely because he is the Creator and the covenant Lord, would one day, the day of YHWH, act to put the whole cosmos right and place his elect people in a right relation to himself freed from all oppression and tribulation.

What we need to be aware of, as we reflect on the origin of the doctrine of the Holy Trinity, is that it is this very Jewish belief and worldview of monotheism, which caused the majority of Jews to reject not only the claims of Christianity but also the claims of Stoicism, Epicureanism, paganism, and Gnosticism as well in the first century. Because Jewish monotheism emphasized so intently the unity and oneness of YHWH, it could not entertain the claim that the man, Jesus Christ, actually is the complete self-revelation of God. So the Jewish rabbis said of Christians that they both know YHWH and at the same time deny him!

Certainly Christianity possessed the same Scriptures as did Judaism and certainly Christianity believed in YHWH, the one God, as did Judaism. However, Christians read the Scriptures as those who believed not only that Jesus of Nazareth is the Messiah of the Jews, but that he is also the full revelation of God in human flesh. By his resurrection from the dead, he has been vindicated as the Messiah by YHWH, and he has been raised to the right hand of the Father in heaven. In fact, we can state that the Christian claim from the beginning was that YHWH, the Creator of the world, who is the God of Abraham, Moses, and Elijah, has revealed himself uniquely through Jesus in a way which necessarily sets aside both pagan claims concerning the gods and Jewish definitions of the Unity of YHWH.

At this point and before we turn to the Old Testament to look for any indication of YHWH as a Trinity in Unity therein, we need to be aware of the discussion among scholars concerning Jewish teaching about possible intermediaries between God and his covenant people. One major question in debate has been whether Jewish monotheism was compromised by reason of teaching in the intertestamental period concerning: (a) the personification and/or hypostatization of the Word and Wisdom of God; (b) the development of belief in the hierarchy of angels and archangels; and (c) the attributing to great patriarchs of the past (e.g., Enoch and Moses) a present mediating role before God in heaven. Another question in debate has been whether or not the confession of the resurrected Jesus as the exalted Lord and Mediator by the first Christians was basically a continuation of the supposed Jewish doctrine of divine agents as intermediaries.

The position adopted in this book (following Larry Hurtado and N.T. Wright) is that, after the exile in Babylon and under the Greek and Roman Empires, there was certainly an increase in Jewish speculation concerning the Word and Wisdom of God as well as concerning intercessory and mediating roles for patriarchs and angels. However, this absorbing interest does not in any obvious way diminish the transcendence, majesty, and Unity of the One God. Rather, it highlights and underlines the immanence and omnipresence of this One living God in his creation — present through his Spirit, Word, Wisdom, messengers, and intercessors. Further, this speculative teaching serves to illustrate the search for the truth of God, who he really is; and, in doing so, it points to the culmination of that search in the Revelation by God himself through Jesus Christ that he, YHWH, is a Plurality in Unity, the Holy Trinity.

In this chapter our subject matter will necessarily include focusing upon "the angel of the Lord." And my position will be essentially that of George F. Knight who wrote:

There is no evidence in the OT that the conception of angels is a late one. Some scholars have maintained that in the post-exilic period the God of the Hebrews grew more and more remote from Israel and finally became transcendent alone. The conception of intermediaries between God and man, they maintain, had to be introduced. It is true that a proliferation of angels is a mark of the period of the apocryphal books, and that the hierarchical ranks and even the names of leading angels may have entered Judaism from the east through Persian influence. . . . But the conception that God could be represented on earth by an angel is as old as some of the oldest extant literature of the OT that we possess.[1]

Thus we proceed on the assumption that angels and in particular, the "angel of the Lord," truly appeared to the patriarchs.

TWO APPROACHES TO THE OLD TESTAMENT

In the last decade of the twentieth century, many Christians are not sure how they should read the Old Testament. Are they to read it on its own terms according to the principles of historical science, or as a kind of preparatory book for the New Testament? To read it on its own terms seems to harmonize with our modern sense of development and progress in history; and virtually all the academic books devoted to the study of the Old Testament appear to point in this direction. From this "scientific" perspective, to read the Old Testament as preparation for the New Testament can seem to be unscientific and irrational as well as overly spiritual or pietistic. However, in the historic churches where an ancient Liturgy is used and the Old Testament is read according to the traditional Lectionary, then the operative principle is that the Old Testament definitely contains a preparation for Jesus Christ, and is rightly understood in this way.

We note then that there are two basic ways of reading those books which Christians call the Old Testament, and we assert that both may be used by those who are willing to make the effort to do so. The simultaneous use of the two ways is perhaps the surest way for Christians today to be "modern" and "Christian."

The way which is most common in theological education and modern Old Testament scholarship is to read the books according to the historical-critical method. Here the attempt is being made to understand their content solely or primarily in terms of their own times and context. This approach, in one or another of its forms, dominates the reading and study of the Bible in virtually all academic circles in the Western world.

The other is to adopt the approach of the major biblical exegetes of the early church and see the Old Testament as preparation for the New Testament. One way of putting this is to say: "The New is in the Old concealed; the Old is by the New revealed." (Or, "Latent in the Old Testament is the New, patent in the New Testament is the Old.") Here it is understood that the One and the Same living God revealed himself by word and deed through history; thus what he reveals himself to be in the later revelation he actually was/is in the earlier revelation. Therefore, in the earlier self-disclosure by God one may expect hints of the fuller character and nature of God which are made clear in the later revelation.

There are, of course, clear pointers in the New Testament which lead to the Christian reading of the Old Testament — as we indicated in chapter 1. For example, the inspiration upon the Old Testament prophets is declared to be from the Holy Trinity by one writer:

> The prophets who prophesied of the grace that was to be yours searched and inquired about this salvation; they inquired what person or time was indicated by the Spirit of Christ within them when predicting the sufferings of Christ and the subsequent glory. It was revealed to them that they were serving not themselves but you, in the things which have now been announced to you by those who preached the good news to you through the Holy Spirit sent from heaven, things into which angels long to look (1 Peter 1:10-12).

Christ is viewed as being already alive in the prophets, and the Holy Spirit, who brings the Word from heaven, is nothing less than God. The presence of the Father is supplied by the context in which this passage occurs.

So this principle of the New being concealed in the Old obviously applies to the doctrine of God as Holy Trinity — Three Persons, One God. However, if we read the books of the Old Testament in terms of modern biblical criticism — literary, source, form, and redaction criticism — then we should not expect to find anything which points obviously to the One God as a Plurality in Unity. The major textbooks on the theology of the Old Testament have little or nothing to say of God as the Holy and Undivided Trinity. For, as we all know, such a doctrine was only specifically known in the period after the incarnation of the Son of God. Thus what is seen in the Old Testament by this historical-critical method is the gradual recognition by the Israelites that Yahweh-Elohim, the Lord God, is not only the supreme God among the gods of the nations, but the one and only LORD God (1 Kings 8:60).

On the other hand, if we read the Old Testament after having first read and believed the content of the books of the New Testament and adopted the Christian Creed (Apostles' and Nicene), then we see in the words of the text more meaning than we would see if we were reading it solely in terms of its original, historical context. This richer meaning has been associated historically within the church with what is often called the fourfold sense of Scripture. It is well captured in the medieval distich:

Littera gesta docet, quid credas allegoria, Moralis quid agas, quo tendas anagogia. ("The letter teaches what took place, the allegory what to believe, the moral what to do, the anagogy what goal to strive for.")

First of all, in the *literal* sense, the Scriptures tell us what happened and how God has intervened in human history. Thus the literal and historical sense are interchangeable. Next, the literal reading suggests and the *allegorical* supplies what to believe. (The word *allegory* reflects the days when Scripture for the early church meant what we now call the Old Testament. To use allegory then was to go beyond the literal significance of the Old Testament texts to find in them the mysteries revealed in the New Testament. It was also to affirm the unity of the two testaments.) This fullness of belief, sometimes called the mystical sense, is the totality of truths concerning Christ and his church, prefigured in the Old and present in the New Testament. Thirdly, arising from the literal and allegorical meanings, is the *moral sense* — what you must do as a Christian to love, trust, and obey God. Finally, *anagogy* points to what goals to strive for as a Christian. The anagogical meaning is also the eschatological meaning.

The best example of the fourfold sense is the word, "Jerusalem." It is (a) the historical city; (b) the church, a mystical city; (c) the individual soul; and (d) the heavenly Jerusalem, the church above.

To summarize, the historical-critical method seeks to state what was intended and understood by those to whom the Revelation was originally given; in contrast, the patristic and medieval method seeks to state what is veiled but nevertheless present to the eyes of faith and by the design of God within the historically given Revelation. In this chapter, we shall use both methods, applying them specifically to the records of God's self-disclosure to the patriarchs and to Moses. In terms of the fourfold sense, our interest is primarily with the *allegorical* since our topic is definitely doctrinal.

Therefore, we shall look at God's encounter with Moses from two perspectives. In each case we shall first follow the modern historical-critical method and then, secondly, note the way the same texts were read and understood by the Fathers.

YAHWEH-ELOHIM VISITS THE PATRIARCHS

God Speaks to and Meets with Abraham and Jacob

In the Book of Genesis there is a series of accounts of encounters between the God (Elohim), who is later known as YHWH, Yahweh, the Elohim of Israel (Ex. 6:3), and the patriarchs, Abraham and Jacob. Modern scholarship sees these scriptural accounts as the careful and creative weaving together of previously existing oral and written traditions concerning the patriarchs and their God. Our limited task here is only to note the content of the final text. It is not to inquire into the prehistory of the contents of the text.

The call of Abraham (Gen. 12:1-6) contains no visual or visible appearance by God to the patriarch. Abraham is recorded as hearing a word from the invisible Yahweh. It is, however, a remarkable word, taking us from the local to the universal. He is commanded to leave his home, clan, and country and go to another land. There God will richly bless him and make him a blessing to all the families of the earth.

The covenant between Yahweh and Abraham is described in Genesis 15:1-21. The word of God came to him "in a vision" but no visual perception is recorded. Rather it is Yahweh, the invisible but speaking God, who confronts Abraham. Though the patriarch has no heir, Yahweh promised him that his seed would be as countless as the stars in the heavens. In response, we read that "Abraham had faith on Yahweh, who imputed it to him for righteousness." Obviously Abraham took God at his word and truly believed the promise made to him. At the same time Yahweh placed Abraham in a relation of communion and friendship (justification in Pauline terms) with himself.

In Genesis 18 we find the superb and intriguing account of the visit of the three strangers to Abraham and Sarah by the Oaks of Mamre. As we read what appears at first to be a simple, moving story we begin to see that it is rich and complex. First of all, Abraham addressed only one of the visitors, but offered hospitality to all three. Then all three asked him about Sarah, his wife, but only one of them, who is identified as Yahweh, announced the forthcoming birth of a son to Abraham and Sarah. Hearing this, Sarah, now past the age of child-bearing, laughed. Thus Yahweh spoke again (vv. 13-14) assuring Abraham that Sarah would truly bear him a son.

Abraham accompanied the three men as they left, traveling toward Sodom (v. 16). At this point in the narrative we hear a soliloquy from Yahweh (vv. 17-19) concerning his plans for Abraham, followed by a word (which Abraham was intended to hear?) concerning Sodom and Gomorrah. Then follows the moving intercession by Abraham, addressed to Yahweh, on behalf of Sodom (vv. 20-31). Next we hear of the visit of two angels to Sodom where they meet Lot, enter his house, strike unwelcome visitors with blindness, cause Lot to leave and then execute the judgment of the Lord upon Sodom and Gomorrah (19:1ff).

Yet another engaging story is that of the testing of Abraham's faith in Genesis 22. The words, "Take your son, your only son

Isaac, whom you love, and go to the land of Moriah and offer him there as a burnt offering upon one of the mountains" (v. 2) have made profound impressions on many souls.

In this visitation we have both the direct word of God and the word of God via an angel heard by Abraham. Further, we have the last-minute provision of a sacrifice in place of Isaac. Abraham has shown that "he fears God." Such fear, or supreme devotion, is the very essence of true religion for the Old Testament. It is trust in, and love for, the God who is both far and near and who, in this particular episode, conceals his own divine nature in what seems to be hostility toward the man of his choice!

As we meditate upon the accounts of Abraham's encounter with Yahweh, we recognize that Yahweh is a *self-concealing God.* In the words of Isaiah: "Verily, thou art a God that hidest thyself, O God of Israel, the Savior" (45:15, KJV). Certainly God speaks and certainly God appears, but at the same time he remains elusive. He cannot be located at any one place or shrine and his full identity is never revealed.

Yahweh, as the self-concealing God, also revealed himself to Jacob both in the dream of the heavenly stairway (Gen. 28:10-22) and in the wrestling with the stranger by night (Gen. 32:22-32). From Genesis 28 we learn that communion with God is real and that God's plan is to bless the whole world through the seed of Abraham (Jacob). Further, from Genesis 32 we learn that the stranger with whom Jacob fought was, in an elusive and veiled way, the God of Abraham. Jacob won the fight; however, he remained forever afterward a maimed man, who knew that there is forgiveness with the Lord. In fact, Jacob only became the new man, Israel, when he recognized in his adversary, the presence of God himself. "I have seen Elohim face to face" (v. 30). (The word *'elohim* is the standard word for "God." Although the noun is plural in form it usually takes the singular verb. In contrast, other Semitic languages have retained a singular noun for "God.")

The Holy Trinity Encounters Abraham and Jacob
When we read the patristic theological interpretation of the revelation of God to the patriarchs, we realize that we are in a

different thought world than that of modern commentators on the Pentateuch. The early fathers, as many commentators after them, came to the text as Trinitarians. They believed in God the Father, His Son Jesus Christ our Lord, and the Holy Spirit, who proceeds from the Father (and the Son). They confessed One God in Trinity and a Trinity in Unity. Nevertheless, as we would expect, they differed as to how far there is a veiled Revelation of the Holy Trinity in the Old Testament. All believed that the "angel of the Lord" was the Second Person, the eternal Word, who was to be, in the fullness of the times, born of the Virgin Mary. Some also believed that here and there God actually revealed himself (howbeit in an indirect manner) to be the Three in One and One in Three.

The late William G.T. Shedd in his editing of the text of Augustine's classic study, *De Trinitate*, wrote these words:

> The theophanies of the Pentateuch are trinitarian in their implication. They involve distinctions in God — God sending, and God sent; God speaking of God, and God speaking to God. The trinitarianism of the Old Testament has been lost sight of to some extent in the modern [i.e., late 19th century] construction of the doctrine. The patristic, medieval and reformation theologies worked this vein with thoroughness, and the analysis of Augustine in this respect is worthy of careful study.[2]

We may add that in the modern era (i.e., late twentieth century) the trinitarianism of the Old Testament has been lost sight of to an even greater degree than in 1887 when Shedd wrote these words. The sole use of the historical-critical method serves to hide the Holy Trinity from view.

Shedd's observation appears as a footnote in the text of *De Trinitate* where Augustine of Hippo is discussing first the visit of the Lord God (which is also the visit of the three men) to Abraham and Sarah at the Oaks of Mamre and then, secondly, the appearance to Lot (in Gen. 18–19). Augustine was obviously deeply intrigued by the three who speak as One and then later the two who speak as One. Here it was not simply the Second Person accommodating himself to the likeness of man. His thought was that:

Since three men appeared, and no one of them is said to be greater than the rest either in form, or age, or power, why should we not here understand, as visibly intimated by the visible creature, the equality of the Trinity, and one and the same substance in Three Persons?[3]

With respect to the two who visited Lot, Augustine concluded his thoughts with these words:

But which two Persons do we here understand? — of the Father and of the Son, or of the Father and of the Holy Spirit, or of the Son and of the Holy Spirit? The last, perhaps, is the most suitable; for they said of themselves that they were sent, which is that which we say of the Son and of the Holy Spirit. For we find nowhere in the Scriptures that the Father was sent.[4]

Some may regard Augustine's approach as too speculative or fanciful. What is clear, however, to anyone who will carefully read Genesis 18–19, is that the interchange of the singular and plural is most striking and intriguing.

The trinitarian interpretation of this incident is most beautifully presented in pictorial form by the late fourteenth or early fifteenth-century icon by Andrej Rublev, *The Holy Trinity*, which is in the Tretyakov Gallery, Moscow. Rublev was not innovating but drawing on a long iconographic and exegetical tradition, when he undertook to paint the Trinity in terms of three angels at a table on which were the consecrated bread and wine. The Three are at the one table and their communion (*circumincession or perichōrēsis*) is represented by the one bread and one cup.

Hilary of Poitiers, who wrote his book *The Trinity* between 356 and 360 (some sixty years before Augustine wrote his), did not speak of a Revelation of the Holy Trinity. He saw one of the three as "the angel of the Lord" and discerned two meanings in this expression — "he himself who is, and he of whom he is." Thus "he who is God from God is also the angel of God." Or, "Although Abraham saw him as a man, he adored him as the Lord; that is, he recognized the mystery of the future Incarnation."[5]

In the sixteenth century, John Calvin made it clear how he

read and thought others should read the references to the "angel of Yahweh" in the "Books of Moses" and in Judges (see e.g., Jud. 6:11-22). In his classic exposition of the Apostles' Creed, *The Institutes of the Christian Religion,* he wrote this of the "angel of the eternal God."

> The orthodox doctors of the Church have rightly and prudently interpreted the chief angel to be God's Word, who already at that time, as a sort of foretaste, began to fulfil the office of Mediator. For even though he was not yet clothed with flesh, he came down, so to speak, as an intermediary, in order to approach believers more intimately. Therefore this closer intercourse gave him the name of angel. Meanwhile what was his he retained, that as God he might be of ineffable glory. The same thing is meant by Hosea, who, after recounting Jacob's struggle with the angel, says, "Jehovah, the God of Hosts, Jehovah, his name is a remembrance" (Hos. 12:5, Vulgate). . . . Hence, also, that saying of Paul's that Christ was the leader of the people in the wilderness (1 Cor. 10:4), because even though the time of humbling had not yet arrived, that eternal Word nevertheless set forth a figure of the office to which he had been destined.[6]

Those who know Calvin's commentaries will be aware that this principle of the "angel" as the "Word," together with his use of typology (i.e., that the ceremonies enjoined in the Law were "foreshadowings" of the full and clear revelation of the Gospel, in which the ceremonies cease), were very important to him as an exegete of the sacred text.

In his *Commentary upon Genesis,* however, Calvin does not follow either the Western or Eastern Christian traditions in seeing a Revelation of the Trinity at the Oaks of Mamre and in Sodom (Gen. 18–19). In fact, he referred to this interpretation as "frivolous." What Calvin saw was the Word (the Second Person), not yet made flesh, appearing with two angels to Abraham and Sarah, and then just the two angels appearing to Lot in Sodom and there executing the judgment of the Lord upon the city. Obviously, Calvin respected traditional exegesis and interpretations, but he also felt free to depart from them when necessary.

THE THEOPHANIES OF YAHWEH-ELOHIM[7] AT THE MOUNTAIN

God Appears to and Speaks with Moses

Near to the mountain (called both Horeb and Sinai) Moses was grazing his flock. At first he heard no voice, rather he beheld a wondrous sight. He saw a messenger of Yahweh in a fiery flame in the middle of a bush. Turning to look more closely, Moses was directly addressed by Yahweh who told him that he stood on holy ground and that he who spoke to him was none other than the God of the patriarchs. Appropriately, "Moses hid his face for he was afraid to look upon God" (Ex. 3:6, KJV).

Yahweh addressed Moses giving him a mission and promising to be with him in that mission. He who had escaped from Egypt was to go to Pharaoh to lead God's people out of Egypt to a good and large land flowing with milk and honey. Yet he would not go alone for Yahweh's commitment of communion with him was clear: "I will be with thee" (Ex. 3:12, KJV).

The promise of the presence of God encouraged Moses to continue the dialogue and to be bold to ask this God what is his name. This request was made because he had been given a commission and because he wanted to succeed in it. Leading slaves out of Egypt was no simple task.

The answer given to Moses by the God of Abraham and Jacob at the foot of the mountain has been recorded in these words (3:14-15):

> And Elohim said to Moses, " *'Eheyeh 'asher 'eheyeh.*" And he said, "Say to the people of Israel, *'Eheyeh* has sent me to you." Elohim also said to Moses, "Say this to the people of Israel, *'Yahweh,* the Elohim of your fathers, the Elohim of Abraham, the Elohim of Isaac, and the Elohim of Jacob has sent me to you': this is my name for ever, and thus am I to be remembered throughout all generations."

The divine name is YHWH (Yahweh), which is placed in parallel to *'Eheyeh* and which in turn is related to the longer *'Eheyeh 'asher 'eheyeh.* The usual translation of the latter three Hebrew words is "I am that I am." So we are to hold in parallel three statements concerning the name of the God (Elohim) of the patriarchs: "I am that I am," and "I am" and "Yahweh." Therefore, the meaning of the name, *Yahweh,* the God of Abraham and Israel, is related to the verb "to be." Whether *'Eheyeh* is read as present tense, "I am who I am," or future tense, "I shall be who I shall be," or even as the causative-factitive, "I cause to be whatever I cause to be" (or even as all three tenses) is a matter of scholarly debate. The majority view is that we have the Hebrew verb in the imperfect tense which translates into the present or future tenses in English. Further, Semitic verbs are inflected for the gender of the subject as well as for person and number; here, as elsewhere, the form of the verb which is God's name, is masculine! Likewise, in the Hebrew Bible every adjective, every pronoun, and every participle which refers to YHWH is also unmistakably masculine.

The God, Elohim, who is always "I AM" is obviously the God who does not change and who will therefore always be there as the God of Israel. Thus "memorial" is placed in parallel to "name" in order to emphasize hope, that the intentions of Yahweh for Moses and the people of Israel shall surely come to pass.

We know from the contents of Exodus 4 through 18 that the intentions of Yahweh did come to pass. Thus in chapter 19 we find the tribes of Israel camped before the mountain of God. The people of Israel not only witness the solitary figure of Moses going to meet with God, but they also see nature in apparent tumult. They come to see that the Exodus and crossing of the Red Sea, though manifestations of the presence and power of Yahweh, which they had experienced, were only a prelude for the theophany on the mountain.

Yahweh, descending upon the mountain, called to Moses and gave him a message for "the house of Jacob," addressing the people in the second person plural. "If you obey my voice and keep my covenant, you will be for me, out of all peoples, a peculiar treasure, for the whole earth is mine" (Ex. 19:5). Israel is loved in order to become the priestly kingdom of Yahweh in human history. Israel as a whole is before God a holy nation and a royal priesthood.

Yet Israel needs to know the power and the glory of Yahweh.

Thus we have the description of the theophany in Exodus 19:16ff. As Yahweh descended there was thunder, lightning, thick cloud, and the sound of a very loud trumpet. The mountain was set on fire and there was much smoke. From within this wondrous tumult of nature, Yahweh spoke to Moses and gave him the content of the covenant.

As the climax of this theophany (Ex. 24:1-11), Moses with the priests, Aaron, Nadab, and Abihu, together with seventy elders of Israel, "saw the God of Israel" (stated twice, vv. 10 and 11). Under his feet, it seemed, was a pavement of sapphire stone, like heaven in purity. God is not hidden in darkness but by dazzling light! The onlookers are blinded by the power of pure light.

In Exodus 33 we read of Moses in conversation with God before he leaves the area of Horeb-Sinai. Moses made three requests of Yahweh — to know his way in order to know him, to be assured of his continuing presence as they leave Sinai, and to see his glory (the innermost secret of the Godhead). The last request was denied; but, as a divine concession, Moses was allowed to see the goodness and "the back" of Yahweh rather than his "face" (33:23). Here "the back" of God is a way of speaking of the self-revelation of God in the proclamation of his name, Yahweh, and the unfolding of his ways with respect to Israel, in ongoing historical experience.

How God is toward Israel is proclaimed in these words: "Yahweh passed before him, and proclaimed, 'Yahweh, Yahweh, a God merciful and gracious, slow to anger, and abounding in steadfast love and faithfulness, keeping steadfast love for thousands, forgiving iniquity and transgression and sin'" (Ex. 34:6-7). Here God's relation with Israel and his ways with men is declared.

Common to all the theophanies preserved in the Book of Exodus is the proclamation by God, Elohim, of his name of Yahweh. Not surprisingly the third of the Ten Words (Ten Commandments) is: "Thou shalt not invoke the name of Yahweh thy Elohim in vain." Yahweh is the sovereign Lord of the universe. He is the Lord of history and thus transcends nature, mankind, and sexuality.

While it is correct exegetically to see in the name of YHWH the embodiment of God's promise to be actively with and for his covenant people, it is also permissible for us to understand the Name in ontological terms as well. In saying, "I am who I am," Yahweh is also affirming that he is the Absolutely Existent One to whose Being there is no limit and no restriction. In the Septuagint the rendering is, "I am he who is," suggesting that the Hebrew mind has been touched by the Greek mind to see the metaphysical significance of the Name.

Returning to the content of Exodus 3, it may be claimed that theologically we are given a threefold revelation – of God's immanence in history ("I shall be there"); of God's transcendence to history ("I shall be there as who I am"); and of God's transparence through history ("As who I am shall I be there"). Yahweh is the God-with-his-people; Yahweh is present in sovereign freedom; Yahweh does not reveal the inner secret of his Being to his people, but they are privileged to know him, as through his mighty works and words he becomes known to them. However, in the end, only God knows who God is. The Name of Yahweh is ineffable.

The Holy Trinity Appears to and Speaks with Moses

Calvin had no doubt but that "the angel of the Lord," who spoke from the burning bush, was the "eternal Word of God, of one Godhead with the Father." The Word, said Calvin, assumed the name of "the Angel" on the ground of his future mission. Augustine also favored the identification of the angel with the eternal Son who is called by the Prophet Isaiah, "the Angel of the Great Counsel" (Isa. 9:6).

However, when the question is asked of Augustine, "Which Person descended upon Mount Sinai in cloud and with fire?" we find that he provides – after some discussion – the following answer:

> If it is allowable, without rash assertion, to venture upon a modest and hesitating conjecture from this passage [Ex. 19], if it is possible to understand it of one person of the Trinity, why do we not rather understand the Holy Spirit to be spoken of, since the Law itself also, which was given there, is said to have been written upon tables of stone with the "finger of God" [Ex. 21:18], by which name we know the Holy Spirit to be signified in the Gospel [Luke 11:20].[8]

Again, Augustine may be judged to be speculative, even though what he says does make good sense.

Normally, the early fathers, and especially the Greek fathers, thought of the Father as being the Lord God, the Kyrios-Theos of the Septuagint. However, in thinking of the Father, they did not think of the Father as being alone, for he is always the Father of the eternally begotten Son and the Father from whom the eternal Spirit is spirated. So for them Yahweh/Kyrios meant the Father, or the Three Persons acting as One, or one of the other Persons. Normally, however, Yahweh/Kyrios of the Old Testament is the Father.

What must be made clear is that both the Latin and the Greek fathers denied that in any of these visitations, revelations, and theophanies of the Old Testament was the essential nature or the very substance of God actually seen by the patriarchs or Moses. What was seen by these holy men of God was One of the Persons of the Holy Trinity accommodating himself to the understanding and senses of man through the creative use of both nature and of man himself, God's creature. The Creator was making use of his creation for his own ends.

Whether or not we, as moderns, are moved by the results of the patristic reading of the Old Testament, we are the inheritors of this approach, even if we are Protestants and not Roman Catholics or Greek Orthodox. Further, we are also the inheritors in Western Christianity of the patristic interpretation of the full identity of the Word, the Wisdom, and the Spirit of God in the old covenant. And it is to there and to related themes, including the revealed name and nature of God, that we turn in the next chapter.

APPENDIX: THE ANGEL OF THE LORD

Since the identification of "the angel of the Lord" with the Second Person of the Holy Trinity is basic to Patristic, Medieval, and Reformation exegesis, those theophanies which include the angel of the Lord are here listed. Virtually all are from the early period of the history of Israel.

(a) Genesis 16:7-14. The angel finds Hagar and addresses her. She recognizes that it is Yahweh who speaks to her.

(b) Genesis 18:1-22. The three visitors are addressed as "My Lord."

(c) Genesis 19. The two messengers in Sodom, who are addressed as "My Lord."

(d) Genesis 21:17-19. The angel, who is identified with God, visits Hagar.

(e) Genesis 22:11-18. The angel summons Abraham to sacrifice Isaac and speaks as God.

(f) Genesis 31:11-13. The angel declares to Jacob that he is God.

(g) Genesis 32:24-30. Jacob wrestles with the angel (God).

(h) Genesis 48:15-16. Jacob blesses his sons and declares that it was an angel who had redeemed him from all evil. Much later Isaiah declared that "Yahweh became their Savior . . . the angel of his presence saved them" (Isa. 63:8-9).

(i) Exodus 3:2-6. The call of Moses by the angel (Yahweh).

(j) Exodus 14:19-22. The angel of the Lord, who is here distinguished from Yahweh, goes before the camp of Israel. However, in the previous chapter (13:21) it is Yahweh himself who goes before the camp in a pillar of a cloud and a pillar of a fire. Further, in 14:24, Yahweh himself is clearly identified with the cloud and fire (cf., Num. 20:16).

(k) Joshua 5:13-16. Joshua meets a man who is "the captain of the host of Yahweh." The "man" conveys the presence of Yahweh for he tells Joshua that he stands on holy ground.

(l) Judges 2:1-5. The angel of Yahweh speaks as the One who has brought the Israelite tribes out of Egypt and as the One who will not annul his covenant with them.

(m) Judges 6:11-14. Here Gideon's heavenly visitor is first of all separate from Yahweh and then becomes Yahweh (cf. vv. 12, 14, and see v. 22).

(n) Judges 13:2-23. Here Manoah's heavenly visitor, who brings good tidings of the birth of a son, is never as such identified with Yahweh. However, after the visits of the angel, Manoah confesses: "We are doomed to die, because we have seen God (*'elohim*)."

And from the postexilic period:

(o) Ezekiel 40:1–47:12. While it is the angel who guides Ezekiel on a tour of the new temple, from time to time it is Yahweh himself (as the angel) who speaks to him (e.g., 44:4ff).

(p) Zechariah 1:1–6:8. While it is the angel who speaks often to Zechariah and also addresses Yahweh (1:12-13), it is the same angel who speaks as the mouthpiece of Yahweh (3:6-10).

(Note: The angel as representing or actually being Yahweh may be seen as an example of an "Extension" of Yahweh's Personality. For discussion of this concept see Aubrey R. Johnson, *The One and the Many in the Israelite Conception of God* (1961), pp. 28–32. We shall return to the subject of Angelology and Christology in chapter 6. The chapter entitled, "The Trinity and Angelology" (pp. 117–46), in Jean Daniélou, *The Theology of Jewish Christianity*, is a valuable study of angelomorphic language in early Christian texts. Further, the chapter entitled, "Principal Angels" (pp. 71–92), in *One God, One Lord: Early Christian Devotion and Ancient Jewish Monotheism*, by Larry W. Hurtado is a fine survey of the place of angels in postexilic Judaism.)

FOR FURTHER READING

Augustine. *On the Holy Trinity*. Vol. 3 of A Select Library of Nicene and Post Nicene Fathers. Grand Rapids: Eerdmans, 1956.

Calvin, John. *Commentaries on the Book of Genesis*. Grand Rapids: Baker, 1981.

Calvin, John. *Commentaries on the Four Last Books of Moses*. Grand Rapids: Baker, 1981.

Daniélou, Jean. *The Theology of Jewish Christianity*. Philadelphia: Westminster, 1964.

Eichrodt, Walther. *Theology of the Old Testament*, 2 vols. London: SCM, 1967.

Fossum, J.E. *The Name of God and the Angel of the Lord: The Origins of Intermediation in Gnosticism*, Tubingen, Germany: J.C.B. Mohr (Paul Siebeck), 1985.

Hurtado, Larry W. *One God, One Lord: Early Christian Devotion and Ancient Jewish Monotheism*. Philadelphia: Fortress, 1988.

Hilary of Poitiers, *The Trinity*. Vol. 25 of The Fathers of the Church. New York: Fathers of the Church, 1954.

Johnson, Aubrey R. *The One and the Many in the Israelite Conception of God*. Cardiff: Univ. of Wales Press, 1961.

Knight, George A.F. *A Christian Theology of the Old Testament*. Richmond, Va.: John Knox, 1964.

Mettinger, Tryggve N.D., *In Search of God: The Meaning and Message of the Everlasting Names*. Philadelphia: Fortress, 1988.

Terrien, Samuel. *The Elusive Presence: Towards a New Biblical Theology*. San Francisco: Harper & Row, 1978.

Vriezen, Theodorus. *An Outline of Old Testament Theology*, rev. ed. Oxford: Basil Blackwell, 1970.

Wright, N.T. *The New Testament and the People of God*. Minneapolis: Fortress, 1992.

5

YHWH—
PLURALITY IN UNITY

In the last chapter we noted the appearances of God in the early history of Israel, and we noted the revelation of the Name, YHWH, of the God of Israel. In this chapter we must now continue our study of the Name of Yahweh and also of his Wisdom, Word, and Spirit. With respect to the latter the insightful words of Aubrey Johnson are worth noting:

> In Israelite thought, while man was conceived, not in some analytical fashion as "soul" and "body," but synthetically as a psychical whole and a unit of vital power, this power was found to reach far beyond the contour of the body and to make itself felt through indefinable "extensions" of personality. Now the same idea is quite clearly present in the conception of the Godhead.[1]

It is present, he claims, in the Spirit, the Word, the Name, and the Angel of Yahweh. We looked at the Angel in the last chapter. Here we shall examine the Name, the Spirit, the Wisdom, and the Word of Yahweh. As we do so, we shall gain insights into the nature of the Godhead of Yahweh and see that He is a marvelous mystery, a plurality in unity, and a unity in plurality.

THE TETRAGRAMMATON

Three words — LORD, Jehovah, and Yahweh — are used in English to render the tetragrammaton, the four Hebrew consonants, YHWH, which is the unique Name of the God of Israel. As this Name was treated with ever more and more reverence, the Jews ceased to pronounce it during the latter part of the Old Testament period. So we are not completely sure today just how it was originally pronounced.

In the synagogue the Name of YHWH, which was too sacred to utter, was replaced by the word "Adonay," which means "my Lord," in the reading of the Hebrew Scriptures. Then, later, (after A.D. 500) to avoid the risk of false readings, Jews vocalized the "YHWH" with the vowels of "Adonay" (and sometimes of "Elohim") and these are the vowels found in the markings of the Masoretic text.

"Jehovah" came into use in the Middle Ages but it is an artificial form, which bears no relation to how YHWH was originally pronounced. The word, "Yahweh," represents the generally accepted modern attempt to recover the original pronunciation of the tetragrammaton. This is based upon the available evidence which includes Hebrew theophoric names, Amorite onomastics, Greek transliterations in the magical papyri of the Graeco-Roman period, and testimony of the church fathers, especially Clement of Alexandria.

Though in the Hebrew Bible the Name of YHWH is used from Genesis through to Malachi, it was not known and used by the tribes of Israel before the time of Moses. Naturally, once known, it was not only used in the present but when referring to the past — for YHWH was one and the same God of Abraham and Moses. Thus YHWH appears in the narratives of Genesis as well as Exodus.

In the Book of Exodus are two key passages, both of which associate the Name of YHWH with the time of Moses. Already we have looked at the first of these, 3:14-15, in chapter 4. The second is in 6:2-3 and occurs when Yahweh is addressing Moses in Egypt.

> I am the Lord. I appeared to Abraham, to Isaac, and to Jacob, as "God Almighty" [El Shaddai], but by my Name "the Lord" [YHWH] I did not make myself known to them.

God had been known by other names than YHWH in the patriarchal age. Only from the theophany and visitation at the burning bush on Sinai did the God of the patriarchs declare himself to be YHWH.

The content of Exodus 3:14, as well as recent scholarly research, indicate that YHWH is to be taken as a form of the verb *haya*, "to be." In the light of this it is appropriate to see two meanings arising out of this name. First of all, from Exodus 3:14-15, YHWH as a Name is a positive assurance of God's acting, aiding, and communing presence. The "I AM" will be always with his covenant people. He who is now will be also. In the second place, and based on the declarations of Deuteronomy 4:39, 1 Kings 8:60, and Isaiah 45:21-22, YHWH is the only God who actually exists and there is no other. YHWH is the one and only deity, who is both above and within his creation; all other gods are but creatures or the projections of human imagination.

In Israel the name of a man was regarded as an exact picture of the one who owned it. So the name summed up all that its owner is: the name is, as it were, the definition of the person. In other words, the name was the person himself in the form of an alter ego, which represented him, exhibited him, and was him. In like manner the Name of God stood for God himself — "the Name of the God of Jacob protect you!" (Ps. 20:1) and "the Name of the LORD is a strong tower" (Prov. 18:10). The place where Yahweh chose to put his Name was "his habitation" (Deut. 12:5, 11; 14:23-24; 16:6; 26:2). Further, the Name of Yahweh was in his angel: "Behold, I send an angel before you, to guard you on the way and to bring you to the place which I have prepared. Give heed to him and hearken to his voice, do not rebel against him, for he will not pardon your transgression; for my name is in him" (Ex. 23:20-21). The "Name" is an important "extension" of Yahweh's personality, claims Johnson, who also points to the cultic use of the expression "to call upon the Name," where the Name is Yahweh himself.[2]

PLURALITY IN UNITY

Probably the most well-known text in Judaism is the *Shema* of Deuteronomy 6:4-5:

Hear, O Israel: Yahweh, our Elohim, Yahweh is One, and
thou shalt love Yahweh thy Elohim with all thine heart,
and with all thy soul and with all thy might (KJV).

The Hebrew word for "one" here is *ehadh,* which is derived
from a verb form having the meaning of to unify. It is the same
word used in the expression, "they become one flesh" in marriage (Gen. 2:24). Obviously the unity of and in marriage is a
unity which contains a plurality — that is, a duality. So likewise,
as Christians will come to say, the unity of God is not that of a
simple monad, but is a oneness which allows for and contains a
plurality. (We need to be aware that the other Hebrew word for
one where one means unique, the only one of a class, is *yahidh.*
It is used of Isaac "the *only* son" in the testing of Abraham:
"Take your . . . only son, Isaac, whom you love" (Gen. 22:2). Both
Hebrew words for "one" are found in Zechariah 14:9. "On that
day, Yahweh will be *ehadh* and his name *yahidh.*")

The concept of Plurality in Unity is also suggested to Christian readers of the Hebrew Bible by the word *'elohim,* God. In
grammatical terms, it may be called a quantitative plural or a
plural of intensity (cf., such plural words as *mayim* for water and
shamayim for heaven). In view of the emphatic monotheism of
the Hebrew Bible, it is (to say the very least) a striking linguistic
use. It is only in the quoted speeches of pagans that *'elohim* is
used as an actual plural word in referring to the God of Israel
and/or gods (1 Sam. 4:8, cf. Deut. 5:26; 2 Sam. 7:23; Ps. 58:11).

But we are going ahead too quickly. It is necessary to ponder
for a while what the confession in the *Shema* contains. Here the
words of Walter Kasper are helpful in clarifying our thinking.

The singleness and uniqueness of God is qualitative. God
is not only one (*unus*) but also unique (*unicus*); he is as it
were unqualified uniqueness. For by his very nature God
is such that there is only one of him. From the nature of
God as the reality that determines and includes everything his uniqueness follows with intrinsic necessity. If
God is not one, then there is no God. Only one God can
be infinite and all inclusive; two Gods would limit one
another even if they were somehow interpenetrated.
Conversely: as the one God, God is also the only God.

The singleness of God is therefore not just one of the attributes of God; rather his singleness is given directly with his very essence. Therefore, too, the oneness and uniqueness of the biblical God is anything but evidence of narrow-mindedness. On the contrary, for precisely as the one and only God, he is the Lord of all peoples and of all history. He is the First and the Last (Isa. 41:4; 43:10f; 44:6; 48:12; Rev. 1:4, 8, 17).[3]

The commitment to monotheism in contrast to henotheism obviously links Christianity to Judaism, as we have noted above.

However, the further confession of Unity in Trinity by Christianity raises a question. Has Christianity by its confession of the Trinity proved unfaithful to its confession of the One God? Obviously if the statement of the Trinity were as clear in the Hebrew Bible as is the statement of the Unity of Yahweh then such a question would not be asked. Therefore, the Christian claim has been that within the Old Testament there are significant bases and hints concerning the trinitarian nature of God, but that they are of such a nature as only to be so recognized after the revelation of the New Testament is known.

Kasper suggests that one such base is the conviction and clear statement that the God of Israel is the living God. "I am Yahweh, and there is no other, besides me there is no God" (Isa. 45:5; 46:9). Yahweh swears by himself, " 'As I live,' says the LORD" (Isa. 49:18), since he can swear by no one or nothing greater than himself. Yahweh differs radically from creatures in that he possesses his existence in himself, not from another. Therefore, God in his oneness and uniqueness is simultaneously the fullness of life: "As the hart longs for flowing streams, so longs my soul for thee, O God. My soul thirsts for God, for the living God" (Ps. 42:1-2); and "My soul longs, yea, faints for the courts of the LORD; my heart and flesh sing for joy to the living God" (84:2).

Jeremiah declared that "Yahweh is the true God; he is the living God and the everlasting King" (Jer. 10:10). And he bemoaned the fact that Israel had forsaken Yahweh, "the fountain of living water" (17:13).

According to the Book of Daniel, King Darius wrote a letter to all peoples telling them that under his rule men tremble and fear before the God of Daniel, for he is the living God, enduring for ever; his kingdom shall never be destroyed, and his dominion shall be to the end. He delivers and rescues, he works signs and wonders in heaven and on earth, he who has saved Daniel from the power of the lions (Dan. 6:26-27).

As the living God, Yahweh is able to give and save life for he is life, real life, himself!

Because Yahweh is superabundant fullness of life and plenitude of Being he is portrayed as taking counsel with himself and engaging in soliloquy. What has been called the "plural of deliberation" is evident in such passages as these:

Then God said, "Let us make man in our image, after our likeness" (Gen. 1:26).

Then the LORD God said, "Behold, the man has become like one of us, knowing good and evil" (Gen. 3:22).

And the LORD said ". . . Come, let us go down, and there confuse their language" (Gen. 11:6-7).

It is of interest to note that it is *'elohim* who speaks in Genesis 1:26 but Yahweh in 11:7 — where a plural verb is used with the singular Yahweh. Thus both Yahweh and *'elohim* here speak in the plural. (It will be recalled that *'elohim* is the standard and normal Hebrew word for the divine Being, that it is plural in form and that usually it takes the singular verb.)

Though these significant texts containing the "let us" are not developed in a trinitarian way in the documents of the New Testament, by the second century such an interpretation had become the norm in the churches. For example, commenting on Genesis 1:26 Irenaeus wrote:

Now man is a mixed organization of soul and flesh, who was formed after the likeness of God [the Father], and molded by his hands, that is, by the Son and the Holy Spirit, to whom also he said, "Let us make man."[4]

For with him [the Father] were always present the Word

and Wisdom, the Son and the Spirit, by whom and in whom freely and spontaneously, he made all things, to whom also he speaks, saying, "Let us make man after our image and likeness."[5]

Here, for Irenaeus, the plurality of deliberation is certainly the Holy Trinity. In contrast, we know that Jewish writers did their best to hide or negate this plurality in order to emphasize the unity of God.[6]

Another place where there is both the plural of deliberation and the triple recital of "Holy" is the account of the call of Isaiah. First of all, we read of the seraphim declaring the holiness of Yahweh.

Holy, holy, holy is the LORD of hosts; the whole earth is full of his glory (Isa. 6:3).

Then after his cleansing with the burning coal from the altar, Isaiah hears the voice of the Lord saying:

Whom shall I send, and who will go for us? (6:8)

It did not take the church long to interpret the triple recital of "holy" as being addressed by the heavenly host to the Father, the Son, and the Holy Spirit—especially when the triple recital also occurs in Revelation 4:8. The *Trisagion* quickly became a part of the Liturgy of the churches of the East and West and it remains in most Liturgies today. Likewise the singular "I" and the plural "us" were soon read as pointing to the unity and plurality of the Holy Trinity.

Referring to this Christian interpretation of Isaiah 6, Kasper writes: "It has great symbolic importance, for in its own way it shows that in the time of the church fathers the trinitarian confession did not originate in pure theory and abstract speculation but rather had its vital context in the doxology, that is, in the liturgical glorification of God."[7]

Another Roman Catholic theologian, Bertrand de Margerie, S.J., commenting in his book, *The Christian Trinity in History*, upon the plural of deity (in Gen. 1:26; 3:22; 11:7; and Isa. 6:8) asks:

Does this Divine "we" evoke a polytheistic age anterior to the Bible? Or a deliberation of God with his angelic court? Or does it not rather indicate the interior richness of the divinity? How does it happen that only in these four passages the plural form of the name *Elohim* used here has influenced the verb, which is plural only here? And what is more extraordinary is that these plural forms are introduced by formulas in the singular: "Elohim says" or "Yahweh says" (Gen. 1:26; 3:22; 11:6).[8]

At least we can say that the plural and singular forms of the verb are intriguing, whether or not we see (in the intention of God who inspired the writing of the text) the Holy Trinity veiled here.

What is also intriguing is the threefold structure of the priestly blessing in Numbers 6:22-26.

Yahweh said to Moses, "Say to Aaron and his sons, Thus you shall bless the people of Israel: you shall say to them, *Yahweh bless you and keep you: Yahweh make his face to shine upon you, and be gracious to you:* Yahweh lift up his countenance upon you and give you peace.

In view of the enormous significance of the Name in Israelite religion, Yahweh's emphatic comment on the priestly blessing in verse 27 is significant: "So shall they put my Name upon the people of Israel, and I will bless them." Since Jesus told his apostles to baptize in the Name (Yahweh) "of the Father and the Son and the Holy Spirit," the early church naturally came to read this threefold blessing as not only pointing to, but also coming from, the Three Persons of the Holy Trinity.

It is perhaps also worth noting that there are passages where Yahweh, his Word/Angel of the Presence, and Spirit are named together as co-causes of effects (cf. Ps. 33:6; Isa. 61:1; 63:9-12; Hag. 2:5-6). Naturally such texts were read through Christian eyes as referring to the Holy Trinity.

Finally, the possible connection between the Trinity and the central theological theme of the Old Testament, expressed in the tripartite formula, "I will be your God; you shall be my people, and I will dwell in the midst of you," also is worthy of notice. This threefold formula is made up of (1) the basic promise of Genesis 17:7-8 and 28:21 where Yahweh establishes his covenant "to be God to you and to your descendants after you"; (2) the additional promise after the Exodus of being not merely God's people but also of being known as God's son — "Israel is my first-born son" (Ex. 4:22); and (3) the further promise by God to dwell in the midst of his covenant people — "I will dwell among the people of Israel and will be their God" (Ex. 29:45). As a Trinitarian believer the Christian holds that the Father establishes the covenant of grace and sends the Son; the Son is incarnate and is both the new Adam and the new Israel, God's true Son, so that all who come to the Father come in and through the Son; and the Holy Spirit is sent by the Father and the Son to dwell in the people who are the new Israel.

Only Yahweh in whom is plenitude of being could fulfill such a tripartite promise. Only Yahweh who possesses Wisdom, who speaks the living Word, and who acts as Holy Spirit could make and keep such a promise. Thus we move on to look at this plenitude of life of Yahweh, the living God, in the Wisdom, the Word, and the Spirit of God.

THE WISDOM OF GOD

The Hebrew Bible is familiar with wisdom as both a human and a divine attribute, for some men are said to be wise and God is declared always to be wise. However, in Proverbs 1–9, *hokmah* is not merely an attribute of God, it also appears to become in some sense actually distinct from God, without being other than God. In fact it is in 1:20-23 and especially in 8:22-36 that wisdom seems to have become an elaborate personification — a divine agent.

The relation of Wisdom to Yahweh in the creation of the world is set forth in these words.

The LORD created me at the beginning of his work, the first of his acts of old. Ages ago I was set up, at the first, before the beginning of the earth. When there were no depths I was brought forth, when there were no springs abounding with water. Before the mountains had been shaped, before the hills, I was brought forth; before he had made the earth with its fields, or the first of the dust of the world. When he established the heavens, I was there, when he drew a circle on the face of the deep, when he made firm the skies above, when he established the fountains of the deep, when he assigned to the sea its limit, so that the waters might not transgress his command, when he marked out the foundations of the earth, then I was beside him, like a master workman; and I was daily his delight, rejoicing before him always, rejoicing in his inhabited world and delighting in the sons of men (Prov. 8:22-31).

Here wisdom is what Yahweh, the Creator, reckoned primary and indispensable. Wisdom is both older than the universe and is fundamental to it, for nothing came into existence without it. Thus wisdom is the spring of joy.

Commenting upon this passage, Derek Kidner explains that the context within the Book of Proverbs points not to wisdom as a hypostasis (a heavenly being related to but distinct from God) but as a vivid personification of wisdom. "Not only does the next chapter proceed immediately to a fresh portrait of wisdom, in a new guise (as a great lady [9:1-6] whose rival is certainly no hypostasis)," writes Kidner, "but the present passage makes excellent sense at the level of metaphor: i.e., as a powerful way of saying that if *we* must do nothing without wisdom, God himself has made and done nothing without it. The wisdom by which the world is rightly ruled is none other than the wisdom by which it exists."[9] However, Kidner does not stop here; he recognizes a wider setting. The New Testament shows by its allusions to this passage (see Col. 1:15-17; 2:3; Rev. 3:14) that the personifying of wisdom, far from overshooting the literal truth, was a preparation for its full statement. That is, the agent of creation was no mere activity or attribute of God but the Son, the eternal Word and Wisdom (see John 1:1-14; 1 Cor. 1:24, 30; Heb. 1:1-14).

In the centuries before the birth of Jesus, the Jews showed great interest in divine wisdom. The evidence of this is to be found, for example, in the amount of material on wisdom in the books of the Apocrypha—e.g., in The Wisdom of Solomon and Ecclesiasticus (the Wisdom of Jesus Son of Sirach). Here we meet again the personification of wisdom.

For she is a breath of the power of God, And a pure emanation of the glory of the Almighty; therefore nothing defiled gains entrance into her. For she is a reflection of light, a spotless mirror of the working of God, and an image of his goodness (Wisd. 7:25-26).

Wisdom will praise herself, and will glory in the midst of her people. In the assembly of the Most High she will open her mouth, and in the presence of his host she will glory: "I came forth from the mouth of the Most High, and covered the earth like a mist. I dwelt in high places, and my throne was in a pillar of cloud. Alone I have made the circuit of the vault of heaven and have walked in the depths of the abyss" (Ecclus. 24:1-5).

In the early church such passages from the deuterocanonical books (found in the Septuagint), along with passages in Proverbs (e.g., 8:22-36) and in the Psalter (e.g., 85:10-13), were read as pointing to Jesus Christ, the Wisdom of God.

Recently, much attention has been focused by the feminist movement upon the fact that the word for wisdom in both Greek (*sophia*) and in Hebrew (*hokmah*) is in the feminine gender. It has been claimed that these words refer to a female deity. However, such a claim confuses grammatical gender with physical sexuality! (See chapter 1.) Nevertheless, much has been made of the supposed feminine nature of Wisdom by some feminist theologians. Elisabeth Schüssler Fiorenza has popularized the expressions "gracious Sophia-God" for Yahweh of the Old Testament, and the "Sophia-God of Jesus" for "the God and Father of our Lord Jesus Christ" of the New Testament. One of her much-repeated statements is: "Divine Sophia is Israel's God in the language and *Gestalt* of the Goddess."[10] Apart from confusing grammatical gender with sexuality, this way of thinking gets close to the Gnosticism (in which male and female supernatural beings are paired).

THE WORD OF GOD

According to the Old Testament, Yahweh is certainly the speaking God! From the first chapter of Genesis through to the last

words of Malachi, we read of what God has said. The word of the
Lord is a mighty and efficacious word which creates the cosmos,
establishes the covenant with Israel, and comes to the prophet to
be heard by the people through him.

> By the word of the LORD the heavens were made, and all
> their host by the breath of his mouth. He gathered the
> waters of the sea as in a bottle; he put the deeps in
> storehouses. Let all the earth fear the LORD, let all the
> inhabitants of the world stand in awe of him! For he
> spoke, and it came to be; he commanded, and it stood
> forth (Ps. 33:6-9).

> For as the rain and the snow come down from heaven,
> and return not thither but water the earth, making it
> bring forth and sprout, giving seed to the sower and
> bread to the eater, so shall my word be that goes forth
> from my mouth; it shall not return to me empty, but it
> shall accomplish that which I [Yahweh] purpose, and
> prosper in the thing for which I sent it (Isa. 55:10-11).

There are examples of the personification of the word of God
at various points in the Hebrew Bible. For example:

> [The LORD] sent forth his word and healed them, and
> delivered them from destruction (Ps. 107:20).

> For ever, O LORD, thy word is firmly fixed in the heav-
> ens (119:89).

> He sends forth his command to the earth; his word runs
> swiftly (147:15).

> The LORD has sent a word against Jacob, and it will light
> upon Israel (Isa. 9:8).

However, in the Apocrypha there is a remarkable passage
wherein the word of God is more obviously personified.

> All things were lying in peace and silence, and night in
> her swift course was half-spent, when thy all-powerful

word leapt from thy royal throne in heaven into the midst of that doomed land like a relentless warrior, bearing the sharp sword of thy inflexible decree; with his head touching the heavens and his feet on earth, he stood and spread death everywhere (Wisd. 18:15-16).

Christians in the early church reading such passages saw them as pointing to the full personification of the Word of God as a hypostasis, which is presented in the prologue of the Gospel of John. "In the beginning was the Word, and the Word was with God, and the Word was God. He was in the beginning with God [the Father]; all things were made through him, and without him was not anything made that was made" (1:1-3).

THE SPIRIT OF GOD

The Spirit (lit., the wind and/or the breath) of Yahweh is God present and active upon, around, and within that which Yahweh had made — the world and human beings. In fact, the Spirit was active in the actual creation of the world — "the Spirit of God was moving over the face of the waters" (Gen. 1:2).

The psalmist, addressing Yahweh, said:

When thou sendest forth thy Spirit [breath], they are created; and thou renewest the face of the ground (Ps. 104:30).

There is no place within the created order from where the Spirit of Yahweh and thus Yahweh himself is absent.

Whither shall I go from thy Spirit? Or whither shall I flee from thy presence? If I ascend to heaven, thou art there! If I make my bed in Sheol, thou art there! If I take the wings of the morning and dwell in the uttermost parts of the sea, even there thy hand shall lead me, and thy right hand shall hold me (139:7-10).

The breath of God causes the rhythms of nature:

The grass withers, the flower fades, when the breath of the LORD blows upon it (Isa. 40:7).

Apart from the general presence of the Spirit throughout the created order, there is the specific or intensified presence of the Spirit to add to the natural powers of man. Thus Joseph was enabled by the Spirit to interpret Pharaoh's dream (Gen. 41:38), and Moses and the seventy elders were able to prophesy. "Then the LORD came down in the cloud and spoke to [Moses], and took some of the Spirit that was upon him and put it upon the seventy elders; and when the Spirit rested upon them, they prophesied" (Num. 11:25). Further, Moses later laid his hands upon Joshua and he was filled with the Spirit of wisdom (Deut. 34:9). At a very practical level, the skill of Bezaleel in constructing the tabernacle occurred because the Spirit came upon him (Ex. 31:3; 35:31). And Zerubbabel found that he could only rebuild the temple after the exile by the Spirit of the Lord: "Not by might, nor by power, but by my Spirit, says the LORD of hosts" (Zech. 4:6).

Therefore, it is not surprising that the prophets, who spoke as they were moved by the Spirit of Yahweh (Isa. 59:21; Micah 3:8), declared that the Messiah to come would be the servant of God upon whom the Spirit uniquely rested and in whom the Spirit dwelt (Isa. 11:2; 42:1; 61:1). Likewise in the messianic age there would be an outpouring of the prophetic Spirit upon all the people: "I will pour out my Spirit upon all flesh; your sons and your daughters shall prophesy, your old men shall dream dreams, and your young men shall see visions. Even upon the menservants and maidservants in those days, I will pour out my Spirit" (Joel 2:28-29).

There is a further dimension of the presence and work of the Spirit, and this is the corporate and personal area of holiness and communion with God. A typical prayer was:

Teach me to do thy will, for thou art my God! Let thy good spirit lead me on a level path (Ps. 143:10).

And also:

Create in me a clean heart, O God, and put a new and right spirit within me. Cast me not away from thy presence, and take not thy holy Spirit from me. Restore to me

the joy of thy salvation, and uphold me with a willing
spirit (Ps. 51:10-12).

There could be no true revival without the Spirit: "I will put
my Spirit within you, and you shall live, and I will place you in
your own land" (Ezek. 37:14). "A new heart I will give you, and a
new spirit I will put within you; and I will take out of your flesh
the heart of stone and give you a heart of flesh. And I will put
my spirit within you, and cause you to walk in my statutes and
be careful to observe my ordinances" (36:26-27). Isaiah spoke for
Yahweh: "I will pour water on the thirsty land, and streams on
the dry ground; I will pour my Spirit upon your descendants,
and my blessing on your offspring" (Isa. 44:3).

So the Spirit of YHWH is present in the created order, in the
giving of outstanding gifts to people, in prophecy, and as an
essential part of the future hope of the Messiah and the new age.
George A.F. Knight has remarked that "since the Spirit of God is
no less than God himself acting in accordance with his essential
nature, Spirit actually comes to be pictured in a manner that is
virtually parallel to the pictorial concept of the angelic activity"[11]
which we examined in the last chapter. As in the Old Testament,
so in the New Testament, the Holy Spirit is always present and
invisible but usually "anonymous" and thus not mentioned.

Between the Testaments and particularly within Hellenistic
or Diaspora Judaism, certain developments concerning the Spirit
of Yahweh occurred. First of all, and this was new for the Greek
language, *pneuma* came to cover the broad range of meaning
which *ruach* bears in the Hebrew Bible. This occurred because
of the influence of the Septuagint where *pneuma* was used to
translate *ruach*. Not surprisingly there developed in this context
the teaching that not only were the prophets inspired by the
Spirit to speak God's word, but those who wrote the text of the
Old Testament were also inspired by the Spirit to write down
God's word.

There also developed in Alexandrian Judaism a linking of
God's *pneuma* with his *sophia*. This is seen in the Wisdom of
Solomon, where this *sophia/pneuma* is portrayed as present
throughout the universe and distinctively present and operative
in "the wise" and "the righteous" (Wisd. 1:4-8; 7:21-30). While

this development does not seem to have affected the presentation and development of pneumatology in the New Testament, it certainly affected Christology (e.g., Heb. 1:2-3). Later, however, in the fourth century when the deity of the Spirit was under discussion these Wisdom texts from the Septuagint were used by the fathers in support of orthodoxy.

IN CONCLUSION

Reflecting upon the Christian reading of the Old Testament under the illumination of the revelation recorded in the New Testament, B.B. Warfield wrote:

> The Old Testament may be likened to a chamber richly furnished but dimly lighted; the introduction of light brings into it nothing which was not in it before; but it brings out into clearer view much of what is in it but was only dimly or even not at all perceived before. The mystery of the Trinity is not revealed in the Old Testament revelation; but the mystery of the Trinity underlies the Old Testament revelation, and here and there almost comes into view. Thus the Old Testament revelation of God is not corrected by the fuller revelation which follows it, but only perfected, extended and enlarged.[12]

There is an old saying that what becomes patent in the New Testament was latent in the Old Testament. Thus we have seen how the early Christians saw in Yahweh the Triune God whom they worshiped and served. Yahweh, the God of the Old Testament, was their God and their God was a Holy Trinity.

This said, we need also to be reminded by Knight that

> none of these pictorial concepts [e.g., Word, Spirit] . . . acts as a kind of intermediary, a hypostasis, between the life of God and the life of man. God's assuming a form, whether that of Angel or as his own Holy Spirit, has no meaning apart from God himself. Revelation does not mean that the hidden God is resolved into the revealed God in any form whatever. The *Deus Revelatus* actually remains the *Deus Absconditus* throughout the whole OT

from the earliest forms of expression to the latest and profoundest writings in the exilic and post-exilic periods.[13]

In a different vein, but in some ways looking in the same direction as Warfield and Knight, Kasper points out that behind the various hints and indications of pluripersonal fullness of being in Yahweh there is a basic question, "Who is God's appropriate *vis-a-vis?*"[14] To speak of an I without a Thou (in and for Yahweh) is unthinkable! But is the highest creature, man, a proper *vis-a-vis* for Yahweh? Of course not! Man is a creature loved by Yahweh with an everlasting love. We conclude that the "Thou" is only revealed in the New Testament — the Son, the Lord Jesus Christ.

FOR FURTHER READING

Caird, George B. *The Language and Imagery of the Bible*. Philadelphia: Westminster, 1980.

Hurtado, Larry W. *One God, One Lord: Early Christian Devotion and Ancient Jewish Monotheism*. Philadelphia: Fortress, 1988.

Irenaeus, *Against Heresies*. Vol. 1 of *The Ante Nicene Fathers*. Edited by Alexander Roberts and James Donaldson, Grand Rapids: Eerdmans, 1953.

Isaacs, M.E., *The Concept of Spirit: A Study in Hellenistic Judaism and Its Bearing on the New Testament*. London: Heythrop College, 1976.

Johnson, Aubrey R. *The One and the Many in the Israelite Conception of God*. Cardiff: Univ. of Wales Press, 1961.

Kidner, Derek. *The Proverbs: An Introduction and Commentary*, London: Tyndale, 1972.

Kasper, Walter, *The God of Jesus Christ*, New York: Crossroad, 1984.

Knight, George A.F. *A Christian Theology of the Old Testament*, Richmond, Va.: John Knox, 1959.

De Margerie, Bertrand. *The Christian Trinity in History*. Still River, Mass.: St. Bede's, 1982.

Mettinger, Tryggve N.D. *In Search of God: The Meaning and Message of the Everlasting Names*. Philadelphia: Fortress, 1988.

Montague, George T. *The Holy Spirit: Growth of a Biblical Tradition. A Commentary on the Principal Texts of the Old and New Testaments*. New York: Paulist, 1976.

Von Rad, G., *Old Testament Theology*, 2 vols. New York: Harper, 1975.

Schüssler, Elisabeth Fiorenza. *In Memory of Her: A Feminist Theological Reconstruction of Christian Origins*. New York: Crossroad, 1985.

Segal, A.F. *Two Powers in Heaven*. Leiden: E.J. Brill, 1978.

Wainwright, Arthur W. *The Trinity in the New Testament*. London: SPCK, 1969.

Warfield, Benjamin B. "The Biblical Doctrine of the Trinity." In *Biblical and Theological Studies*. Philadelphia: Presbyterian and Reformed, 1968.

6

MUTATION IN MONOTHEISM

The first Christians, apostles and disciples, were thoroughly committed to the living God, to his unity and his uniqueness. Yet very quickly and without losing their passionate commitment to the unity of YHWH, they began to speak of and worship the resurrected, ascended, and glorified Lord Jesus Christ in such a way as to confess that he is divine as is the Father. This belief and conviction has been called binitarianism by various New Testament scholars. In this chapter we shall follow the attractive presentation of binitarianism by Larry W. Hurtado in his book, *One God, One Lord.* Also we shall note briefly the criticism of Hurtado's thesis by James D.G. Dunn in his fascinating book, *The Parting of the Ways between Christianity and Judaism.* Then we shall suggest, giving reasons, that the consciousness (in contrast to the explicit confession) of the first Christians was not merely binitarian but truly trinitarian, without ceasing to be monotheistic.

However, we begin with the simple task of noticing the clear commitment to monotheism within the New Testament. The tetragram, YHWH, is avoided as in Judaism but the confession of Deuteronomy 6:4, "Hear, O Israel: The Lord our God is one Lord," is accepted and confirmed by Jesus (Mark 12:29; Matt.

22:37; Luke 10:26) and by his apostles (e.g., Rom. 3:30; 1 Cor. 8:4, 6; Gal. 3:20). A careful reading of the Temptation narratives (Matt. 4:1-10; Luke 4:1-12) reveals that they take the form of a midrash on Deuteronomy 6–8, in which chapters is the clear statement of the unity and uniqueness of God. In fact, the climax of the response of Jesus to his testing is to cite Deuteronomy 6:13, "You shall worship the Lord your God and him only shall you serve" (Matt. 4:10). Equally striking is the answer of Jesus to the rich young man, "No one is good but God alone" (Mark 10:18).

Everywhere in the New Testament the truth of the monotheistic formula is taken for granted—"God is one—*eis o theos.*" In fact, God is "the only true God" (John 17:3); he is "the only God, our Savior" (Jude 25) and "the only wise God" (Rom. 16:27). So "to the King of ages, immortal, invisible, the only God, be honor and glory for ever and ever. Amen" (1 Tim. 1:17).

THE MUTATION

A major part of Hurtado's book, *One God, One Lord,* is a study of divine agency in postexilic Judaism, especially the intertestamental period. (In contrast, most of the material used in chapters 4 and 5 to illustrate the "Extension of Divine Personality" is taken from the preexilic period of Israel's history.) It is well-known in academic circles that the texts of Judaism of the postexilic period contain many references to a variety of heavenly figures, who are presented as serving God in his rule over the world and the redemption of the elect. These examples of divine agency may be classified under three general types, according to Hurtado. First, divine attributes and powers (e.g., Wisdom and Logos); secondly exalted patriarchs (e.g., Moses and Enoch); and thirdly, principal angels (e.g., Michael and Yahoel). What they have in common is that they are all pictured as being heavenly in origin or having been exalted to a heavenly position close to God. In fact, they represent God in a unique capacity and are second only to him in the created universe.

After careful study of these types of divine agency in the period immediately before, and contemporaneous with, the birth of Christianity, Hurtado presents what he calls "the Christian mutation." He means that the earliest Christian devotion was a direct outgrowth from, and indeed a variety of, the ancient Jewish tradition; further, this devotion exhibited at an early stage a sudden and significant difference in character and content from the related Jewish devotion. The place of the exalted Jesus in the religious life, devotion, and piety of the first Christians was strikingly different from the Jewish belief in and attitude toward divine agents. The difference was both in how Jesus is named and in the relation/attitude of Christians to him.

The exalted Jesus was given the devotional attention which was reserved only for God himself in the Jewish tradition. Yet this was done in such a way that there was no competition between Jesus and God for the loyalty and devotion of the first Christians. Hurtado comments:

We are dealing with a redefinition of Jewish monotheistic devotion by a group that has to be seen as a movement within Jewish tradition of the early first century C.E. The binitarian shape of early Christian devotion did not result from a clumsy crossbreeding of Jewish monotheism and pagan polytheism under the influence of gentile Christians too ill-informed about the Jewish heritage to preserve its [monotheistic] character. Rather in its crucial first stages, we have a significantly new but essentially internal development within the Jewish monotheistic tradition, a mutation within that species of religious devotion.[1]

In order to demonstrate the new binitarian monotheism of primitive Christianity, Hurtado carefully examines six features of early Christian devotion — hymns, prayer, use of the name of Christ, the Lord's Supper, confession of faith in Jesus, and prophetic pronouncements of the risen Christ.

According to Hurtado, the result of his examination of these features within the New Testament is twofold:

(a) that early Christian devotion can be accurately described as binitarian in shape, with a prominent place being given to the risen Christ alongside God; and (b) that this binitarian shape is distinctive in the broad and

diverse Jewish monotheistic tradition that was the immediate background of the first Christians, among whom
these devotional practices [the six features] had their beginnings.[2]

It is important to recognize, says Hurtado, that the concept
of divine agency, and the widespread acceptance of a chief agent
position in heaven, provided the early Christians with important
conceptual resources for accommodating the exalted Christ within Jewish monotheism. However, Christian binitarianism is not a
simple development from Jewish divine agency doctrine, it is a
major mutation.

In attempting to explain the causes of this major mutation,
Hurtado points to (1) the impact of the ministry of Jesus upon his
followers; (2) the conviction that Jesus had been raised from the
dead and exalted into heaven as the agent of God's eschatological
salvation; and (3) opposition to the new movement from Judaism,
causing Christians to state explicitly the implications of their
devotion to the exalted Jesus. Whatever were the conditioning
factors and causes, the result of them is clear—Jesus was seen
not merely as a divine agent, but as One to whom a loyalty,
devotion, and worship, which properly belongs to God, is due.

Hurtado does not go on to examine the whole of the New
Testament and so it is not clear whether he thinks that there is a
Trinitarianism in say, the Johannine corpus. What in fact he does
in his book, and does well, is to present a hypothesis to explain
the amazing fact that Jewish monotheists, who were disciples of
the resurrected Jesus, came to address and worship Jesus as truly
divine.

His study may be judged a necessary one because of two
generally held views found in recent New Testament studies.
First, it has been widely held (e.g., by Wilhelm Bousset and his
disciples) that Judaism had lessened its hold on pure monotheism in the postexilic period because of its belief in divine agency—angelology, for example; and, secondly, it has been assumed
that the development of doctrine concerning Jesus as divine occurred not in the original Jewish context of Christianity but
within Gentile Christianity.

In facing the question as to whether there is a unitarian,

binitarian, or trinitarian expression of Christian Faith in the books of the New Testament, we need to make certain distinctions. First of all, there is a legitimate and necessary task of seeking to trace the actual development of both Christian devotion/worship and of Christian thinking in the early church in the light of the events of the Resurrection and the Descent of the Holy Spirit. Hurtado's book belongs to this sphere of academic endeavor. Then there is the task of determining what kind of consciousness or mind-set is presupposed by the actual existence and contents of the books of the New Testament. To determine how Christian worship and thinking developed within monotheism is one thing: to ask what is the result of the development or mutation as presupposed by the canon of the New Testament is another.

Further, what appears at an early stage in the self-consciousness of Jewish Christianity to be binitarian in terms of its explicit devotion may well have arisen from within what may be described as a basically trinitarian consciousness and knowledge (where knowledge is the Hebraic knowing a person[s] relationally rather than knowing objective facts). There was no doubt in the mind of the first Christians that Jesus was a real Person, for they had been with him. His Personhood was indelibly written into their memories and experience. In contrast, by the very nature of things, the Holy Spirit, who is not incarnate but invisible Holy Spirit, could not be thought of at first as being a distinct Person or hypostasis in the same way as was the Lord Jesus. However, the dynamic experience of the amazing and awesome Descent of the Spirit at the Feast of Pentecost, and the further evidence of his presence and activity in the early church, was the experience of One, who was God unto them as invisible, and he was known primarily through the effects of his presence.

Now it is wholly possible — indeed probable — that while the explicit confession of the early Christians may be termed binitarian their experiential knowing of God was trinitarian — knowing the Father through the Lord Jesus and in/by the Holy Spirit. In fact, it may be said that underlying the words of the Gospels and the New Testament letters is a basic trinitarian consciousness, and that this consciousness comes to the surface here and there in an explicit way, sometimes in a binitarian and sometimes trinitarian manner, depending upon the context. The fact that it is sometimes binitarian is often simply because the active relation to God is "to the Father through Jesus Christ"; yet here, it may be suggested, the Holy Spirit is present anonymously and invisibly as the One who makes this relation possible and effective.

BINITARIANISM

We now proceed to look at the evidence adduced by Hurtado for what looks like, or is on its way toward, binitarianism.

Hymns to and about Jesus

When the first Christians met together as an assembly, they celebrated God's presence as they sang hymns as well as exercised charismatic gifts (1 Cor. 14:26). While the singing would certainly have included psalms, especially those which were seen as prophetic of Jesus Christ (e.g., Ps. 110), the hymns that were sung to or about Jesus were essentially new compositions. The believers were making melody to the Lord with all their heart (Eph. 5:19). Examples of such hymns are seen by scholars as embedded in the New Testament at such places as John 1:1-18, Colossians 1:15-20, and Philippians 2:5-11. Fragments of hymns are seen in other places — Ephesians 2:14-16; 5:14; 1 Timothy 3:16; 1 Peter 3:18-22; and Hebrews 1:3.

An examination of all these reveals that they are devoted to the true significance and the saving work of Jesus. "They all celebrate Christ as the supreme agent of God, whether in creation (e.g., Col. 1:15-17; Heb. 1:3; John 1:1-3), earthly obedience (Phil. 2:5-8), redemptive suffering (Rev. 5:9-10), or eschatological triumph (Phil. 2:9-11; Col. 1:20). In short, and most important, they show that the devotional life of early Christianity involved the hymnic celebration of the risen Christ in the corporate worship setting. This is a clear indication of the binitarian shape of early Christian devotion, most likely from the earliest years of the movement."[3]

Dunn is not persuaded that Hurtado is wholly right for he writes: "The earliest hymns of those cited (Phil. 2:6-11 and Col. 1:15-20) are hymns *about* Christ, not hymns *to* Christ. The earliest clear examples of worship of Christ do not appear until the hymns in the Revelation of John, one of the latest documents in the NT (e.g., Rev. 5:8-10)."[4] So what Dunn sees is early Christian devotion to the exalted Christ on the way to full-scale Christian worship of Christ as God.

Prayer to Christ

The early Christians naturally prayed to God, YHWH, whom they called "the Father." However, from time to time, when the occasion seemed to demand it, they prayed to Jesus as "Lord." The best known example is the prayer of the martyr Stephen as he died: "Lord Jesus, receive my spirit" (Acts 7:59). Another occasion, from the personal life of the Apostle Paul, is his beseeching "the Lord" three times concerning his "thorn in the flesh" (2 Cor. 12:8).

There are occasions when prayer is directed both to the Father and to the Lord Jesus: "Now may our God and Father himself, and our Lord Jesus, direct our way to you; and may the Lord make you increase and abound in love to one another and to all men" (1 Thes. 3:11-12). Further, there are many places where "grace and peace" from God the Father and the Lord Jesus Christ are requested for the Christian congregations (e.g., Rom. 1:7; 1 Cor. 1:3). Finally, prayer to Jesus is reflected in the Jewish Christian and Aramaic expression, *maranatha* (1 Cor. 16:22), which means "O Lord [our Lord] come."

"The evidence indicates," says Hurtado, "that the heavenly Christ was regularly invoked and appealed to in prayer and that this practice began among Jewish Christians in an Aramaic-speaking setting, probably the first stratum of the Christian movement."[5] Prayer to Christ is for Hurtado an indication of binitarian devotion. Again, Dunn has reservations about claiming too much for the early stage, insisting that more typical of Paul's understanding of prayer is prayer to God the Father through Christ (see e.g., Rom. 1:8; 7:25; 2 Cor. 1:20; Col. 3:17).

Calling upon the Name

The calling "upon the name" of the Lord (Jesus) of which the Book of Acts speaks (9:14, 21; 22:16) is apparently derived from the calling "upon the name" of the LORD, *Yahweh* (e.g., Pss.

99:6; 105:1; Joel 2:32). It probably had reference to baptism. According to Paul, believers are those who "call on the name of the Lord Jesus Christ" (1 Cor. 1:2) and, further, they are washed, sanctified, and justified "in the name of the Lord Jesus Christ" (1 Cor. 6:11). In a strict monotheistic tradition, such usage is an innovation! It points clearly to binitarianism, says Hurtado.

The Lord's Supper

The sacred meal described in 1 Corinthians 11:23-26 which had been in existence before Paul's conversion is a remarkable phenomenon. Common meals were known in Judaism — for example, in the Jewish sect at Qumran — but this is different. It is "the Lord's Supper"! It is a meal specifically designed for the purpose of proclaiming Jesus' redemptive death, celebrating his victory, and communing with him as Lord. Within monotheism, this, for Hurtado, means binitarianism!

Confessing Jesus

Here the emphasis is upon the widespread use of the verb, *homologeo* (to confess) in the New Testament. To confess Jesus was more than to name or refer to him. It was to speak of him as unique in either testimony to others or in affirming one's faith with others in the assembly of the faithful. To be a Christian was to confess that Jesus is Lord (Rom. 10:9-13). The devotion of the Christian congregation inspired by the Holy Spirit was also to confess Jesus as Lord (1 Cor. 12:1-3). And the solemn duty of the whole creation at the end of the age is also to confess that Jesus, the Christ, is Lord (Phil. 2:9-11).

In contrast, while the Qumran sect referred to a heavenly figure (Michael/Melchizedec), whom they believed would be God's agent in redemption in the eschaton, they did not "confess" him. Confession of Jesus thus points again to binitarianism, claims Hurtado.

Prophecy from the Exalted Christ

The words of Jesus Christ in the first-person singular are spoken by a Christian "prophet" in Revelation 1:17–3:22. He addresses each of the seven churches saying, "I know your works." Probably this points to a reasonably common phenomenon in the churches, where a prophet, "in the Spirit," would address the assembly with a message from the exalted Lord Jesus. For Hurtado such words and such practice point clearly to a binitarian devotion.

In summary, there is much evidence, says Hurtado, which points to the giving of a unique place and devotion to the exalted Lord Jesus alongside God, the Father. Jesus is viewed as being a Person and as also being divine. This is seen very clearly in the statement of Paul. "For us there is one God, the Father, from whom are all things and for whom we exist, and one Lord, Jesus Christ, through whom are all things and through whom we exist" (1 Cor. 8:6). However, as Hurtado admits, at this stage the ontological and metaphysical implications of this form of confession are not addressed.

In contrast, Dunn is hesitant to see binitarianism except in the very latest development of Christian devotion and thinking found in the books of the New Testament. That is, only in the Gospel of John and the Book of Revelation can there be found evidence of a decisive move *outside* the possible categories of divine agency in Jewish monotheism to produce a new form of Christian monotheism in which the confession of the one God includes the confession of the deity of the exalted Lord Jesus Christ (and the deity of the Holy Spirit?). All the early devotion to the exalted Jesus can be contained with the divine agency thought of postexilic Judaism, even though the latter is stretched to the limits. For Dunn, in contrast to Hurtado, the new wine has not yet burst out of the old wineskins.

Certainly one great value of Dunn's book is that he makes very clear that the evidence in the New Testament (within the context of contemporary Judaism) reveals a development of Christology taking place in the early church within the givenness and total acceptance of monotheism. The belief in one and one only YHWH is always foundational to any confession of the exalted Lord Christ and the Holy Spirit.

TRINITARIAN CONSCIOUSNESS

We now proceed to look for what may be called the expression of a trinitarian consciousness, conviction, and vision which (it is here being suggested) undergirded and/or accompanied the implicit or explicit binitarian confession, which Hurtado and others have noticed — either at any early or a later stage of the period in which the books of the New Testament were written. That is, we search for evidence not only that the apostles and disciples of the exalted Lord Jesus had a trinitarian consciousness, but that they also found that to deal adequately, meaningfully, or even reasonably with the total impact of the LORD God upon them since the Day of Pentecost (Acts 2), they had to speak from time to time (out of this deep knowledge in their souls) of the Triad — of the Father, of his Son, and of his Spirit (but not necessarily in this order). To look and search for such evidence of a trinitarian consciousness will not appear foolish or even illogical, if we recognize one simple fact. The Holy Spirit is both invisible and anonymous and thus his elusive presence will not normally be noted, even when it is known that he is present.

Experience of the Spirit

No one has ever seen the Holy Spirit, but his presence is known by what he does. As the wind blows and we know it blows through its effects, so the Holy Spirit (who is the "breath/wind" of the Father) is present and active, and we know this through his effects. The first Christians knew the presence and effects of the Holy Spirit in a dynamic way fifty days after the Resurrection, at the Feast of Pentecost. Acts 2 provides us with the description of the Descent of the Spirit from the Father and from the exalted Lord Jesus, of the signs and wonders caused by his appearance, and of the dramatic effect he had through the preaching of Peter upon the hearers. All this is seen as fulfilling the promise of God made through the Prophet Joel. In the rest of Acts, the presence and power of the same Holy Spirit is presupposed (even though he is not seen), and we hear of this Holy Spirit speaking to the apostles and evangelists (8:29, 39; 10:19; 11:12) as well as specifically guiding them (16:7; 21:4). (We shall return to this theme in chapter 9.)

The deep sensitivity of the early church to the presence of the invisible Spirit of God may be seen in a simple statistic. In the whole of the Hebrew (Masoretic) text of the Bible (O.T.) the word *ruach* occurs only about 90 times as referring to the Spirit of God, while in the Septuagint *pneuma* occurs only about 100 times. But in the letters of Paul, which are only a fraction of the size of the Hebrew Bible and the Greek Septuagint, *pneuma* referring to the Holy Spirit occurs about 115 times!

If we then ask what accounts for this tremendous increase in references to the Spirit of God, we find that the answer is that Paul and his converts, the early Christians, were very conscious of his presence and power in and with them — as the letters make clear. In fact, they held that the presence of the Holy Spirit was absolutely necessary in order to place a repentant believing sinner in union with the Lord Jesus and thus with the Father. "No one can say 'Jesus is Lord' except by the Holy Spirit" (1 Cor. 12:3). So with an explicit binitarianism went an implicit trinitarianism; for the Lord Jesus is seen not only as inseparable from his Father, but also inseparable from the Spirit of the Father.

The early Christians believed that the Holy Spirit indwelt them and their bodies were the temple of the Spirit; that their fellowship one with another and with the Father through the Son was in and by the Spirit; that the Spirit gave spiritual gifts to the church in order to build up the members in the Faith; that the Spirit sanctified their lives so that they should adorn the Gospel; that the Spirit guided them in daily living in practical ways; that the Spirit gave them joy to rejoice in tribulation and difficult circumstances; that the Spirit gave them boldness to proclaim the Gospel and confess Jesus as Lord in a hostile world; that the Spirit opened the hearts and minds of listeners to the Gospel so that they would repent and believe the Gospel; that the Spirit enabled them to worship and pray in a manner pleasing to God; and that the Spirit kept them in a dynamic relation to Jesus Christ.

However, when the first Christians worshiped the Father through the Son, the Lord Jesus Christ, and when they preached the Gospel of the Father concerning the Son and his Resurrection, they did not normally speak of the Holy Spirit (even though they knew that they worshiped and prayed in the Spirit and that they proclaimed the Gospel in the power of the Spirit). As they exercised various forms of ministry, using the supernatural gifts of the Spirit given unto them, they did not usually speak of the Spirit who gave and sustained the gifts within them. Instead they spoke of the Lord Jesus and his Father. Thus what has been called binitarianism is normally undergirded by a trinitarian consciousness. And the invisible and anonymous Spirit is doing what the Father sent him to do—to glorify the Son!

Triadic Statements

The illustration of the iceberg, most of which is under the water and little of which is visible at sea level, helps to make the point concerning the trinitarian consciousness of the apostles and disciples. In the New Testament we encounter here and there formulae or statements concerning the Father, his Son, and his Spirit. Yet we do not have any sense that they are odd, out of place, or wrong, for they seem quite natural. This is because they arise out of a trinitarian consciousness. Further, as we reflect upon the general content of the books of the New Testament we form the impression that everything is from the Father through the Son and in/by the Spirit, and that all returns to the Father through the Son and in/by the Spirit.

Here are some of these threefold statements from Pauline letters.

I appeal to you, brethren, by our Lord Jesus Christ and by the love of the Spirit, to strive together with me in your prayers to God [the Father] on my behalf (Rom. 15:30).

Now there are varieties of gifts, but the same Spirit; and there are varieties of service, but the same Lord; and there are varieties of working, but it is the same God [the Father] who inspires them all in every one (1 Cor. 12:4-6).

The grace of the Lord Jesus Christ and the love of God [the Father] and the fellowship of the Holy Spirit be with you all (2 Cor. 13:14).

When the time had fully come, God [the Father] sent forth his Son, born of woman, born under the law, to redeem those who were under the law, so that we might receive adoption as sons. And because you are sons, God [the Father] has sent the Spirit of his Son into our hearts, crying, "Abba! Father!" (Gal. 4:4-6)

For through him [the Lord Jesus Christ] we both [Jew and Gentile] have access in one Spirit to the Father (Eph. 2:18).

We always thank God, the Father of our Lord Jesus Christ, when we pray for you, because we have heard of your faith in Christ Jesus and of the love which you have for all the saints. . . . Epaphras . . . has made known to us your love in the Spirit (Col. 1:3-8).

We are bound to give thanks to God always for you, brethren beloved by the Lord, because God [the Father] chose you from the beginning to be saved, through sanctification by the Spirit and belief in the truth. To this he called you through our gospel, so that you may obtain the glory of our Lord Jesus Christ (2 Thes. 2:13-14).

When the goodness and loving kindness of God [the Father] our Savior appeared, he saved us, not because of deeds done by us in righteousness, but in virtue of his own mercy, by the washing of regeneration and renewal in the Holy Spirit, which he poured out upon us richly through Jesus Christ our Savior, so that we might be justified by his grace and become heirs in hope of eternal life (Titus 3:4-7).

If these are joined to others from Paul's letters as well as those texts in the rest of the New Testament which we have not cited, they point to something more than a binitarian consciousness.

The texts point to a general trinitarian consciousness out of which there arises an implicit trinitarianism. An explicit binitarianism and an implicit trinitarianism can therefore be seen to belong to the same Faith. For only a dogmatic binitarianism denies a trinitarian consciousness and an implicit trinitarianism. An experiential and practical binitarianism is wholly compatible with an experiential implicit trinitarianism, because by the latter the Holy Spirit is known to be present, but present as the anonymous, elusive, and invisible personal Spirit from the Father and from the exalted Christ.

At the end of his little book, *Holy Spirit: A Biblical Study,* the late Michael Ramsey, Archbishop of Canterbury, expressed what we have been calling an implicit trinitarianism. He explained that the first Christians began with the monotheism of Israel, and without abandoning that monotheism, were led by the impact of Jesus upon them to worship Jesus as divine and did so as they were conscious that the divine Spirit within them enabled both their access to God the Father and their response to Jesus as the Lord. Then he wrote:

Often we have noticed that the Holy Spirit is described as the Spirit of God and the Spirit of Christ. Yet to say only that the Spirit is the impact of God or the impact of Jesus is to do less than justice to the Christian experience, for the Holy Spirit was felt to be one who from within the Christians' own lives makes response to Jesus and to the Father. "Deep answers unto deep. The deep of God above us and around us is inaudible save as it is answered by the deep of God within us." It is here that the doctrine of the triune God begins to emerge, not only as a mode of the divine activity but as a relationship within the life of deity. In knowing "the grace of the Lord Jesus Christ and the love of God and the fellowship of the Holy Spirit" (2 Cor. 13:14), and in having access through Jesus "in one Spirit to the Father" (Eph. 2:18), the Christians were encountering not only their own relation to God but the relation of God to God. When the Spirit cries in us, "Abba, Father" and prompts us to say, "Jesus is Lord," there is God within responding to God beyond. The fourth Gospel takes the further step of suggesting that the divine relationship, known in the historic mission of Jesus and its sequel, reflects the being of God in eternity. Here the key is found in John's concept of the glory. The glory of the self-giving love in the passion and the mission of the Paraclete is one with the glory of God before the world began.[6]

"Deep answering unto deep" — this is a thought to ponder as one contemplates the glory of God in the face of Jesus Christ by the illumination of the Holy Spirit. "In thy light do we see light" (Ps. 36:9) is true at all levels of communion with the Father, through the Son, and in the Holy Spirit.

In later chapters we shall be looking at the Personhood (hypostasis) of the Father, the Son, and the Holy Spirit in greater detail than we have yet done. Here, in closing this chapter, it may be useful to observe that if the words attributed to the resurrected Jesus at the end of Matthew's Gospel were truly said by him as the resurrected Lord (and not attributed to him later by a church that had developed an implicit trinitarian doctrine), then the possession of a trinitarian consciousness in his apostles and disciples is a real probability — perhaps a necessity.

Jesus is recorded as saying: "Go therefore and make disciples of all nations, baptizing them in the name of the Father and of the Son and of the Holy Spirit" (Matt. 28:19). If such a command constantly rang in their ears from the depth of the memories, then the apostles must have had some kind of a trinitarian consciousness. Probably this was in terms of what was later called the economic Trinity: "from the Father through the exalted Christ and by the Spirit" as the movement from God to man and then "to the Father through the exalted Christ in, by and through the Holy Spirit" from man to God. That is, they would have thought of the one, unique God, Yahweh, as somehow truly a plurality in unity and in their relation to him they spoke of coming to the Father through the Son by the Spirit (see further chapter 11). In this sense it can be said that they spoke of the Trinity — yet not of *theos* as a Trinity because for them God, *theos*, was (with a few exceptions, as we shall see in chapter 8) always the Father. We may also recall that the baptism of Jesus himself revealed the presence of the Three — the Father spoke, the Spirit descended, and the Son received (cf. Matt. 3:13-17). So it was not strange that baptism should be in the Name of the Three.

The famous Princeton theologian, B.B. Warfield, made the case for this basic trinitarian consciousness and implicit trinitarianism as strongly as it can be stated when he wrote about eighty years ago these words in his essay, "The Biblical Doctrine of the Trinity":

The simplicity and assurance with which the New Testament writers speak of God as a Trinity have, however, a further implication. If they betray no sense of novelty in so speaking of him, this is undoubtedly in part because it was no longer a novelty so to speak of him. It is clear, in other words, that, as we read the New Testament, we are not witnessing the birth of a new conception of God. What we meet with in its pages is a firmly established conception of God underlying and giving its tone to the whole fabric. It is not in a text here and there that the New Testament bears its testimony to the doctrine of the Trinity. The whole book is Trinitarian to the core; all its teaching is built on the assumption of the Trinity; and its allusions to the Trinity are frequent, cursory, easy, and confident. It is with a view to the cursoriness of the allusions to it in the New Testament that it has been remarked that "the doctrine of the Trinity is not so much heard as overheard in the statement of Scripture." It would be more exact to say that it is not so much inculcated as presupposed. The doctrine of the Trinity does not appear in the New Testament in the making, but as already made.[7]

Warfield does not mean that the ecclesiastical dogma of the Holy Trinity is found in the New Testament. He refers to the doctrine that our creation and salvation is of YHWH who is the Father, the Son, and the Holy Spirit. Further, the Princeton theologian is deeply impressed by the remarkable fact that this experiential knowledge and implicit confession of the Holy Trinity took its place without struggle and without controversy among accepted Christian truths in the Christian fellowship. So he wrote:

> The explanation of this remarkable phenomenon is, however, simple. Our New Testament is not a record of the development of the doctrine or of its assimilation. It everywhere presupposes the doctrine as the fixed possession of the Christian community; and the process by which it became the possession of the Christian community lies behind the New Testament.[8]

My only comment on this claim that the confession of the Holy Trinity occurred before the writing of the New Testament actually occurred is this. Each of the different writers of the books of the New Testament has his own (inspired) way of speaking of the Father, Son, and Holy Spirit, and thus there is not the kind of uniformity in Scripture which occurred after the ecclesial dogma had been set forth and embraced in the liturgies and doctrines of the church. Further, I would prefer to speak of a vision, or conviction, or a consciousness of the Trinity rather than a doctrine of the Trinity being present as the background of the existence of the New Testament.

What Warfield is right to emphasize, I believe, is that the revelation of the Holy Trinity was made in the first place not in word but in deed. It was made in the Incarnation of the Son of the Father and in the outpouring of the Spirit of the Father. So the revelation of the Trinity was, as he says, incidental to, and the inevitable effect of, the accomplishment of our redemption. Thus "the doctrine of the Trinity is simply the modification wrought in the conception of the one, only God by his complete revelation of himself in the redemptive process. It necessarily waited, therefore, upon the redemptive process for its revelation, and its revelation, as necessarily, lay complete in the redemptive process."[9] Today we would perhaps (as those who are more conditioned by the use of the historical-critical method) want to say that the explicit statement of the implicit trinitarian consciousness took longer than Warfield assumed; and, further, that there is evidence (as Hurtado and Dunn show) of the gradual move from Jewish to Christian monotheism in the pages of the New Testament, but that this move in no way takes away from the basic trinitarian consciousness underlying the New Testament.

FOR FURTHER READING

De Margerie, Bertrand. *The Christian Trinity in History*. Still River, Mass.: St. Bede's, 1982.

Dunn, James D.G. *The Parting of the Ways between Christianity and Judaism, and Their Significance for the Character of Christianity*. Philadelphia: Trinity, 1991.

Hurtado, Larry W. *One God, One Lord: Early Christian Devotion* and *Ancient Jewish Monotheism*. Philadelphia: Fortress, 1988.

Ramsey, Michael. *Holy Spirit: A Biblical Study*. London: SPCK, 1977.

Schaberg, J. *The Father, the Son and the Holy Spirit: The Triadic Phrase in Matthew 28:19b*. Chico, Calif.: Scholars, 1982.

Wainwright, Arthur W. *The Trinity in the New Testament*. London: SPCK, 1975.

Warfield, B.B., "The Biblical Doctrine of the Trinity." In *Biblical and Theological Studies*. Philadelphia: Presbyterian and Reformed, 1968, 22–59.

PART THREE

THE WITNESS
OF THE
NEW TESTAMENT

7

THE FATHER

In antiquity it was common to call both god and king by the name of father. This is not surprising when one recalls that the father in a family was seen as its protector, nourisher, and the begetter of the children. Our task is to notice specifically the way in which YHWH is called Father in the Old Testament, how Jesus addressed God as "my Father," and how the Apostle Paul spoke of the "God and Father of the Lord Jesus Christ." Then we shall reflect upon the nature of the word "Father" and its contemporary appropriateness in the light of modern sensitivities.

YAHWEH AS A FATHER

From the beginning, there is in the religion of Israel a clear and precise yet limited confession of the fatherhood of Yahweh. To appreciate this belief and its expression in words it needs to be seen in the context of the polytheistic mythologies that surrounded it. Within these mythologies sexual potency and fertility were ritually divinized; the gods were portrayed as sexual beings who lust, mate, and give birth. Further, the god who was called *'ab* (father) was nothing like the patriarchal figure which feminist rhetoric has depicted. Most often, the father god in ancient Near Eastern mythologies is incompetent, ineffective, and inert while the divine activity is conducted by his wife or consort or son or daughter.

In contrast, Yahweh's fatherhood is wholly removed from the notion of physical procreation. In fact, it has been well said that the loudest silence of the Hebrew Bible is the absence of a consort for Yahweh. He is utterly and completely alone! Perhaps Yahweh's solitude is the most distinctive thing about him, for to be Semitic he needs a female consort and he does not have one! Amazing! Yahweh is male and beyond sexuality!

Yahweh's fatherhood is best described as supervenient, for Yahweh deliberately and mercifully comes upon and makes Israel into his "firstborn son." When Moses was instructed by Yahweh to return to Egypt he was told to say to Pharaoh, "Thus says the LORD, Israel is my first-born son, and I say to you, 'Let my son go that he may serve me'; if you refuse to let him go, behold, I will slay your first-born son" (Ex. 4:22-23). Yahweh as Father exercises his fatherhood by creating a specific relation with an already existing people. His fatherhood is a supervenient intrusion into the life of an historical people.

This message is clear in Deuteronomy, where Moses addressed the assembly of Israel and said:

> Do you thus requite Yahweh, you foolish and senseless people? Is not he your father, who created you, who made you and established you? (32:6)

> For the Lord's portion is his people, Jacob his allotted heritage (32:9).

And using the image of begetting, Moses further said:

> You were unmindful of the Rock that begot you, and you forgot the God who gave you birth (32:18).

By divine election, Yahweh made this people his people. The deep impression of this fatherhood in terms of election is seen vividly in the Book of Hosea, where Yahweh speaks in great tenderness of his son.

When Israel was a child, I loved him, and out of Egypt I called my son. The more I called them, the more they went from me; they kept sacrificing to the Ba'als, and burning incense to idols.

Yet it was I who taught Ephraim to walk, I took them up in my arms; but they did not know that I healed them. I led them with cords of compassion, with the bands of love, and I became to them as one who eases the yoke on their jaws, and I bent down to them and fed them (11:1-4).

Commenting on this text, Paul Mankowski expresses the view that the picture here is not of a father teaching his own infant son to take his first steps. Rather it is "of one who is helping an injured youth, most probably a slave lamed by mistreatment, to regain the power to walk. God comes upon Israel enslaved in Egypt the way a man walking in the countryside might come upon a young beaten slave, whom he nurses and takes to his bosom as a son."[1] Thus again fatherhood for Yahweh is a purely gratuitous extension of partiality: "Out of Egypt I called my son" (Hosea 11:1).

Jeremiah also uses the image of the fatherhood of Yahweh along with the image of God as the Bridegroom both to describe the unfaithfulness and to call the elect people back to loyalty to their God. Israel has polluted the land with vile harlotry and as faithless children have forsaken Yahweh, who says:

Have you not just now called to me, "My father, thou art the friend of my youth" (Jer. 3:4).

Later, speaking of the future, Yahweh declares,

And I thought you would call me, My Father, and would not turn from following me (3:19).

God's love and favor met Israel's disobedience and ingratitude. They would not match their words with their deeds! Yet Yahweh remained their Father.

Speaking for his people and addressing Yahweh, Isaiah lamented:

Look down from heaven and see, from thy holy and glorious habitation. Where are thy zeal and thy might? The yearning of thy heart and thy compassion are withheld from me. For thou art our Father, though Abraham does not know us and Israel does not acknowledge us; thou, O Yahweh, art our Father, our Redeemer from of old is thy name (Isa. 63:15-16).

Yet, O Yahweh, thou art our Father; we are the clay, and thou art our potter; we are all the work of thy hand (64:8).

The same kind of appeal and thought is found in the work of the Prophet Malachi (1:6; 2:10). Such speech was not borrowed from its Semitic neighbors by Israel and it was not the projection of patriarchalism into the nature and character of Yahweh. No! Rather it was the confession of a faith in the one God as solitary, active, generous, and compassionate, whose fatherhood consists in adopting a people and making them his own.

As part of his fatherhood of the whole people, Yahweh is also "Father of the fatherless and protector of widows" (Ps. 68:5). In fact, "as a father pities his children, so Yahweh pities those who fear him" (Ps. 103:13).

Alongside the confession of faith in Yahweh as Father through election, we meet in the Old Testament the proclamation that Yahweh is the Father of the king. This is found first of all in the oracle of Nathan the prophet addressed to David and concerning his son, Solomon:

When your days are fulfilled and you lie down with your fathers, I will raise up your offspring after you, who shall come forth from your body, and I will establish his kingdom. He shall build a house for my name, and I will establish the throne of his kingdom for ever. I will be his father, and he shall be my son (2 Sam. 7:12-14).

This oracle is repeated in 1 Chronicles (17:13; 22:10; 28:6) and in two Psalms.

I will tell of the decree of Yahweh: He said to me, "You are my son, today I have begotten you" (Ps. 2:7).

And with reference to David and his house:

He shall cry to me, "Thou art my Father, my God, and the Rock of my salvation." And I will make him the firstborn, the highest of the kings of the earth (89:26-27).

Here the king is created or made "son of God" by Yahweh when he is crowned. As the whole people is Yahweh's firstborn son by election (Ex. 4:22-24), so the king, who represents the people, is adopted and appointed son of God by election. In Canaanite religion and culture, the king was believed to be an offspring of the gods and to have been suckled at divine breasts. In contrast, within the Hebrew Bible no claims are made for the king's divinity and, furthermore, no prophet is ever recorded as condemning any Hebrew king or kingship on this ground.

Naturally these texts concerning the Son were interpreted by the early church as pointing to the coronation of Jesus in his resurrection and exaltation as the Messiah and as the true Son of God (see Acts 13:33; Heb. 1:5).

In Proverbs there is a further reference to an individual man as a son of God in terms of beneficent, divine discipline.

My son, do not despise Yahweh's discipline or be weary of his reproof, for Yahweh reproves him whom he loves, as a father the son in whom he delights (Prov. 3:11-12).

However, the idea that Yahweh is "my father" reappears in the deuterocanonical literature (see Sir. 23:1, 4; 51:10; Wisd. 2:16-18; 5:5; 14:3; Tob. 14:3).

If personal names are any indication of the faith of a people then it is significant that while there are no personal names which are compounds of the word "mother" in biblical Hebrew, there are at least eight persons (six men and two women) who are called 'abiyya ("Yahweh is my father" — 1 Sam. 8:2; 1 Kings 14:1; 2 Kings 18:2; Neh. 12:2; 1 Chron. 2:24; 7:8; 24:10; 2 Chron. 11:20) and three who are called Yo'ab ("Yahweh is father" — 1 Sam. 26:6; 1 Chron. 4:14; Ezra 2:6). In addition, the word 'El for God occurs in compounds of the same kind, confessing God as Father — e.g., 'eli'ab (Num. 1:9; 16:1; 1 Sam. 16:6; 1 Chron. 12:9; 15:8) and 'abi'el (1 Sam. 9:1).

In order to understand what Israelites had in mind when they used the word "father," it is instructive to note what is both presupposed and taught concerning the place and roles of a father in the Torah and Wisdom literature of the Hebrew Bible. Here John Miller's book, *Biblical Faith and Fathering*, is very useful in showing how Israel's understanding of God produced a new kind of human fatherhood for the ancient world.[2] What Miller makes clear is that (contrary to feminist claims — for which see below) the word "father" was not forged as a legitimation of coercive power in Israel, but rather was an expression of a caring, educative, and committed authority (where authority is not conceived as coercive as in much modern thought!).

YHWH AS FATHER IN EARLY JUDAISM

A careful study of *The Apocrypha and Pseudepigrapha of the Old Testament*[3] reveals that in both Palestinian and Hellenistic Judaism the term "father" was used only rarely of YHWH — six times in Palestinian and seven times in Hellenistic texts. For example, in the Hellenistic Tobit comes the confession: "For he is our Lord and God, he is our Father forever" (13:4).

Further, there is only one example in the Qumran texts (1QH9:35f.). The supplicant (relating to Ps. 22:11) states: "My [human] father has renounced me and my mother has abandoned me to thee. Yet thou art a Father to all who know thy truth. Thou wilt rejoice over them like a mother over her infant."

In the Rabbinic Judaism of the first century the use of the name of Father for YHWH (e.g., as "Father in heaven," emphasizing his transcendence) increased; even so, it is still far less frequently used than other standard Old Testament terms and names. It is possible that in the time of Jesus, Jews were addressing YHWH in the Jewish New Year Liturgy as "Our Father, our King."

Commenting upon this evidence, Robert Hamerton-Kelly notes that the simple invocation "Father" does not occur in the extant prayer sources of Judaism. (To make this statement he has with other scholars to read Sirach 23:1, 4 as originally stating in Hebrew, "God of my father and God [Master] of my life," instead of via the Greek as, "Lord, Father and Master of my life.") Then he concludes: "Therefore, although early Judaism differs from the Old Testament by invoking God as Father, this invocation does not indicate a personal intimacy with God of the kind that is the hallmark of Jesus' use of 'Father' in his prayers."[4] YHWH is the Father in the sense of the heavenly, transcendent, patriarchal Father. The connection between YHWH and Father is bound here, as in the Jewish Bible, by the ties of election, covenant, and the promise of salvation.

In general agreement with the Protestant Hamerton-Kelly, the Dominican biblical scholar, Francis Martin, writes that the material "indicates that God was spoken of as Father and addressed as such in both Greek- and Hebrew-speaking Jewish milieu. The paucity of references, however, also indicates that while such language was intelligible and acceptable, it was quite rare."[5]

THE ABBA OF JESUS IN MATTHEW, MARK, AND LUKE

It seems clear that Jesus often addressed God, YHWH, as *abba*. This is an Aramaic word with a warm familiar ring to it and seems to have originated as a word used by small children of their fathers. It is not inflected and takes none of the suffixes by which Aramaic indicates the personal and possessive pronouns. Thus *abba* can mean "father," "my father," and "the father." We have no evidence that any Jew before Jesus addressed YHWH as abba. Significantly this Aramaic word occurs three times in the Greek New Testament. First of all, in the mouth of Jesus, *abba* occurs only in the oldest form of the prayer in Gethsemane (Mark 14:36). It is an expression of a childlike trust in God and of obligation to obedience (both aspects being characteristic of the calling of God "Father" in Judaism). Jesus prayed, "Abba, Father, all things are possible to thee; remove this cup from me; yet not what I will, but what thou wilt."

In the light of Mark 14:36, it is probable — but cannot be proved — that the expression, *the father, ho pater*, of Mark 13:32 (Matt. 24:36) as well as the expression *my father, ho pater mou*, in Matthew 16:17 and Luke 22:29 are translations of *abba*. This points both to the general use of this intimate expression by

Jesus and to the preference of Jesus to speak of YHWH as the one and only Father, who is uniquely his Father.

Further, it is difficult to believe that any Christians would have used the word *abba* of God (see Paul's use in Rom. 8:15; Gal. 4:6) had Jesus himself not set the precedent. We can therefore suggest the word *abba* was cherished and remembered by the first Christians because it was expressive of Jesus' own sonship and they wanted to share in that sonship. Probably the "Our Father" was originally addressed to *Abba*.

In the Synoptic Gospels Jesus himself is reported as speaking of God as "Father," *Pater,* on various occasions. From these we can choose three brief sayings which modern scholars generally accept are authentic words of Jesus (in contrast to words placed on the lips of Jesus by the evangelists). We should assume that Jesus originally said *Abba*.

(1) After the confession by Peter that Jesus is the Messiah, Jesus said to him: "Blessed are you, Simon Bar-Jona! For flesh and blood has not revealed this to you, but my Father who is in heaven" (Matt. 16:17).

(2) Speaking of the end of the age, Jesus said: "Of that day or that hour no one knows, not even the angels in heaven, nor the Son, but only the Father" (Mark 13:32; cf. Matt. 24:36).

(3) Addressing his disciples in the upper room at the Passover, Jesus said to them: "As my Father appointed a kingdom for me, so do I appoint for you that you may eat and drink at my table in my kingdom" (Luke 22:29-30).

Whether it is "my Father" or "the Father" there is a certain intimacy with God who is in heaven (transcendent and all-glorious) communicated by this form of speech. However, it is certainly not irreverent. It is probably to be seen as an intensification in terms of personal relationship of the reality of the divine fatherhood known in Judaism. What is hinted at and experienced before is wholly surpassed in the knowledge and experience of God by Jesus, the Servant-Messiah and Son.

To these three sayings must be added, also from the Synoptic Gospels, a further, longer saying. This is found in both Matthew and Luke and is also usually reckoned as being an original saying of Jesus. It has been called "the Johannine logion" because it sounds as if it could belong to the Gospel of John.

I thank thee, Father, Lord of heaven and earth, that thou hast hidden these things from the wise and understanding and revealed them to babes; yea, Father, for such was thy gracious will. All things have been delivered to me by my Father; and no one knows the Son except the Father, and no one knows the Father except the Son and anyone to whom the Son chooses to reveal him (Matt. 11:25-27; Luke 10:21-22).

To address YHWH as "Lord of heaven and earth" was common in Jewish prayer, but to combine with this the more intimate, *Abba*, "Father," was to move into the unfamiliar. The addressing of God as "Father" appears to be closely related to the revelation of God's will to the disciples of the kingdom of heaven. In the second half of this logion Jesus speaks specifically of "the Father" and "the Son" (note the definite articles) as well as of the unique and intimate knowledge between them. He is the Son who reveals the Father.

The distinction between the "my Father" of Jesus and the "your [heavenly] Father" of his disciples is maintained in the Synoptic Gospels. They pray "Our Father," knowing that "[their] your Father is merciful/perfect" (Matt. 6:9; 5:48; Luke 6:36). The disciples never address the Father together with Jesus for the simple reason that their relation to the Father is dependent upon and derivative from his own unique relation to the Father.

An "astonishing fact" is often noted by modern biblical scholars concerning Jesus' prayers as recorded in the five layers of the Gospel tradition (Mark, Q, Matthew, Luke, and John). With one exception, Jesus always addressed God as "Father"; and the one exception is a quotation from Psalm 22:1, which was prayed by Jesus on his Cross at Calvary (Mark 15:34; Matt. 27:46)—"My God, My God, why hast thou forsaken me?"

Hamerton-Kelly summarizes the three levels of intimacy on which Jesus used "Father" according to the Synoptic Gospels:

"My Father" when he prayed and when he revealed his identity as the Son to his disciples; "your Father" when he taught his disciples how to pray to a God who cared for them with compassion and forgiveness . . . "the Father" when defending his message against doubters and attack.[6]

In comparison with the Judaism of his time, Jesus' teaching on God as his/our/the Father is remarkable — most probably unique.

THE ABBA OF JESUS IN THE GOSPEL OF JOHN

In the Gospel of John the expression "Father" for *Theos* occurs 122 times, which is more than the total number in the other three Gospels (Matthew—44; Mark—5; and Luke—17). Here is a list and summary of the major occurrences of the name of "Father" in John's Gospel.

1:14: The Father has an "only-begotten Son."

1:18: No one has ever seen God — the Father. The only-begotten Son is in his bosom (i.e., in an intimate relation with him).

2:16: The temple in Jerusalem is (says Jesus) "my Father's house."

3:35: The Father loves the Son and has given all things into his hands as the Mediator between God and man.

4:23: The Father seeks those who will worship him in spirit and in truth.

5:17-23: Jesus calls God his Father and also claims that the Father loves the Son and shows him all that he himself does. Also the Father shares with his Son his prerogatives of raising the dead and judging the world.

5:26: The Father has life in himself, and this prerogative he shares with his Son.

5:36: The Father has given to the Son works to complete.

6:57: The living Father sent the Son, who has life through the Father — and this life is given to those who "eat" the Son.

8:38-44: Jesus has come forth from God, his Father, and bears the Father's authority.

10:30: Jesus and the Father are One.

10:38: The Father is in the Son, and the Son is in the Father.

14:2: In the Father's house, in which the Son stays forever, there are many places to stay.

14:6: No one goes to the Father except through Jesus, the Son, who is the way, the truth, and the life.

14:9-11: To see the Son is to see the Father, for the Father is in the Son and the Son in the Father. So the Father works in and through the Son.

15:1: The Father is the cultivator of the real vine, which is Jesus, the Son.

16:26-28: The Son came out from the Father into the world and he is leaving the world and going to the Father.

17:1: Jesus prays to the Father asking him to glorify his Son so that the Son may glorify the Father.

17:5: Jesus prays that he as the Son will be glorified in the presence of the Father with the glory which he had with the Father before the world existed.

17:21: Jesus prays that his disciples will be one as he the Son is one with the Father. The mutual glorification of the Father and the Son implies a unity in which the disciples are to share.

18:11: The Father has given to Jesus, the Son, a "cup" to drink.

20:17: Jesus is ascending to his Father and his God.

20:21: As the Father has sent Jesus into the world, so Jesus sends his disciples into the world.

A first impression on looking through these verses is that they tell us more about the Son than the Father. And, since the Son reveals the Father, and the Son is visible and the Father is invisible, this is an appropriate impression. However, we do learn some things about the Father. Yahweh-Elohim is the Father, and he is called the Father because he has an only-begotten Son who is one with him and shares his eternal glory and his prerogatives. The Son perfectly loves and obeys his Father, doing the work given to him on earth. So, in the first place, this heavenly fatherhood is by its very nature to be understood only in reference to the eternal relation of Yahweh to the Logos, the incarnate Son, Jesus. It is not a fatherhood whose first reference is to creatures. Further, "Father" is a proper name: it is the literal name of *Theos* for Jesus, who is the only Son. Finally, the disciples of Jesus are "children of God" (1:12; 11:52), who call God "Father" because of their union with the only Son.

THE ABBA OF THE EARLY CHRISTIANS

In the letters of Paul God is said to be "Father" about forty times. A common way of speaking of YHWH is "the God and Father of our Lord Jesus Christ" (Rom. 15:6; 2 Cor. 1:3; 11:31; Eph. 1:3; Col. 1:3). Yet YHWH, *Theos*, is also the Father of believers and thus "our Father" (1 Cor. 1:3; 8:6; 2 Cor. 1:2; Gal. 1:4; Eph. 1:1; Phil. 1:2; 4:20; Col. 1:2; 1 Thes. 1:3; 3:11, 13; 2 Thes. 1:1; 2:16; Phile. 3). "For us there is but one God, the Father" (1 Cor. 8:6).

It is obvious that the early Christians did not so much speak of God as Father but rather they addressed him as "Father." They knew YHWH, *Abba*, through Jesus and in the Spirit as their Father by adoption through grace. In fact, they knew that they had received the Spirit of adoption and were able to cry out in prayer, "*Abba*, Father" (Gal. 4:6-7; Rom. 8:14-17). Being in vital union with the Lord Jesus they had the great privilege of joining him in his way of addressing YHWH. The Fatherhood is not a fact of nature but it is a miracle of grace.

In 1 John, YHWH remains as "the Father" (1:2; 3:1; 4:14) while God's fatherhood of believers is interpreted through the concept of begetting. Christians are God's children because they have been begotten by him (3:9). The origin of their new being is wholly from God himself (4:4). So they have fellowship with him and he abides in them (4:16) and they abide in his love (3:16-17).

It would appear that alongside this distinctive naming of YHWH as the Father of the Lord Jesus Christ, and the Father of those whom he calls, adopts, and begets through Christ, there is also the naming of YHWH as "the Father" in a related but different sense. "I bow my knees before the Father, from whom every family in heaven and on earth is named" (Eph. 3:14-15). Here the universe is not a Greek cosmos but a Palestinian and Jewish cosmos, where God, the Father, is the Father of both the upper cosmos of the angelic world and the lower cosmos of the human world. The Father is the Master of the whole house, of the invisible and visible worlds. It is possible that "Fatherhood" is here understood as inherent in the nature of God and thus it is wholly appropriate to see Yahweh-Elohim, the Father, as the archetype, origin, and source of all fatherhood in the created realm.

The writer of Hebrews asks: "Shall we not much more be subject to the Father of spirits and live?" Again the reference is to the Lordship of YHWH over both heaven and earth and is dependent upon the way Yahweh-Elohim is described in Numbers 16:22 and 27:16. And James, using a phrase which was familiar in the liturgy of the synagogues, wrote of blessings coming down from heaven "from the Father of lights with whom there is no variation or shadow due to change" (1:17).

INCLUSIVE LANGUAGE

There is a significant minority of people within the Christian church in the West who are hesitant, or not prepared, to call God (however they define God) by the name of "Father." In chapter 1 we noted the nature of the feminist challenge to orthodox Christianity. The material presented in this chapter makes it clear that the name of "the Father" when used of YHWH has a major place in the Christian Scriptures, especially in the New Testament. Thus to cease to use the name of the Father or to replace it by another name would be to impose a major change in the way Christians think about, name, and address God. Further, it would mean that the revealed name and nature of God was probably giving way to an identity projected from below upon the God-head out of human experience—a theology from below in contrast to a theology from above.

Perhaps we need to note that the word "Father" as used of God functions at different levels in the Christian Bible. First of all, it can be a simile, where God is likened to this or that aspect of human fatherhood. For example, the psalmist claimed that "as a father pities his children so YHWH pities those who fear him" (Ps. 103:13). In the second place, it can be a metaphor, where God is given the name of Father. This is a stronger meaning than the simile. When the writers of the Old Testament speak of YHWH as the Father of the nation and the Father of the king they use metaphor. Here God's relation to his chosen people in the created order is being described through a well-known picture drawn from human experience. God is not in all respects exactly the same as a human father—for example, he does not sexually beget his children—but his care is sufficiently similar to that of the care of a good, patriarchal father for his family that he can be called "Father."

There is the third level of the literal statement—God is truly and really "the Father." This is not found in the Old Testament and occurs only in the New Testament where God is naming himself through self-revelation. Thus *Theos* is literally "the Father" and he is the Father of "the only begotten Son" and the Father from whom comes "the Holy Spirit." What "the Father" means here is not to be gained by studying human fatherhood and projecting that information into God so as to name and understand him. Rather, this is God's self-revealed name and what it means is revealed by the One who is his "Son" and by the One who is his "Holy Spirit." Converts to Christianity were to be baptized into the fully revealed Name (YHWH) of "the Father and the Son and the Holy Spirit" (Matt. 28:19). In the Old Testament YHWH is the literal Name of the living God. In the New Testament the literal Name of the living God is spelled out more: "the Father and the Son and the Holy Spirit." The literal Name of God is most clearly revealed in the Gospel of John, but it is not absent from the rest of the New Testament as we noted above.

It is a mistake to treat this third level merely as a specific form of metaphor. For while the actual name of "the Father" is certainly a word taken from the language of mortal men, the content of what Fatherhood means is wholly revealed. As the Son who has been given complete knowledge of the Father (John 3:35; 10:15; 16:15), Jesus reveals the Father (John 1:18; 8:26-29; 12:49-50; 14:7, 9). When Jesus addressed his Father he was not using a metaphor drawn from human experience. He was speaking in the literal mode according to personal knowledge.

Now if we take the word "mother" and ask whether or not it can be a substitute for "father" in these three levels we discover interesting results. First of all, God is likened to a mother (human or animal) in both the Old and New Testaments. Here are some examples. First of all, God is like a protective mother bird:

> Like an eagle that stirs up its nest, that flutters over its young, spreading out its wings, catching them, bearing them on its pinions, YHWH alone did lead him (Deut. 32:11-12).

and,

> Like birds hovering, so the LORD of hosts will protect Jerusalem; he will protect and deliver it, he will spare and rescue it (Isa. 31:5).

Further, in delivering the tribes of Israel from Egypt YHWH described his action thus: "I bore you on eagles' wings and brought you to myself" (Ex. 19:4). Jesus, the Son, also used this simile, likening himself in his relation to the holy city, Jerusalem, to a mother bird. "O Jerusalem. . . . How often would I have gathered your children together as a hen gathers her brood under her wings, and you would not" (Matt. 23:37; Luke 13:34).

The clearest examples of feminine images for God in the Old Testament occur in Isaiah. In none of them is YHWH called or addressed as "Mother," but the image of motherhood is used to dramatic effect by the prophet through simile:

(1) 42:13-14: Having been bottled up, Yahweh's war cry bursts forth like the cries, gasps, and groans of a woman in labor.

YHWH goes forth like a mighty man, like a man of war he stirs up his fury; he cries out, he shouts aloud, he shows himself mighty against his foes. For a long time I have held my peace, I have kept still and restrained myself; now I will cry out like a woman in travail, I will gasp and pant.

(2) 45:9-10: YHWH is likened first to a potter, then to a father, and finally to a mother, as a woe is pronounced upon anyone who resists his God.

Woe to him who strives with his Maker, an earthen vessel with the potter! . . . Woe to him who says to a father, "What are you begetting?" or to a woman, "With what are you in travail?"

(3) 49:14-15: YHWH is first presented as the bridegroom of the bride (Zion) and then as the mother of the child (Zion).

But Zion said, "YHWH has forsaken me, my Lord has forgotten me." "Can a woman forget her sucking child, that she should have no compassion on the son of her womb?" Even these may forget, yet I will not forget you.

(4) 66:13: Yahweh is like a mother who comforts her child.

As one whom his mother comforts, so I will comfort you; you shall be comforted in Jerusalem.

While this image of motherly care conveys a vital sense of the compassion of YHWH for his people, it occurs only rarely in the Old Testament and is thus never developed into a metaphor, where God is said to be "a" or "the" Mother.[7]

IN CONCLUSION

The early church confessed that *Theos* is the Father and the Father is the *Pantokrator*, whose divine action, creative and provident, is universal in scope. This teaching entered the Niceno-Constantinopolitan Creed, whose first paragraph is brief and reads: "We believe in one God the Father Almighty (*pantokrator*), Creator of heaven and earth, and of all things visible and invisible." In the second paragraph, which is devoted to the Son, the relation of the Son to the Father is set forth and thus the reason why the Father is called the Father becomes clear. The one God is the Father because he has a Son begotten before all ages, who is consubstantial with him.

The German Protestant theologian, Jürgen Moltmann, explained the identity of "the Father" in this way:

> The first person of the Trinity is *the Father* only in respect of the Son, that is, in the eternal begetting of the Son. God the Father is *the Father of the Son.* He is never simply "universal Father," like Zeus, Jupiter, Vishnu or Wotan. He is not called *Father* merely because he is the unique cause on whom all things depend. Nor is it for the sake of the authority and power which all authorities and powers in heaven and on earth, in religion, state and family, hold from him. It is solely and exclusively in the eternal begetting of the eternal Son that God shows himself as *the Father.* He is uniquely "the Father of Jesus Christ" and only through Christ, the only-begotten Son, and in the fellowship of this "firstborn" among many brothers and sisters, is he also "our Father."[8]

In order to maintain this crucial distinction, Moltmann continued in his lecture (paper) to speak emphatically of "the Father of the Son."

The Jesuit theologian, Bertrand de Margerie, summarized the teaching of the western medieval councils on the identity of "the Father" within the Blessed and Holy Trinity in these words.

> The Father is the foundation and principle of intra-divine unity. It is the Father, and not the divine essence considered abstractly, who is the principle of the Son and of the Spirit; and a principle without principle, for the Father himself does not spring from some mysterious impersonal essence. The Council of Florence says formally: "All that the Father is, and all that he has, he does not derive from another, but from himself; he is the principle that has no principle." The Father is *ex se*, he cannot then be *ab ilio.* Much earlier a local council of Toledo had pro-

claimed the Father "source and origin of the whole divinity,"—*fons et origo totius divinitatis*. An incomprehensible abyss of affirmation, the Father is eternally plenitude as source, *fontalis plenitudo*, without receiving anything from anyone, not only uncreated but also unbegotten.

And he continues:

The Father gives to the Son and to their Spirit his substance or nature without losing it, and in giving it, and in giving it totally, he gives himself. Thus he gives and he retains. He remains in the Son and in the Spirit to whom he is essentially relative, at the same time that he communicates to them his essence and gives himself personally to them.[9]

Therefore the Father is "the summit of the Holy Trinity" and the Son and the Spirit, within the immanent Trinity, are truly consubstantial with him because they receive from him their substance/essence.

Yet the truth of the matter is that we can only name, address, and know the Father because of our Lord Jesus Christ who is God, the Son incarnate. So it must be our task in the next chapter to investigate the identity and the nature of this unique and only-begotten Son of God the Father. The fact of the matter is that we only know the Father in, through, and by the Son, Jesus of Nazareth, who addressed God as *Abba*.

FOR FURTHER READING

Achtemeier, Elizabeth. "Exchanging God for 'No Gods': A Discussion of Female Language for God." In *Speaking the Christian God: The Holy Trinity and the Challenge of Feminism*, edited by Alvin F. Kimel, Jr. Grand Rapids: Eerdmans, 1992.

Barr, James. "Abba Isn't 'Daddy.' " *Journal of Theological Studies* 39 (1988): 28–47.

De Margerie, Bernard. *The Christian Trinity in History*. Still River, Mass.: St. Bede's, 1982.

Dunn, James D.G. *The Parting of the Ways between Christianity and Judaism*. Philadelphia: Trinity, 1991.

Hamerton-Kelly, Robert. *God the Father: Theology and Patriarchy in the Teaching of Jesus*. Philadelphia: Fortress, 1979.

Jeremias, Joachim. *The Prayers of Jesus*. London: SCM, 1967.

_____. *New Testament Theology. Volume 1: The Proclamation of Jesus*. New York: Scribner's, 1971.

Mankowski, Paul V. "Old Testament Iconology and the Nature of God." In *The Politics of Prayer*, edited by H.H. Hitchcock. San Francisco: Ignatius Press, 1992.

Martin, Francis. *The Feminist Question*. Grand Rapids: Eerdmans, 1994.

Miller, John W. *Biblical Faith and Fathering*. New York: Paulist, 1989.

Moltmann, Jürgen. "Theological Proposals." In *Spirit of God, Spirit of Christ*, Faith and Order Paper, WCC, no. 103. London: SPCK, 1981.

Toon, Peter. *Yesterday, Today and Forever: Jesus Christ and the Holy Trinity in the Teaching of the Seven Ecumenical Councils*. Swedesboro, N.J.: Preservation, 1995.

See also the articles on *abba* and *pater* and *theos* in Horst Balz and Gerhard Schneider, eds., *Exegetical Dictionary of the New Testament*, 3 vols. (Grand Rapids: Eerdmans, 1990, 1991, 1993).

8

THE SON

One thing is clear. Because Jesus himself addressed *Elohim, ho Theos,* God, as *ho Pater, Abba,* Father, Christians have spoken of God as the Father—as the Apostles' and Nicene Creeds, with their "I believe in God the Father almighty . . ." have long declared. In this chapter we shall continue to reflect upon the implications of Jesus using the word *Abba.* Further we shall examine several Christological titles used or given to Jesus in the New Testament. Hopefully this will lead us into an appreciation of the filial relation of Jesus Christ to the Father.

THE SELF-CONSCIOUSNESS OF JESUS HIMSELF

Serious readers of the four Gospels find it difficult to escape the conclusion that Jesus had a relation to God which is impossible to fit into regular human ways of describing the relation of a man to God. His disciples sensed this unique relation, relatedness, and relationship of Jesus to the God of their fathers. Jesus' relation was not merely that of a prophet to Yahweh-Elohim or of a member of the righteous remnant, the "poor of the Lord," in his humility before God; it was different from that of the devoted priest in the temple, waiting upon God in faithful service; and it was not like that of the Pharisee, devoted to God through meticulous obedience to the Law. In terms of the external manner and events of his ministry, Jesus fits into various categories—prophet, rabbi, miracle-worker, exorcist, and healer. Yet in terms of his inner life—as reflected in his prayer and in his naming of the living God, Yahweh-Elohim as *Abba*—Jesus of Nazareth cannot easily be fitted in any category. In fact, he fits into no obvious category.

Already, in the last chapter, we noted the rare but extremely important occurrences of the Aramaic word, *Abba*, in the New Testament—on the lips of Jesus and as the cry of the Spirit of Jesus in the hearts of baptized believers. We recognized that the retention of this Aramaic word within the Greek New Testament pointed to *Abba* being the word specifically chosen and used by Jesus to express his own, unique relation to the living God, YHWH. Further, we noticed that the way it is used by the Apostle Paul of the intimate sense of union with the Father of Jesus Christ enjoyed by believers also points to the unique use of this word by Jesus himself (Gal. 4:16; Rom. 8:15). Paul did not use the word in other places (e.g., doxologies) and, as far as we can tell, the word was not used in any of the early liturgies of the church (i.e., as we know of them via the anonymous *Didache* and the writings of Justin Martyr and Hippolytus of Rome).

It is possible to see Jesus' use of *Abba* as merely reflecting his creativity, independence of thought, boldness of expression, and freedom from Jewish traditionalism. Certainly there was no precedent in his religious and devotional heritage for calling the God of Jewish monotheism *Abba*. However, the wiser and better way is to see in Jesus' adoption of this startling form of address indications of not only his own true identity, but also the true identity of Yahweh-Elohim. In fact, one might say that Jesus chose the word *Abba* because his own relation to, and experience of, the living God could not adequately be expressed in any of the ways of speaking of Elohim/Theos provided in the Jewish Scriptures or the Jewish tradition of worship.

Of course, when he was at the synagogue and in the temple Jesus prayed as a Jew with Jews and used the traditional forms of worship and prayer. Yet, at the personal level, such was his unique relation, relatedness, and relationship to YHWH that he had to create his own verbal expression, using his own vocabulary. The One whom Jesus addresses as *Abba* is certainly Yahweh-Elohim and Theos; yet he is known, experienced, and addressed in a more intimate way by Jesus than had ever been the case on earth before.

Without denying the Hebraic and Jewish tradition of prayer and covenantal communion with Yahweh, and without setting aside the Torah, Jesus moves on into new spiritual territory. For what God was/is to him, God was/is to no one else. In fact (as later Christology will make clear), Jesus spoke from within Divinity — from inside the Godhead. He experienced fully the divine Filiation. To pray privately addressing the Deity as Elohim or to Yahweh or to Adonai would have been to pray to himself! So he prays to *Abba* as the Son praying to the Father, where both Father and Son together (in the unity of the Holy Spirit) are Yahweh-Elohim, the one unique God, who is a plurality in unity!

The Jesus of the Synoptic Gospels is conscious of a personal intimacy with the Father, knows that YHWH is his Father and Father of his disciples in different but related ways, and is wholly dedicated as the Son-Servant to be the Suffering Servant in absolute obedience to the will of God. All this is clear in the Gospel of Mark which begins with the statement, "The beginning of the gospel of Jesus Christ, the Son of God," and then quickly moves to the baptism, where Jesus is told by the Father that he is the Son and his vocation is that of the Suffering Servant.

Obviously, the implications of Jesus' choice and use of *Abba* only became clear to his apostles and disciples after his resurrection and after their reception of the gift of the Holy Spirit. This means that the Gospels were written by those who had this insight and knowledge. So it is the Synoptic Gospels and Mark in particular (14:36) which provide the clues concerning Jesus' original use of *Abba*, as we noticed in the last chapter. However, being written in Greek they use *ho Pater* all the time, with Matthew's Gospel containing the greatest frequency of use of the words "Father" and "Son" in the Synoptics. In fact, Matthew makes it clear that "Son of God" is the only adequate title of

Jesus and that to recognize Jesus as truly the Son of God requires divine revelation. Even Peter the apostle needed illumination from heaven (see Matt. 16:13-17; cf. 27:51-54). Further, in this Gospel, the sonship of Jesus is presented primarily in terms of obedience to the Father, his readiness to suffer and die in order to fulfill all righteousness (3:15). Because of this total, loving obedience, the Father raised him from the dead and exalted him, giving him "all authority in heaven and on earth" (28:18). Now he reigns as the Son (28:19; 24:36) and will return to the earth in glory as the only Son of the Father (10:32; 16:27; 25:31-46).

There are, of course, all kinds of indications in the Gospels that Jesus is unique in his knowing of God. One such is his relation to the Torah, which he claimed to revise and fulfill as though he were its original giver (Matt. 5). He acted according to who he is — the maker and therefore the reviser of the Torah. Further, as Raymond E. Brown, the distinguished Catholic biblical scholar, writes: "Jesus could and did declare sins forgiven, modify the Law of Moses, violate Sabbath ordinances, offend against the proprieties (eat with tax collectors and sinners), make stringent demands (forbid divorce; challenge to celibacy and to leave family ties), defy common sense (encouragement to turn the other cheek) — in short, teach as no teacher of his time taught. . . . Moreover, the certainty with which Jesus spoke and acted implies a consciousness of a unique relationship to God."[1]

The kingdom of God (= kingdom of heaven), which was the focal point of his ministry, is never described by Jesus for it is beyond description — ineffable. Yet all kinds of hints were given by Jesus in his parables and actions for those who had ears to hear. In terms of the perspective of Jesus himself George Tavard writes:

The kingdom of *Elohim,* the kingdom of the heavens, must have, as it were, two levels. As the kingdom of *Abba,* it belongs to the One who is beyond *Yahweh-Elohim,* whom the Jewish hearers of Jesus did not know because he was yet unrevealed in their life. Into this kingdom no one can enter except the Son, who comes from it without having left it. In the mouth of Jesus, the

parables of the kingdom reveal first of all that there exists a realm so far unsuspected, an impenetrable aura of
divinity, which no one has ever entered since no one can
see God and live, yet of which he, Jesus, can speak, since
he belongs to it, and soon will return to it. But Jesus
cannot describe it, cannot even conceptualize it, because
no words in any language can formulate this experience
of being the Son.

This is the first level, the level into which the prayer to *Abba*
is addressed. Then there is the second level.

There is, accordingly, another level . . . the kingdom of
Elohim, of which Jesus speaks, is the kingdom of himself,
of which he is the king, an aura of Divinity around Jesus
closely related to what the Old Testament had called the
Spirit of God. This is the kingdom of the One whom the
gospel of John calls the *Logos*, whom Paul calls the
Kyrios, of the One who gave the Law, who spoke in the
prophets and who sent the Apostles. Thus the parables of
the kingdom are Jesus' mythical presentation of himself
and of his mission on earth. To say that Jesus has a
kingdom is, on the analogy of the Old Testament, to
imply the he has a Spirit, that this Spirit seeks those who
belong to Jesus and brings them into his joy.[2]

There are other indications in the Synoptic Gospels of the
profound sense enjoyed by Jesus of an intimate communion with
the Father in heaven. In the last chapter we noted some of the
recorded words of Jesus where he spoke of his unique relation to
the Father (e.g., Matt. 11:27; Mark 12:6; 13:32; Luke 10:22;
20:13). To these can be added the words Jesus uttered at the age
of twelve when he was in the temple in Jerusalem. Addressing
Joseph and Mary who were earnestly and urgently looking for
him he said, "How is it that you sought me? Did you not know
that I must be in my Father's house?" (Luke 2:49) Luke's comment on this early expression of filial consciousness in Jesus is:
"And they did not understand the saying which he spoke to
them" (v. 50).

When we look at the Synoptic Gospels and ask what further

evidence within them points to a unique relation of Jesus to Yahweh-Elohim and harmonizes with Jesus' own sense of *Abba,* we cannot avoid examining the narratives of the conception and birth of Jesus in Matthew and Luke, and the descriptions of the baptism and Transfiguration in Matthew, Mark, and Luke. Later we shall return to these important events to seek evidence of the revelation of the Trinity, but here our only concern is with Jesus as the unique Son of the Father.

Though the Matthean and Lucan infancy narratives are very different, they agree on two facts. First of all, in terms of his human identity, Joseph is his legal father and thus Jesus is of the House of David (Matt. 1:20; Luke 1:27). In the second place, in terms of his divine identity, he was conceived by Mary without a human father through the unique act of the Holy Spirit (Matt. 1:20; Luke 1:35)—therefore, God is his Father. So Jesus is Emmanuel (God with us) and God's Son (Matt. 1:23; Luke 1:32). We must presume that sooner or later Mary told Jesus that Joseph was not his father. What Jesus knew innately within himself was surely confirmed by this knowledge of his origins.

The three Synoptic Gospels present us with accounts of both the baptism and the Transfiguration of Jesus. At the baptism, the beginning of his public ministry, the voice of the Father from heaven tells Jesus that he is "my beloved Son" (Mark 1:11; Matt. 3:17; Luke 3:22); then, again, at the Transfiguration, as he turned his face toward Jerusalem, the city of God, the voice of the Father from heaven tells Moses, Elijah, and the disciples, "This is my beloved Son" (Mark 9:7; Matt. 17:5; Luke 9:35). Again we have to say that only he to whom and about whom such heavenly words are said could pray in a wholly natural way, *Abba.*

THE IMPACT OF THE RESURRECTION

We possess what we now call the New Testament because the apostles and disciples of Jesus believed that God the Father by the Holy Spirit had raised Jesus of Nazareth from the dead and exalted him into heaven to his right hand. This message resounds in the early chapters of Acts where we are told of the first preaching in Jerusalem, "This Jesus God raised up, and of that we all are witnesses . . . God has made him both Lord and

Christ, this Jesus whom you crucified" (2:32, 36). "The God of our fathers raised Jesus . . . God exalted him at his right hand as Leader and Savior, to give repentance to Israel and forgiveness of sins" (5:30-31).

Undoubtedly the Resurrection is the major event in Jesus' revelation of the divine life, that is, of the full identity of YHWH. In terms of the revelation of God as Holy Trinity, we may say that the revelation was incidental to, and the inevitable effect of, the accomplishment of redemption—first in the resurrection of the crucified Jesus (who was raised by the Holy Spirit) and then in the gift of the Holy Spirit to the waiting disciples (for which see chapter 9).

The books of the New Testament were certainly written by men who believed that Jesus was truly raised from the dead in a bodily resurrection, left behind an empty tomb, and ascended into heaven in his glorified human nature/body. Further, the conviction of these authors that the resurrection of Jesus demonstrated that he is truly the Messiah of the Jews, the Son of God, and the Lord resounds through their writings. Therefore, even the Gospels, as they tell of the ministry of Jesus before his death and resurrection, show that they were written from within a profound faith in the living, exalted Lord Jesus Christ, Messiah, and Son. This is especially true of the Gospel of John where the full identity of Jesus, known after the Resurrection, is used in a more intense and obvious way to inform the narrative of events and the sayings of Jesus before the crucifixion and Resurrection.

It is because the Gospels were written from within commitment to the exalted, living Lord Jesus, that it is (for modern scholars) exceedingly difficult to determine what impact this faith and knowledge had on the actual reporting of the words and works of Jesus during his public ministry. So it is not surprising that in academia there has been the "quest for the historical Jesus"—the search for the "Jesus of history" freed from interpretations based on "the Christ of faith." There are, of course, legitimate and interesting questions raised by biblical scholars concerning whether or not we can ever surely know precisely what Jesus originally knew, felt, and said. Obviously we are dependent on the memory of faithful disciples for what he said and did; and happily they lived in a culture where accurate memory was taken for granted. Yet the impact of the Resurrection, by which the glory of his full identity began to dawn upon them, must have caused them to see in his remembered words and works meaning which was earlier, during the period of the public ministry, far from obvious to them.

It may be claimed that their memory remained accurate but their interpretation of the content of memory enlarged and developed under the guidance of the Holy Spirit. And it is reasonable to assume that their insight into the full identity of Jesus and the total meaning of his time on earth grew and matured as the days and years went by. However, admitting all this, we do also need to take into account the basic honesty of the writers of the Gospels as reporters of past words and events—and thus affirm the historical reliability not only of the Synoptic Gospels but also, in a different but complementary way, of the Gospel of John. The latter was written on its own admission "that you may believe that Jesus is the Christ, the Son of God, and that believing you may have life in his name" (20:31).

JESUS IS THE SON OF GOD—
THE GOSPEL OF JOHN

In the last chapter, we noted how the word "Father" is used of God as a simile, a metaphor, and in the New Testament only, in a profound literal sense in the Bible. Here we must also note that the expression, "Son of God," has various meanings in the Bible. In the Old Testament, as we already noted in chapter 7, both the king (2 Sam. 7:14; Ps. 2:7) and Israel (Ex. 4:22-23; Hosea 11:1) are presented as sons. Further, angels are also called sons of God (Gen. 6:2; Job 1:6; Dan. 3:25). In the New Testament the confession of Jesus as "Son of God" is sometimes a way of speaking of Jesus as the Davidic Messiah. Jesus is raised from the dead, exalted into heaven, and enthroned as the "Son"—in fulfillment of the prophetic words of Psalm 2:7. For example, in Acts 13 Luke presents Paul as preaching in the synagogue at Antioch of Pisidia. In his address he said:

We bring you the good news that what God promised to the fathers, this he has fulfilled to us their children by raising Jesus; as also it is written in the second psalm, "Thou art my Son, today I have begotten thee" (Acts 13:32-33).

Here Paul is certainly thinking of the enthronement of Jesus as the Son through his exaltation from death to the right hand of the Father in heaven. Psalm 2:7 is seen as being fulfilled. It is not clear whether or not there is also the further insight (which becomes clear in other places in Paul's writings) that he is the Son of God before the Resurrection and that his being raised is a demonstration of his sonship.

When we turn to the Gospel of John we find the teaching that Jesus is the Son of God in a profound, ultimate, and unsurpassable sense. The poetic opening of the Gospel proclaims the *Logos* who was God in the beginning (1:1) and became flesh "and dwelt among us, full of grace and truth . . . the only Son from the Father" (1:14); toward the end of the Gospel, Thomas, one of the Twelve, addresses Jesus as "my Lord and my God" (20:28). In between these statements Jesus is presented as being supremely conscious of his filial relation to the Father as the unique Son of the Father. For example, on the eve of his glorification in Crucifixion (and Exaltation) he told his disciples: "I came from the Father and have come into the world; again, I am leaving the world and going to the Father" (16:28); and he prayed: "Father, glorify thou me in thy own presence with the glory which I had with thee before the world was made" (17:5).

As the Son, Jesus is presented in the Gospel of John as perfectly obeying the will of his Father both in his coming into the world to be incarnate and in his vocation as the Messiah (4:34; 5:30; 6:38; 7:28; 8:42). Further, Jesus is the One who uniquely shares the work of the Father, specifically including those deeds which God alone can do — judging (5:22, 27-29; 8:16) and giving life to the dead (5:21, 24; 6:40). In fact, Jesus says and does nothing unless he has first heard or seen it from the Father (3:32-34; 12:49-50). As the Son, Jesus does the will and the work of the Father because of the unique communion he has with the Father, whom he knows intimately and with whom he is one (1:18; 4:22-23; 6:45-47; 14:13-16; 17:1-5). The unity of the Father and the Son is seen in the holy love of the Father for the Son and the Son for the Father (10:17; 14:31; 17:23).

Jesus is the only Son; he is one of a kind. Certainly his Father has children through divine grace (1:12), but his Father has one and only one Son. This unique status of Jesus and this unique relation with the Father is communicated by the constant use of the definite article — *the* Son of *the* Father — in the Gospel of John. God requires that people come to the Son, believe the Son, and obey the Son and honor the Son (3:36; 5:23; 14:6) in order to receive salvation (5:34) and eternal life (6:40, 47) from the Father and become his children, begotten by his grace.

The preexistence of the Word/the Son (who as the Incarnate God is Jesus of Nazareth) is also made clear in the Gospel of John through the words *ego eimi* (with no predicate) spoken by Jesus. Though in ordinary Greek these words often mean "It is I" or "I am the one," in John's Gospel the meaning is to be fixed through their particular use in the Greek Bible, the Septuagint. Let us first note the significant occurrences of *ego eimi* without a predicate:

> You will die in your sins unless you believe that I AM (8:24).

> When you have lifted up the Son of Man, then you will know that I AM (8:28).

> Truly, truly, I say to you, before Abraham was, I AM (8:58).

> When it does take place you may believe that I AM (13:19).

> Jesus said [to the soldiers], "I AM" (18:5).

Other places where the "I am" of Jesus has the predicate (e.g., when he says he is the good Shepherd, the Light of the world, and so on) are significant; but, they are not of the same profound significance as those without the predicate.

In saying "I AM" and not supplying a predicate, Jesus is speaking in the same way as YHWH speaks in Isaiah 40–55. The Hebrew for "I YHWH" or "I He" is translated in the Septuagint simply as *ego eimi*, and since the predicate is not present, the translation into Greek puts particular emphasis upon existing — the existence of God. Thus in the Hebrew YHWH says *'ani hu'* and in the Greek he says *ego eimi* (see Isa. 41:4; 43:10; 43:25; 46:4; 51:12; 52:6). This way of speaking is to be traced back to Exodus 3:14, where YHWH tells Moses to declare in Egypt that, "I AM has sent me [Moses] to you [Pharaoh]." Commenting on this usage, the Swedish professor Tryggve Mettinger writes: "When Jesus proclaims his 'I AM,' he is unambiguously playing on a formula that recalls the Old Testament text about the revelation of the divine Name. In other words, when a reader of the Bible puts himself in the vantage point of the New Testament 'I AM' expressions and looks backwards to the Old Testament, he sees a line of tradition back to Exodus 3:14. But there is another kind of flashback to Isaiah 40–55."[3] Thus the Father is YHWH and Jesus, the Son of the Father, is YHWH. The rich unity of YHWH has a plurality.

It would be wrong for us to assume that John invented the absolute use of the "I AM," for there are hints of it in the Synoptic Gospels. For example, both Mark and Matthew describe Jesus walking across the water to his disciples and saying to his disciples, "*Ego eimi*, take heart, have no fear" (Matt. 14:27; Mark 6:50; and cf. John 6:20). Though (as we noted above) the Greek may be translated as "It is I" (as in the RSV here and in John 6:20), that the full "I AM" is intended is suggested by the response of the disciples in the boat, "Truly you are the Son of God" (Matt. 14:33). Then, of course, the same Gospel of Matthew contains the command of Jesus that converts be baptized in the Name (YHWH) of the Father, and of the Son, and of the Holy Spirit (28:19).

JESUS IS THE SON OF GOD — FURTHER TESTIMONY

Another book of the New Testament which proclaims that Jesus is Son of God in himself, and not merely Son because of being the enthroned Messiah-Son, is Hebrews. The main theme of 1:1–3:6 is the superiority of Jesus both to the angels and to Moses. He is superior because he is the Son of God, through whom the Father created and sustains the universe. God the Father has spoken "to us by a Son, whom he appointed the heir of all things, through whom also he created the world. He reflects the glory of God and bears the very stamp of his nature, upholding the universe by his word of power" (1:2-3). Of this Son, Scripture not only says (in Ps. 2:7) "You are my Son, today I have begotten you," but also (in Ps. 45:6) "Thy throne, O God, is for ever and ever" (KJV). From earth by faith believers confess that "we see Jesus, who for a little while was made lower than the angels [in his incarnate existence on earth], crowned with glory and honor" (Heb. 2:9).

The Apostle Paul calls Jesus "the Son of God" on four occasions (Rom. 1:4; 2 Cor. 1:9; Gal. 2:20; Eph. 4:13), and on thirteen occasions he speaks of Jesus' divine sonship in such expressions as "his Son" (Rom. 1:3, 9; 5:10; 8:3, 29, 32; 1 Cor. 1:9; 15:28; Gal. 1:16; 4:4, 6; Col. 1:13; 1 Thes. 1:10). It is of interest and theological importance that in all of his seventeen references to the divine sonship of Jesus Paul uses the definite article (which is not always obvious in the English translations). For example, in Romans 1:3 the literal translation is "the Son of him" which the RSV renders as "his Son." By this grammatical means Paul declares that the sonship of Jesus is unique — he is one of a kind. Paul's calling was to proclaim "the Son of him [God the Father]" among the Gentiles (Gal. 1:15-16). The Gospel is the Gospel of God concerning his Son, the Royal Son (Rom. 1:4), the Sacrificed Son (Rom. 8:32), and the Son in and through whom God adopts sons through his grace (Gal. 4:5).

JESUS CHRIST IS GOD

In chapter 7 we noted that *theos* (*elohim*) meaning "God" is normally used of the Father in the New Testament. However, there are several times in the New Testament where Jesus Christ is certainly called, and several when he is apparently called, *theos*, and these we must now examine. We cannot here go into the complex issues of textual variants and syntax, which are raised by the full study of whether and where Jesus is called *theos* by the writers of the New Testament. Happily a recent book, *Jesus as God: The New Testament Use of Theos in Refer-*

ence to Jesus, by the erudite, conservative scholar, Murray J. Harris, covers the technical evidence more than adequately. We shall examine the occurrences as they appear in the order of the books of the New Testament.

(1) "In the beginning was the Word, and the Word was with God, and the Word was *God*" (John 1:1).

(2) "No one has ever seen God; the only Son, who is in the bosom of the Father, he has made him known" (John 1:18). (Instead of "the only Son" we perhaps should read "the only *God*" or "the only-begotten who is God" for this has superior textual support.)

(3) "Thomas answered [Jesus], 'My Lord and My *God!*' " (John 20:28)

(4) "... and of their race, according to the flesh, is the Christ. *God* who is over all be blessed for ever" (Rom. 9:5). (Here the RSV follows the Codex Ephraemi Rescriptus, where a full stop or period is put after flesh. If a full stop is put only after "for ever" and a comma is placed after "Christ" then it reads, "... the Christ according to the flesh, who is over all God blessed for ever.")

(5) "... awaiting our blessed hope, the appearing of the glory of our great *God* and Savior Jesus Christ" (Titus 2:13).

(6) "But of the Son he says, 'Thy throne, O *God*, is for ever and ever' " (Heb. 1:8).

(7) "To those who have obtained a faith of equal standing with ours in the righteousness of our *God* and Savior Jesus Christ" (2 Peter 1:1).

(8) "... in his Son Jesus Christ. This is the true *God* and eternal life" (1 John 5:20).

Of these it may be said that three (1, 3, and 6) contain reasonably sure statements that Jesus is *theos*. In four of the rest (4, 5, 7, and 8) it is possible but unlikely that *theos* refers to God the Father, while in one (2) it is a matter of which textual variant is followed.

What seems clear is that the readiness and tendency to call Jesus *theos* belongs to the latter part of the apostolic age — Romans 9:5 being the earliest possible calling of Jesus *theos.* We know that early in the second century Ignatius of Antioch freely called Jesus *theos,* as his Letters reveal. Further, in the same period the Roman Pliny described the Christians in one of his reports to Rome as those who sang "a hymn to Christ as God."[4]

There are good reasons for thinking that in the first decades of Christianity the Old Testament heritage dominated the use and meaning of *theos.* Only the Father in heaven, the One to whom Jesus prayed, could be *theos.* However, by the 50s and 60s of the Christian era, *theos* began to be used in a fuller, even richer way to reflect the conviction that God had been fully revealed in Jesus. *Theos* now included both the Father and his Son, and so the Son could also be called *theos.* It is perhaps worthy of note that of the eight texts cited above the majority belong to the spirit and content of worship. The calling of Jesus *theos* must have occurred and developed — as Pliny indicates — in worship, where Jesus is addressed as "God-and-Savior."

JESUS CHRIST THE IMAGE OF GOD

When Paul called Christ "the image (*eikon*) of God" the emphasis is upon the equality of the image with the original. The meaning is that Christ shares in God's real Being and is therefore a perfect manifestation of that Being. In 2 Corinthians 4:4 Paul writes of "the glory of Christ, who is the likeness of God." In commenting on this verse Philip E. Hughes wrote:

> St. Paul is not simply saying that Christ is like God or reflects the character of God, or that through his incarnation he is the revealer of God to the world, true though it may be that Christ represents God to us in these respects; for what is stated here is far more than a declaration of the function or effect of the incarnation. It is in the profoundest sense a declaration concerning the essential being of Christ, that is to say, an ontological state-

ment with reference to the Second Person of the Holy Trinity. This conclusion is drawn from the context — a context which speaks (3:7ff.) of the divine glory reflected from the face of Moses but veiled from the people because of their unbelief, and which declares that the divine glory now beams forth, unreflected and unveiled, from the face of Jesus Christ and in the gospel of God's grace, but with transcendent brilliance. The glory of Christ is not a mere reflection or copy of the glory of God; it is identical with it.[5]

This biblical language of image and glory is dynamically equivalent to the "consubstantial" language of the Creed.

In Colossians 1:13-15 Paul writes of God's beloved Son in whom we have redemption, the forgiveness of sins. This Son is "the image of the invisible God." Again, we can benefit from the words of Dr. Hughes.

In the nature of the case, there can be no such thing as a pictorial copy of the invisible; consequently, the term "image" does not mean here simply a visible likeness other than the reality itself. Within the mystery of the infinite trinitarian being of God it is the Son who authentically reveals the divine nature and gives effect to the divine will. Certainly, he does this as the incarnate Son in the perfection of his life and his performance of the work of redemption. He is the image, however, not just temporarily, during the time of his incarnate manifestation here on earth, but eternally; for, as St. Paul goes on to say in this same passage, it was through him and for him who is the image of the invisible God that all things were created (vv. 16f.).[6]

The underlying idea of the image is the manifestation of the hidden and thus Christ is the manifestation of the invisible God. Mankind is not the image of God; rather human beings are made *in* the image of God. Only Jesus Christ is truly and really the eternal *eikon* of God, the Father. As the *eikon* of God, the Son became man to identify fully with man who is originally created *in* (not as) the image of God.

In three other places, Paul uses the word *eikon* in a significant way pointing to the renewal of man through being conformed to the image of the Son of God (Rom. 8:29; 1 Cor. 15:49; Col. 3:10). Made in the image of God but marred through sin, man is renewed in Jesus Christ who is the image of God in which man was first formed!

Related in meaning to *eikon* is the word *morphē*, used by Paul in the important Christological passage, Philippians 2:5-11, where he speaks of the preexistent Christ as being "in the form of God" before he took the "form of a servant." The contrast of the heavenly and earthly existence suggests that *morphē* points to a participation in God which is real, just as partaking in human life and history was real for Jesus. In fact, the meaning is much like that of John 1:1-5, where John speaks of the preexistent Word who became flesh.

JESUS CHRIST IS LORD

Jesus is certainly addressed and described as *kyrios* in the New Testament. But what does *kyrios* mean? Does it have one or a variety of meanings, depending on the context? What we know for sure is that the word *kyrios* was used in Greek in a variety of ways—for example, as a master (owner of slaves), as a polite expression ("Sir"), as a title of gods and heroes, and a title of the Roman Emperor. So shades of these meanings occur throughout the New Testament, for example, in the parables and ministry of Jesus.

Further, scholars are not sure whether in the versions of the Septuagint available in the first century of the Christian era YHWH was usually rendered by *Kyrios*. The earliest major preserved copies of the Septuagint that we possess were prepared by Christians in the fourth and fifth centuries. These certainly use *Kyrios* for YHWH. In fact, *kyrios* occurs about 8,400 times, and of these 6,700 are substitutes for the tetragram, YHWH.

Bearing this in mind, it is not in the least surprising that the Father is often called, *ho kyrios*, "the Lord," in the New Testament—for example, in expressions such as "the angel of the Lord" (Matt. 1:20, 24) and "the name of the Lord" (James 5:10), as well as in the expression, "the Lord God" (Rev. 22:5-6). However, *Kyrios* is used as a title of Jesus in all the books of the New Testament except Titus and 1–3 John.

The early Christian confession, "Jesus is Lord" (1 Cor. 12:3; Rom. 10:9), which Paul inherited from Palestinian Christianity, obviously celebrates Jesus as *kyrios* in a religious sense as the risen and exalted agent of God, by whom comes salvation, and to whom allegiance is owed and given. Paul himself continued to use *kyrios* in the absolute sense of the exalted Jesus in his lordship over both the old and new creations — "for us there is . . . one Lord, Jesus Christ, through whom are all things and through whom we exist" (1 Cor. 8:6).

About 100 times Paul simply calls Jesus "the Lord" (*ho kyrios*) without any other name or title, suggesting perhaps that he received this shorthand name and form of address from Jewish Christianity (from the Aramaic, *marya*; and see also the use of *Maranatha*, "Lord come" in 1 Cor. 16:22). Certainly Jesus is Lord in the sense that he is the Master who is to be served and obeyed with an allegiance which is offered only to God (Rom. 14:1-12). He is also the Lord in the sense that it is he who will appear to judge the world on "the Day of the Lord" (1 Cor. 4:1-5). Thus he acts as YHWH, the Judge. Also he is the Lord who is worshiped in the assembly of Christians, when they meet at the Lord's Table on the Lord's Day (1 Cor. 11:17-22). At the end of the age the whole created order will confess to the glory of God the Father that Jesus is the one and only *Kyrios* (Phil. 2:9-11). So for Paul to call Jesus *ho kyrios* was to identify him in the closest possible way with YHWH, the LORD, and in so doing also identify Jesus in the closest possible way with God the Father, who is YHWH. Thus, to change the title, he is truly *the Son of God.*

OTHER TITLES OF JESUS

Apparently very early *Christos*, a verbal adjective used as a noun, became a proper name or title for Jesus, which Paul received from Christians before him (see 1 Cor. 15:3) and often used. Obviously its early and general use indicated that the first Christians believed that Jesus was the Messiah of Israel and that his resurrection and exaltation proved this to be so. Paul added to this understanding the confession that Christ is also "God blessed forever" — as we saw above in looking at Romans 9:5.

Another indication that for Paul the name of Christ suggests deity is his constant use of the phrase "in Christ" (*en Christo*). It occurs about 170 times in the letters and means much more than the word, *Christianos*, which he does not use at all. For Paul, all baptized believers are "in Christ"; it is only as they are "in Christ" that they can approach the Father, possess the gift of the Spirit, be the adopted sons of God, receive salvation and enter the church which is the body of Christ. All this indicates that Paul thought of Christ as a divine Person in whom all believers everywhere dwell and the One who also dwells by his Spirit in all believers.

The phrase, "Son of Man," is used more often in the Gospels than any other name or title except Jesus, and with one exception (John 12:34) only Jesus speaks of the "Son of Man." Much research and debate among scholars has occurred in the attempt to locate the origin and meaning of this title. It seems generally agreed that in it there is a reference to the "Son of Man" of Daniel 7, who comes from heaven and is therefore, in some sense, divine. However, the actual form of words of the title (see Mark 2:10, 28) also points to manhood — a male man, his father's son. Thus this title conveys the truth that Jesus is both human and divine. As Son of Man he has authority — to forgive sins, as lord of the Sabbath, and as ruler in the kingdom of God. As Son of Man he will come in majesty and glory to judge the people — a coming which stands in contrast to his first coming with its betrayal, rejection, mockery, and injustice, leading to execution and death. The Son of God is the Son of Man for he was incarnate and thus is both God and man.

Finally there is the title, the Word (*logos*). Again there has been much academic interest in the Hellenistic and Jewish background to this word as it is used in the prologue of the Gospel of John. Wherever, precisely, the inspiration for the use of *Logos* came from its meaning in the Gospel of John is clear. The Word is the Person within the Godhead (the only Son) through whom the world was created, who is the source of light and life for mankind and who became flesh that men might become the children of God by grace. In some way the *Logos* is the actual personification of the word and wisdom of God (see chap. 5).

Jesus, the Word, is the express declaration of the divine mind. He is God's utterance to man. He is the Revealer of the will and character of God. He declares, utters, and reveals the Truth!

IN CONCLUSION

Whether Jesus is confessed as "the Son," or "the Lord" or "the Christ," or "the Son of Man," it is clear from the total witness of the New Testament that he is seen as God in the flesh, God with a human nature and body. Further, it is clear that early Christians loved, served, and worshiped him as God incarnate, and did so without in any way setting aside their monotheism, their commitment to YHWH. In worshiping the Father through the Son, the Lord Jesus Christ, they acclaimed the Son as in, with, and through him they praised the Father.

Because of the pressure from feminists today, there is a growing tendency in Christian worship to reduce or take out of the prayers, hymns, and sermons the naming of Jesus as "the Lord," and "the Son," and "the King." In their place are put such words as "Servant" and "Child" so as to avoid charges of sexism and androcentricism. Any careful student of the New Testament knows that to do this kind of thing is to run the risk of losing the heart of the Faith. For it is in the relation of "the Father and the Son" and "the Son and the Father" that the true identity of Jesus is known and salvation is available. To take away the words is also to take away the reality. Christian Trinitarian Theism comes from the Scripture with a specific vocabulary and to change this is to lose that unique monotheism and drift into other forms of belief in God (where "God" becomes grammatically neuter in gender and pantheist in meaning!).

As we observed in chapter 3, the key word which the early church used to establish the full and true deity of Jesus as the only Son of the only Father was *homoousios,* meaning consubstantial with the Father. In so doing the church rejected Arianism, the teaching that Jesus is an inferior form of deity. The paragraph of the Niceno-Constantinopolitan Creed concerning Jesus reads:

> We believe in one Lord Jesus Christ, the only begotten
> Son of God, begotten from the Father before all ages,

light from light, true God from true God, begotten not made, of one substance (*homoousios*) with the Father, through Whom all things came into existence, Who because of us men and because of our salvation came down from heaven, and was incarnate from the Holy Spirit and the Virgin Mary, and became man, and was crucified for us under Pontius Pilate, and suffered and was buried, and rose again on the third day according to the Scriptures and ascended into heaven, and sits on the right hand of the Father, and will come again, with glory, to judge both the living and the dead, of Whose kingdom there will be no end.[7]

Once the deity of Jesus had been established the next major question to answer was the relation within the one Person of the Son, Jesus Christ, of his divine and human natures. Guidelines for answering this question in line with the witness of the New Testament and the Nicene Creed were provided by the Council of Chalcedon (451) in this Declaration:

In agreement, therefore, with the holy fathers, we all unanimously teach that we should confess that our Lord Jesus Christ is one and the same Son, the same perfect in Godhead and the same perfect in manhood, truly God and truly man, the same of a rational soul and body, consubstantial with the Father in Godhead, and the same consubstantial with us in manhood, like us in all things except sin; begotten from the Father before the ages as regards his Godhead, and in the last days, the same, because of us and because of our salvation begotten from the Virgin Mary, the *Theotokos*, as regards his manhood; one and the same Christ, Son, Lord, only-begotten, made known in two natures without confusion, without change, without division, without separation, the difference of the natures being preserved and coalescing in one *prosōpon* and one *hypostasis* — not parted or divided into two *prosōpa*, but one and the same Son, only-begotten, divine Word, the Lord Jesus Christ, as the prophets of old and Jesus Christ himself have taught us about him and the creed of our fathers has handed down.[8]

This doctrine entered into the western Athanasian Creed (the *Quicunque Vult*) and was further refined at the ecumenical Councils of Constantinople (in 553 and 680). Those who desire to maintain that Jesus is one and one only Person, and that he is truly and really God and truly and really man, return often to this statement in order to keep their thinking biblically and patristically orthodox.

Since Jesus Christ, One Person made known in two natures, was filled with the Holy Spirit (in his human nature) and consubstantial with the Father and the Holy Spirit (in his divine nature) his relation to the Holy Spirit belongs both to the very center of both the Trinity and the work of human salvation. Therefore, having studied the identity and nature of the Father and the Son, it is now necessary and appropriate to turn, in the next chapter, to the study of the Holy Spirit.

FOR FURTHER READING

Brown, Raymond E. *An Introduction to New Testament Christology*. New York: Paulist, 1994.

Cullman, Oscar. *The Christology of the New Testament*. London: SCM, 1959.

Dunn, J.D.G. *Christology in the Making*. Philadelphia: Westminster, 1980.

Jeremias, Joachim. *New Testament Theology: The Proclamation of Jesus*. New York: Scribner's, 1971.

Kramer, W. *Christ, Lord, Son of God*. London: SCM, 1966.

Harris, Murray J. *Jesus as God: The New Testament Use of Theos in Reference to Jesus*. Grand Rapids: Baker, 1992.

Hughes, Philip E. *The True Image: The Origin and Destiny of Man in Christ*. Grand Rapids: Eerdmans, 1989.

Mettinger, Tryggve N.D. *In Search of God: The Meaning and Message of the Everlasting Names*. Philadelphia: Fortress, 1988.

Toon, Peter. *Yesterday, Today and Forever: Jesus Christ and the Holy Trinity in the Teaching of the Seven Ecumenical Councils*. Swedesboro, N.J.: Preservation, 1995.

9

THE HOLY SPIRIT

Most of us have no difficulty at all
in thinking of the Spirit of God, or the Holy Spirit, as the general
presence of God in his world or as the specific presence of God
within the church of Jesus Christ and in the hearts of believers.
Thus we are able to appreciate the two general aspects of the
Spirit of YHWH which we encounter in both the Old and New
Testaments. First of all, the Spirit is like wind and fire, a power
which invades a person from without causing him to be moved in
a direction of God's choosing. We read that the Spirit of God
"drove" Jesus into the wilderness after his baptism in the river
Jordan (Mark 1:12); and in Acts the coming of the promised
Spirit is accompanied by wind and fire (Acts 2:1-4). In the second place, the Spirit is like a fluid or substance with which a
person is filled or into which he is immersed so that he has life,
gifts, or virtues from the Spirit. "God anointed Jesus of Nazareth
with the Holy Spirit and with power," said Peter (Acts 10:38).
"Be filled with the Spirit" (Eph. 5:18) and "drink of one Spirit"
(1 Cor. 12:13), writes Paul.

From this perspective, it is quite natural to refer to the Spirit
as "it," just as we refer to the wind or human breath with the
pronoun as neuter. In fact, the Greek word *pneuma* is, in terms

of grammar, neuter gender (in contrast to *ruach* in Hebrew which is feminine gender and *spiritus* in Latin which is masculine gender). Therefore, we find the neuter pronoun used of the Spirit (e.g.,"It had not yet fallen on any of them," Acts 8:16). However, as we shall see below, in the teaching concerning the Holy Spirit as the Paraclete in John's Gospel the Spirit assumes the masculine gender. The Spirit is "he."

THE SYNOPTIC GOSPELS

If we turn to what Jesus is recorded by the Synoptic Gospels as saying concerning the Holy Spirit, we find that, while the concepts he utilized can be contained within inherited Old Testament and Jewish categories, they do point to a more exact definition of the Spirit of YHWH and his relation both to the Father and to Jesus, the Son. This becomes clear in these two examples.

(1) When the Pharisees allege that Jesus cast out demons by the power of Beelzebul, prince of the demons, the response of Jesus includes this terrible saying: "Truly, I say to you, all sins will be forgiven the sons of men, and whatever blasphemies they utter; but whoever blasphemes against the Holy Spirit never has forgiveness, but is guilty of an eternal sin" (Mark 3:28-29). Matthew records these extra words: "And whoever says a word against the Son of man will be forgiven; but whoever speaks against the Holy Spirit will not be forgiven, either in this age or in the age to come" (12:32). The Spirit present and at work in Jesus and his ministry is the Spirit of the age to come—as the Old Testament prophets promised. The Spirit is the "already" of the "not yet" fully arrived kingdom of God. So to deny the presence and activity of God's Spirit in the exorcisms of Jesus and, worse still, to attribute the Spirit's work to Beelzebul is to have no place in the age to come. It is "an aeonian sin," a sin relating to the age to come.

Glimpses of the distinct personhood of the Holy Spirit are contained in the verbs used—to blaspheme against and to speak against the Holy Spirit. In both instances the blaspheming and speaking is obviously against YHWH, but it is also specifically against "the Holy Spirit."

(2) In looking forward to the time when the disciples would

be proclaiming the Gospel and being beaten and arrested, Jesus promised: "When they bring you to trial and deliver you up, do not be anxious beforehand what you are to say; but say whatever is given you in that hour, for it is not you who speak, but the Holy Spirit" (Mark 13:11; cf., Matt. 10:20, where the Spirit is "the Spirit of your Father speaking through you"). Here there is a hint of a distinct identity for the Holy Spirit, who is both the Spirit of prophecy and the Spirit of the Father.

If we move on to examine what is said editorially concerning the relation of the Holy Spirit to Jesus, we find again the heightening and personalizing of the presence and activity of the Holy Spirit in contrast to Jewish thought. This is particularly clear in Luke (at which we shall specifically look), but it is not absent from Matthew. In the latter is the baptism formula of 28:19 containing the words, "the Holy Spirit," after "the Father and the Son." This statement is not in the form of a promise of the Spirit to the disciples, but it is of interest to us as a major hint of an emerging understanding of the Holy Spirit as a distinct identity alongside and in relation to the Father and the Son.

Luke describes the conception of Jesus in the womb of Mary as being directly caused by the Holy Spirit ("the Holy Spirit will come upon you," 1:35). Further, he describes the principal persons in the narrative of the birth of Jesus and John as being "filled with the Spirit" — Mary herself (1:35), John from his mother's womb (1:15), Elizabeth (1:41), and Zechariah (1:67).

After Jesus had been baptized by John and was praying, "the heaven was opened, and the Holy Spirit descended upon [Jesus] in bodily form, as a dove" (3:21-22). Luke draws here upon the imagery of Genesis 1:2 ("the Spirit of God was moving over the face of the waters") in order to emphasize the creative activity of the Holy Spirit. A new thing was being wrought at the baptism comparable with the creation of heaven and earth out of the primeval chaos. The description of the descent of the Holy Spirit upon Jesus, the unique Son, takes us beyond descriptions of his descent upon prophets and moves us, through the dove image, toward an indication of a unique identity for the Spirit in relation both to Jesus and the Father.

Following the baptism we read that Jesus, "full of the Holy Spirit, returned from the Jordan, and was led by the Spirit for forty days in the wilderness, tempted by the devil" (Luke 4:1-2). Here through the theme of the New Exodus is the role of the Spirit entering and filling Jesus, who is the new Israel and Son/Servant of YHWH; and also there is the more personal idea of the same Holy Spirit specifically leading him to where the Father wanted him to be. By the Spirit, Jesus successfully defeats Satan.

Jesus "returned in the power of the Spirit into Galilee" (4:14) and eventually arrived in Nazareth and entered the synagogue. Here Jesus read from Isaiah 61:1-2: "The Spirit of the Lord is upon me, because he [the Lord] has anointed me to preach good news to the poor" (4:18). The descriptions of the Spirit are well within those of the Old Testament. The New Exodus is under way and Jesus in the Spirit as the Son/Servant of YHWH is releasing Israel from Satan's oppression. Such release involves both exorcisms and healings, as well as removing the spiritual and moral blindness of the Jews to God as he is revealed in his Messiah, Jesus.

However, in the next reference to the Spirit we are probably entering into a dimension not found in the old covenant. When the seventy disciples returned from their mission of proclaiming the kingdom of God, rejoicing because of their spiritual success, Jesus himself "rejoiced in the Holy Spirit" as he prayed in intimate terms to his Father in heaven (10:21-22). This is the prayer in which Jesus (as the Son) says that "no one knows who the Son is except the Father and who the Father is except the Son." Is it possible there is here a revelation of the Trinity, specifically the unique communion of the Father and the Son in the Holy Spirit? It is probable that one result of Jesus being "filled with the Spirit" was a heightening awareness of the Father, whose work he as the Son was doing. It has been well said, as we noted in the last two chapters, that it is the interaction of Jesus' filial consciousness and the Spirit, who fills him, that gives Jesus' ministry its distinctive character.

The final reference to the Holy Spirit in Luke is a prediction of what will happen on the Day of Pentecost. "Behold I send the promise of my Father upon you; but stay in the city until you are clothed with power from on high" (24:49). Here the Holy Spirit is called "the promise of my Father" (pointing to Joel's prophecy as cited in Acts 2:17, 33) and "power from on high" and, significantly, Jesus claims to be wholly involved in the sending, along with "my Father."

THE ACTS OF THE APOSTLES

On several occasions it has been claimed in this book that the Holy Trinity is revealed in and through events—the Incarnation and the Descent of the Holy Spirit—before being known by the disciples. It is in Acts 2 that we are given the description of the event of the Holy Spirit—that is, the arrival of the Spirit, who is sent by the Father and by the Son, to the waiting disciples. Though we must assume that the presence of the Spirit brought a tremendous leap forward in the insight and understanding of the apostles and disciples, we have also to recognize that the full spiritual and doctrinal implications of this unique event naturally took time to form and develop in the explicit knowledge of the church. So we look for these implications not only in the Acts but in the rest of the New Testament as well—remembering that the books were written by those who were inspired by and filled with the Holy Spirit.

The Feast of Pentecost had come in Judaism to be a commemoration of the giving of the Law at Sinai. So it is not surprising that the theophany described by Luke in Acts 2:1-3 includes the vivid realities and images of wind and fire—for they were associated (as we saw in chaps. 4 and 5) with the theophanies on Sinai. On Mount Sinai YHWH descended to meet with Moses and the elders of Israel; in Jerusalem as the theophanies of Sinai are remembered, the Spirit of YHWH (who is sent by the Father and the exalted Lord Jesus, the Son) descends not only to rest upon the twelve apostles and the disciples but also to remain with them and to be in them. Therefore, not only are they filled with the Holy Spirit, but they break forth into praise and rejoicing in a variety of languages. Further, they become bold to proclaim the Gospel of God concerning Jesus, Messiah, and Lord.

What happened at this Day of Pentecost was the fulfillment of prophecy—that of Joel in particular. He had prophesied in Yahweh's name that "in the last days . . . I will pour out my

Spirit upon all flesh, and your sons and your daughters shall prophesy, and your young men shall see visions, and your old men shall dream dreams" (Acts 2:17, citing Joel 2:28-32). The "last days" had certainly arrived for the dynamic Sign of the age to come was now gloriously present.

Peter declared to the crowd which assembled the good news concerning Jesus of Nazareth and the Spirit of God. "This Jesus God raised up, and of that we all are witnesses. Being therefore exalted at the right hand of God, and having received from the Father the promise of the Holy Spirit, he has poured out this which you see and hear" (Acts 2:32-33). At the end of his proclamation he called upon his fellow Jews to "repent, and be baptized every one of you in the name of Jesus Christ for the forgiveness of your sins; and you shall receive the gift of the Holy Spirit" (2:38). The gift is given by the crucified and exalted Jesus, whom the Father has declared to be Lord and Christ.

The church now has a mission. It is a mission, like that of the Messiah whom it proclaims, in the power of the Spirit—as the text of Acts makes clear. It is the mission of the Father and of the Son through the church; and the church is to be always filled with the Holy Spirit, who is the gift of the Father and the Son.

If we survey the references to the Holy Spirit in Acts 3–28 we find that they fall into two types, those which continue the traditional biblical (O.T.) way of speaking of the presence and activity of the Spirit, and those which point (dimly but surely) toward the full and distinct personhood of the Spirit within the plurality of the unity of YHWH. It will be sufficient for our purposes to give examples of each type to indicate the fluidity of expression used of the invisible and ineffable Holy Spirit.

First of all, there are texts where the Spirit's coming or presence is presented through the image of filling, as if the Spirit were a heavenly fluid or substance. On a lot of occasions an apostle or disciple is said to be "filled with the Holy Spirit" (e.g., 4:8; 4:31; 6:3; 7:55; 9:17) while on other occasions a person is said to "receive the Spirit" (8:18; 10:47) in becoming a Christian. In the second place, there are occasions when the Spirit is said to act like "a person" in terms of telling Philip what to do (8:29), carrying Philip from one place to another (8:39), explaining to Peter the meaning of his dream (10:19), prompting the church in

Antioch to commission Barnabas and Saul (13:1-4), forbidding the apostles to preach in Asia (16:6), and witnessing to Paul that bonds and afflictions await him in Judea (20:23).

In whatever way and through whatever image we read of the Holy Spirit in the Acts, it (he) is always engaged in continuing the mission of Jesus, now exalted in heaven as the Lord and Christ. There is an obvious but ineffable relation between the Father, the Lord Jesus Christ, and the Holy Spirit.

THE GOSPEL OF JOHN

In the Gospel of John are profound statements and rich teaching concerning the Holy Spirit which are not found in the Synoptic Gospels. It is usual in modern biblical scholarship to attribute this important doctrine not to Jesus himself but to the theological insight of the evangelist, as he reflected upon the experience of the Spirit in the apostolic age. Another way of putting this viewpoint is to say that, having carefully noted what the Spirit was doing from the Day of Pentecost onward, John placed a creative summary of the principles of this action upon the lips of Jesus.

From a more conservative viewpoint, and allowing for the input of the evangelist in filling out the content of the original words of Jesus in the light of the Resurrection, Exaltation, and descent of the Spirit, it is possible to say that Jesus did speak of the Spirit in such a way as to inspire the fuller and developed record of which we read in the Gospel of John. In fact, such is the richness of the content that it makes excellent sense to see the genius of Jesus behind the words.

The most prominent and important teaching on the Spirit is obviously in chapters 14–16. Yet there are important statements concerning the Spirit in earlier chapters. In our own chapter 2 we examined the expression, "God is Spirit" which occurs in 4:23-24, where Jesus is in conversation with the woman of Samaria. To her he spoke of the gift of the Spirit in terms of "a spring of water welling up to eternal life" (v. 14). In John 3:1-8 there is significant teaching on the necessity of being "born from above [i.e., of God]" and "born of the Spirit," an image which points to the personhood of the Holy Spirit, the Begetter. At the end of chapter 3 it is said of the Son: "For he whom God has sent utters the words of God, for it is not by measure that he gives the Spirit" (v. 34). In 7:37-38 we learn that the fullness of the gift of the Spirit (which gift is again presented in terms of "rivers of living water") to the disciples must wait until Jesus is glorified (through his Crucifixion, Resurrection, and Ascension).

So the Jesus who is presented as meeting his disciples in the Upper Room before the feast of the Passover (John 13–17) is the person who both knows all about the Spirit and who has been filled and endowed with the Spirit from the beginning — as John the Baptist perceived (1:32-34). A reader will judge that such must be the case for in chapters 14–16 Jesus speaks in such a way about the Holy Spirit, whom he calls the *Paraklētos* (the Paraclete), as to suggest a holy "familiarity" with him. This said, it needs also to be added that what is taught in these chapters of the work of the Holy Spirit is fully in line with the Jewish understanding of the Spirit as "the Spirit of prophecy" and of the Spirit who inspired and brings the wisdom of YHWH. It is in line with such concepts, but it also extends and deepens that teaching.

In Greek *paraklētos* is formally a passive verbal adjective meaning "one called alongside" (e.g., to assist in a court). So it has often been translated as "Advocate" or "Counselor." The translation of "Comforter" (KJV) is partly generated by the content of John 14–16 (the comfort brought by the Spirit) and by deriving the word from the verb *parakalein,* to encourage.

The future sending of the Paraclete from heaven is the means whereby the Lord Jesus himself returns to the disciples, and in doing so brings glory to the Father. Receiving the Spirit and his ministry, the disciples in turn will know Christ's presence with them on earth. Yet, for all the affinity of the Spirit to Christ, the Spirit is distinct and personal; the emphatic personal pronoun following the neuter noun (*to pneuma — ekeinos*) from 15:26 onward vividly makes this clear. It is the Lord Jesus who will send the Spirit from the Father, and it is also the Father who will send the Spirit in answer to the prayer of the Lord Jesus. In these holy relations between the Father, the Son, and the Holy Spirit we are given an indication of the identity of the Holy Trinity.

In summary, the teaching of Jesus on the *pneuma* and the *paraklētos* in John 14–16 is as follows:

(1) The Paraclete, the Spirit of truth, will indwell the disciples forever (14:15-17).

(2) The Paraclete, whom the Father will send in the name of the Lord Jesus, will teach the disciples all things and bring to their remembrance what he has taught them (14:25-26).

(3) The Paraclete, as the Spirit of Truth from the Father, will bear witness to the Lord Jesus in his ministry to the disciples (15:26-27).

(4) The Paraclete on coming into the world will convince the world of sin and of righteousness and of judgment as he turns people to believe in the Lord Jesus (16:7-11).

(5) The Paraclete as the Spirit of truth will take what belongs to the Lord Jesus and declare it into the disciples; further, he will speak of things that are to come (i.e., the Crucifixion and Resurrection). In all that he says and does he will glorify the Lord Jesus (16:12-15).

To convey adequately what is said of the *pneuma* as *paraklētos* we need probably to use two English words, both of them nouns that apply to persons — Advocate and Comforter. As the *Advocate,* the Holy Spirit continues the work of Jesus himself to persuade people that Jesus is truly the Son of the Father, whom to know is life eternal. The removal of Jesus from earth will leave the disciples as orphans and defenseless. The Spirit comes to be the defense of the disciples as they go forth into the world; the Paraclete takes over Jesus' advocacy of the Father's cause. So the Spirit prosecutes the case against the world. He works through the disciples and their ministry in and upon the minds of people to persuade and to convince them of the truth of the Gospel. "He will convince the world of sin . . . because they do not believe in me [Jesus]; of righteousness because I go to the Father . . . of judgment because the ruler of this world [Satan] is judged" (16:8-11). Thus this great work of the Holy Spirit who comes into the world from the Father, in the name of the Lord

Jesus, is to stir the world's conscience and to confute its errors in order to bring men to conversion (John 12:31-32).

As the *Comforter*, the Holy Spirit brings to the disciples a new and vital communion with the Father and the Son. In this communion there is genuine peace and true joy as there is also comfort in tribulation and trial – "These things I have spoken to you, that my joy may be in you, and that your joy may be full" (15:11); "I have said this to you that in me you may have peace. In the world you have tribulation; but be of good cheer, I have overcome the world" (16:33).

In his mission within the church and within the world, the Holy Spirit will depend upon and listen to the exalted Lord Jesus, who is the Son, just as the Lord Jesus depended (and still depends) and listened (and still listens) to the Father. As the Lord Jesus glorified his Father by declaring the things of the Father as an obedient Son, the Holy Spirit will glorify the Son by declaring the things of the Son to the disciples. In fact, it may be said that the unity of the Son and the Spirit is as permanent and comprehensive as is the unity of the Father and the Son (10:30).

Not only is the personhood of the Holy Spirit as Paraclete indicated by the emphatic personal pronoun *ekeinos* (14:26; 15:26; 16:8, 14) and *autos* (16:7), it is also suggested by means of the parallelism between Jesus and the Spirit. The Paraclete is to Christ as Christ is to the Father. This may be set out as follows:

(1) Both Jesus and the Spirit are sent from the Father into the world (3:16-17 and 16:27-28; 14:26 and 15:26).

(2) Both Jesus and the Spirit are called "holy" (6:69; 14:26) and characterized by "the truth" (14:6; 14:17; 15:26).

(3) Both Jesus and the Spirit teach (13:13-14; 14:26).

(4) Both Jesus and the Spirit are revealers. Jesus bears witness to the Father and reveals all things (4:25-26; cf. 1:18; 3:34-36); the Paraclete witnesses to the Son and reveals him as the glorified Son (15:26-27; 16:13-14).

(5) Both Jesus and the Spirit seek to convince and convict the world (1:12; 16:8-12).

Jesus was the Paraclete until his glorification. The Holy Spirit is the Paraclete from the glorification of Jesus.

Here as well as in chapters 3 and 6 we have noted the possibility that God was conceived as a Binity not a Trinity by the early Christians, Paul in particular. Not surprisingly, the suggestion has been made that because of the way the Paraclete and Jesus are identified in John's Gospel God is here also conceived as a Binity. For example, J.E. Davey has written: "In John, Son and Spirit seem to be aspects of the one Incarnate Divine Life."[1] In contrast, Gary Burge, in his outstanding study of the Spirit in John's Gospel entitled *The Anointed Community*, has written:

> The going/coming texts of John 14 stress that Jesus himself is experienced in the Spirit. Therefore in his eschatology John moves very close to a binitarian theology. To have the Spirit is to have Jesus (and the Father) dwelling within (14:23; cf., 1 John 4:12ff.). But this binitarian danger is only apparent. John understands the Persons of the Godhead as closely unified. The unity and distinction of Jesus and the Spirit is paralleled by the same close relationship between Jesus and the Father. There is oneness (10:30; 14:18, 23) and at the same time there is separation (14:28; 16:7).[2]

Later patristic theology (as we noted in chapter 2) will make use of the concept of *perichoresis* or *circuminsessio* to speak of "merging" (mutual immanence) of the three Persons within the one Godhead.

Finally, let us note that the Gospel of John also provides an account of the occasion when what Jesus had promised in 7:39 at the Feast and in 14-16 to his disciples in the Upper Room actually came to fulfillment. Jesus, the crucified and now resurrected and ascended Lord—and thus according to this Gospel the glorified Lord—went through closed doors to his fearful disciples on the evening of the day of his resurrection. They were obviously glad to see him but were not prepared for what he had to say: "Peace be with you. As the Father has sent me, even so I send you." Then Jesus breathed upon them and said to them, "Receive the Holy Spirit" (20:21-22). Even as Yahweh-Elohim breathed the breath of life into man (Gen. 2:7), so the Lord Jesus breathes his Spirit, his personal life force, into the disciples. Thus a new order, a new epoch, a new creation has come into being with the glorification of Jesus and with the gift of the Spirit. In this new creation the Spirit gives power over sin ("if you forgive the sins of any, they are forgiven," 20:23), since it was sin that brought disorder into the old creation.

It would seem that John intends this account of the giving of the Holy Spirit as a parallel way of stating what Luke does more graphically in Acts 2. What is described certainly appears to be intended to be more than symbolic; but, exactly how Acts 2 and John 20:22 are to be reconciled is very difficult to determine.[3] Certainly both accounts make it very clear that the Holy Spirit comes from the Father and the Son and that he is only given, breathed out, and poured out when the saving work of Jesus on earth is wholly completed.

THE LETTERS OF PAUL

The Apostle Paul had a lot to say about the presence and activity of the Holy Spirit. This Spirit is truly the one and only Spirit of the one and only God. The time for the full expression of his presence and work is in the age to come; however, because of the exalted Jesus Christ the Spirit is present and active on earth in this age as the Spirit of the Father and of the Son to speed along the revelatory, reconciling, and redeeming work of the Son. In the present evil and dark age, true wisdom from God through the Cross of Jesus is desperately needed, but it can only be grasped by the Spirit's illumination and work in human hearts. In fact, because of the sinfulness and weakness of human nature, the making of obedient and holy disciples can only be achieved through the power of the Spirit, who must also guide the Christian mission into and through the evil world. The presence of the Spirit in the lives of believers is also necessary for them to be able to pray and worship aright, to enjoy the reality of Christian fellowship, and to overcome temptations and live victoriously for the sake of Christ and to the glory of God.

It is not part of Paul's task in his letters to argue for and present the personhood of the Holy Spirit. Where he presents suggestions in this connection, they are to be seen as arising from what we called in chapter 6 a general trinitarian conscious-ness and also from the fact that in his experience of God and meditations upon God's grace in Jesus Christ he actually knew the Father, the Lord Jesus Christ, and the Holy Spirit—even if he had no theory concerning their precise relations. So, being very selective from Paul's many references to the Spirit, we shall notice the places where (1) he establishes the closeness of (or the near identity of) Christ and the Spirit and yet he also carefully distinguishes them; (2) he writes of the Spirit in personal terms; and (3) he makes statements which have a trinitarian character.

(1) When Paul writes that Christ as the last Adam "became a life-giving spirit" a question arises as to whether or not he is here (as in other places) identifying the risen, exalted Christ with the Holy Spirit. Then also Paul writes on the one hand of Chris-tians being both "in the Spirit" (Rom. 8:9; Gal. 5:25) and the Spirit being in them (Rom. 8:11; 1 Cor. 3:16; 6:19) and, on the other hand, of their being "in Christ" (2 Cor. 5:17) or having Christ in them (Gal. 2:20). Then in Romans 8:9-11 we read:

> But you are not in the flesh, you are in the Spirit, if the Spirit of God really dwells in you. Any one who does not have the Spirit of Christ does not belong to him. But if Christ is in you, although your bodies are dead because of sin, your spirits are alive because of righteousness. If the Spirit of him who raised Jesus from the dead dwells in you, he who raised Christ Jesus from the dead will give life to your mortal bodies also through his Spirit which dwells in you.

Apparently "the Spirit of God," "the Spirit of Christ," "Christ," and "the Spirit of him who raised up Jesus" all refer to the same reality, the Holy Spirit. He is from the Father, and he acts in the name of Jesus Christ. However, it is clear from the rest of Paul's writing that Christ is not the Holy Spirit, and the Holy Spirit is not Christ. There is, of course, a perfect unity of divine purpose between them (and in terms of later, patristic

Trinitarian theology they share one and the same divinity even though they differ in personhood).

The relation of Christ and the Spirit in these Pauline texts has been well explained by Eduard Schweizer.

> Paul shares with Judaism and the early Christian Church the conception of the Spirit as the gift and power of the last age. His concern is not to replace the concept of "power" by the concept of "person," but to show that this power is not an obscure "something" but is the way and manner in which the Lord of the Church is present. For that reason the Spirit can be placed on a level with the Lord, or subordinated to him, quite indifferently. For that reason also, Paul can occasionally use God, Lord and Spirit interchangeably, simply because their encounter with the believer always takes the same form.[4]

The impact of the risen Christ and the impact of the Holy Spirit upon Christians is the impact of God.

More recently J.D.G. Dunn has surveyed the same Pauline material and written:

> So, in some sense that is not clear, the life-giving Spirit and exalted Christ *merge* in Paul's thinking, the Spirit can now be thought of as the Spirit of Christ—that is, as that power of God which is to be recognized by the consciousness of oneness with Christ (and in Christ) which it engenders and by the impress of the character of Christ which it begins to bring about in the life of the believer.[5]

However, despite the "merging" it is appropriate and possible for us to make conceptual distinctions.

We can distinguish between having personal communion with Jesus Christ and experiencing the presence, witness, and filling of the Holy Spirit in the heart. In terms of both Christ and the Spirit dwelling in the heart or soul, we can say that Christ is the indwelling content while the Spirit is the quickening cause of Christ's indwelling. Finally, Paul's own preference (though not universal usage) seems to be to speak of Christians being "in Christ" and of the Holy Spirit being in Christians: thus to be a

Christian is to be incorporated in Christ and to have the Spirit of Christ within oneself.

If there is one place in Paul's writings where one needs especially to be aware of the "merging" in terms of Jesus and the Spirit it is 2 Corinthians 3:17-18. "Now the Lord is the Spirit, and where the Spirit of the Lord is, there is freedom. And we all, with unveiled face, beholding [or reflecting] the glory of the Lord, are being changed into his likeness from one degree of glory to another; for this comes from the Lord who is the Spirit." In context Paul is saying that when people turn to the Lord Jesus, as Moses turned to Yahweh at Mount Sinai (Ex. 34:34), a veil of spiritual blindness is lifted from their eyes. The removal of this blindness is the spiritual work of the Lord. But which Lord? Perhaps Paul intended the Lord Jesus, who is "a life-giving spirit" (1 Cor. 15:45). So, if we read the word "Spirit" as "spirit" and see it as referring, not to the actual Holy Spirit, but to the spiritual action of the Lord Jesus, the source of life and light in removing blindness, then the text makes perfect sense in terms of grammar and meaning. In other words, there is no specific reference to the Holy Spirit and no equation of the Lord and the Spirit in the first part of the quotation. However, there is certainly a reference to the authority of the Lord Jesus giving light and life in the spiritual realm (where, no doubt, we can say that he is active in and by the Holy Spirit, even though that is not stated in these verses).

Another way of reading the text is to put the first occurrence of the word "Lord" in quotation marks and say that "the Lord" is the Spirit. That is, the Spirit active in the new covenant conforming men to the image of God so that they reflect his glory is truly the dynamic equivalent of "the Lord" (YHWH) in the Moses story; but the difference is one of sovereign power, the transformation of the lives of Christians. Paul is ascribing to the Spirit a work and sovereignty which is wholly divine.

Obviously if it is believed that Jesus Christ is truly alive forevermore, but alive not on earth but in heaven at the Father's right hand as the exalted Lord, then the question of how believers are united to him for salvation and enjoy communion with him is of great importance. Paul's answer to the question is that the union and communion is in and by the Holy Spirit, who is so close to and so identified with Christ in his work within the body of Christ, that it seems at times that they are one and the same "Person."

This "merging" is often referred to when it is being claimed that God is revealed as a Binity not a Trinity in the New Testament. However, to identify closely the presence and work of the Son and the Spirit within the souls of men is not necessarily to identify the personhood of the Son and the Spirit, who are distinct yet acting as one.

(2) Since for Paul the Spirit is the Spirit of Christ, it is not surprising that he is described in personal terms, having "a mind" (Rom. 8:27). Believers are led by the Spirit to produce the fruit of the Spirit (Gal. 5:18), and "all who are led by the Spirit of God are sons of God" (Rom. 8:14). Further, the Spirit reveals the mystery of Christ to believers as they are taught the truth by the Spirit (1 Cor. 2:10-16). Then, also the Spirit is active as the One who witnesses with the spirit of believers and who helps them to pray by interceding from within their souls (Rom. 8:15, 26-27). In fact, so sensitive is the Holy Spirit that he may be grieved by careless Christians (Eph. 4:30).

What we may claim is that the personhood of the Spirit is suggested, not proved, by such forms of speech. However, as we discussed above, when it is recognized that in Paul the Spirit as the active and transforming presence of God is intimately associated with the crucified and exalted Jesus, through whom alone he comes to, and by whom alone, he is defined for Christians, then the personhood of the Spirit becomes more apparent. And this is so even though — in fact, because of the fact that — the Spirit is invisible and anonymous in his presence and work in the church of God. Only the invisible and anonymous Spirit as Person could cause individual Christians as persons to cry out, "Abba, Father!" to the Person of the Father. This is because he is truly "the Spirit of Christ," "the Spirit of God's Son," and "the Spirit of Jesus Christ" (Rom. 8:9; Gal. 4:6; Phil. 1:19; cf., Acts 16:7).

(3) We have already cited various Pauline statements which point to the Holy Trinity and thus to the personhood of the Holy Spirit (see chap. 6). To these can be added the following quotations from Paul:

For the kingdom of God [the Father] does not mean food and drink but righteousness and peace and joy in the Holy Spirit; he who thus serves Christ [the Son] is acceptable to God [the Father] and approved by men (Rom. 14:17-18).

To be a minister of Christ Jesus [the Son] to the Gentiles in the priestly service of the gospel of God [the Father], so that the offering of the Gentiles may be acceptable, sanctified by the Holy Spirit (Rom. 15:16).

But it is God [the Father] who establishes us with you in Christ [the Son], and has commissioned us; he [the Father] has put his seal upon us and given us his Spirit in our hearts as a guarantee (2 Cor. 1:21-22).

You show that you are a letter from Christ [the Son] delivered by us, written not with ink but with the Spirit of the living God [the Father], not on tablets of stone but on tablets of human hearts (2 Cor. 3:3).

Now it is evident that no man is justified before God [the Father] by the law . . . that in Christ Jesus [the Son] the blessing of Abraham might come upon the Gentiles, that we might receive the promise of the Spirit through faith (Gal. 3:11-14).

For this reason I bow my knees before the Father, from whom every family in heaven and on earth is named, that according to the riches of his glory he may grant you to be strengthened with might through his Spirit in the inner man, and that Christ [the Son] may dwell in your hearts through faith (Eph. 3:14-17).

The cumulative force of these threefold formulae is great. In them the Holy Spirit is given a place higher than that afforded to the Spirit in the Old Testament. And the reason for this is his specific relation to the Son. In a real sense the personhood of the Spirit follows from the personhood of the Son.

IN CONCLUSION

As the early Christians engaged in worship, proclaimed the Gospel, and reflected upon their Faith, they came to see that the Holy Spirit is truly a *persona* or *hypostasis*. Yet the personhood of the Holy Spirit is not identical with the personhood of the Son and of the Father. In fact, each of the Three is a "Person" in a unique way; but yet all are Persons. There is a certain "self-effacingness" and other directedness to the Holy Spirit's activity. He is the light who is seen by what (who) he illuminates. His personhood is to point to the person of the incarnate Son and in and though him to the person of the Father.

The early church rejected both Unitarianism and Binitarianism and adopted Trinitarianism. In the words of the ecumenical Niceno-Constantinopolitan Creed, they confessed: "We believe in the Holy Spirit, the Lord and Life-giver, who proceeds from the Father; who with the Father and the Son is together worshiped and glorified, who spoke through the Prophets." The phrase, "and the Son" (*filioque*), was added later in the West (not in the East!) to this Creed—as we noted in chapter 2. Though this creed does not affirm that the Holy Spirit is *consubstantial* with the Father and with the Son, it was certainly understood in this way in both East and West.

The early fathers spent much time meditating upon the possible reason why Jesus had confirmed the name of the divine Third One as "the Holy Spirit/Breath." Augustine gave much thought to the question and wrote:

> The Holy Spirit is a certain unutterable communion of the Father and the Son; and on that account, perhaps, the Holy Spirit bears this name precisely because the Father and the Son can accomodate themselves to it. For in effect we give to him by special title the name we give to them by common title, since the Father is Spirit and the Son is Spirit, the Father is holy and the Son is holy. For thus in order to represent their mutual communion, there is need of a name that is applicable to both of them.[6]

Thus the name of the Holy Spirit points both to the communion of the Father and the Son and to his "procession" from the

Father [and from the Son]—as the Nicene Creed declares.

Writing of the Holy Spirit in Western ecclesiology as influenced by St. Augustine, Bertrand de Margerie said:

> The eternal Spirit of the Father and of the Son, their Communion and their reciprocal Gift, becomes then the Spirit of the Church in time, the temporal Gift which the Father and the Son make to her. The Breath of divine Love becomes the Soul of the universal Church, the Body of Christ. The principle of communion among Christians is at once consubstantial Communion between the Father and the Son and also between the Father and the sons in the Only Son.[7]

The communion of the faithful in the church flows from the communion of the Father and the Son in the Holy Spirit, the Trinity of Holy Love.

In the last three chapters, we have studied and contemplated "The Name [YHWH] of the Father, and of the Son, and of the Holy Spirit." It is now most appropriate to begin to think not of each of the Persons in isolation, but of the Three in One and the One in Three. Therefore, we shall proceed to notice how the Holy Trinity is revealed (1) in the saving deeds of God as they are presented in the New Testament, and (2) in the human (yet divine) work of worship.

FOR FURTHER READING

Augustine. *On the Holy Trinity*. Vol. 3 of A Select Library of Nicene and Post-Nicene Fathers. Grand Rapids: Eerdmans, 1956.

Barrett, C.K. *The Holy Spirit and the Gospel Tradition*. London: SPCK, 1947.

Brown, R.E. *The Gospel According to John*. 2 vols. New York: Doubleday, 1966 and 1970.

Burge, Gary M. *The Anointed Community: The Holy Spirit in the Johannine Tradition*. Grand Rapids: Eerdmans, 1987.

Davey, J.E. *The Jesus of St John: Historical and Christological Studies in the Fourth Gospel*. London: Lutterworth, 1958.

De Margerie, Bertrand. *The Christian Trinity in History*. Still River, Mass.: St. Bede's, 1982.

Dunn, J.D.G. *Jesus and the Spirit*. Philadelphia: Westminster, 1975.

———. *Christology in the Making*. Philadelphia: Westminster, 1980.

Heron, Alisdair. *The Holy Spirit*. London: Marshall, Morgan and Scott, 1983.

Hoskyns, Edwyn Sir. *The Fourth Gospel*. Edited by F.N. Davey. London: Faber and Faber, 1947.

Montague, George T. *The Holy Spirit: Growth of a Biblical Tradition*. New York: Paulist, 1976.

Ramsey, Michael. *Holy Spirit: A Biblical Study*. London: SPCK, 1977.

Schweizer, Eduard. *Spirit of God: Bible Key Words*. London: A & C Black, 1960.

Swete, H.B. *The Holy Spirit in the New Testament*. London: MacMillan, 1909.

Toon, Peter. *Yesterday, Today and Forever: Jesus Christ and the Holy Trinity in the Teaching of the Seven Ecumenical Councils*. Swedesboro, N.J.: Preservation, 1995.

PART FOUR

JOYFUL AND

INFORMED

ORTHODOXY

10

DISCLOSURES OF THE
HOLY TRINITY

Our major task in this chapter is to
examine the primary moments of God's saving deeds recorded in
the New Testament and to see and hear the revelation of the
Trinity in the act of redemption. So we shall look at the conception, baptism, death, and resurrection of Jesus, along with the
descent of the Holy Spirit and the arrival of the New Jerusalem.
In doing so we shall see the truth of the observation made at
various points in the preceding chapters — that the revelation of
the Trinity had to wait for the completion of the saving acts of
the Trinity.

THE CONCEPTION OF JESUS

Here we need to bear in mind three sets of facts before we look
at the narratives in Matthew 1 and Luke 1. In the first place,
Jesus did not exist before he was conceived in the womb of the
Virgin Mary. The existence of Jesus began nine months before his
birth in Bethlehem. Secondly, considered as divine, the Son of God
(or the Word of John 1:1) existed before Mary existed. In the third
place, Mary conceived Jesus without the introduction into her body
of any male semen. She conceived by the Holy Spirit.

What the narratives tell us in their differing ways and emphases is that (1) the Father sent his Son into the created order; (2) the preexisting Son of God took human nature in Mary's womb, and (3) this act of the Son of God occurred because of the act of the Holy Spirit upon and in Mary, who in glad submission to God conceived "by the Holy Spirit."

(1) Matthew tells us that Joseph discovered before their actual marriage and during their betrothal that Mary was pregnant. As he considered what to do, "an angel of the Lord appeared to him in a dream." This heavenly messenger from YHWH said to him, "Joseph, son of David, do not fear to take Mary your wife, for that which is conceived in her is of the Holy Spirit; she will bear a son, and you shall call his name Jesus, for he will save his people from their sins" (1:18-21). We are not told how Joseph understood this remarkable communication. All we know is that he took it at its face value and acted accordingly.

Matthew, who describes Mary as "with child by the Holy Spirit," also declares that her unique conception fulfilled prophecy (Isa. 7:14) and provided the basis for the essential truth concerning Jesus, who is Emmanuel (God with us). Throughout the narrative of Matthew 1 it is understood that this Incarnation occurs because it is the will of YHWH, who sends both his Son and his Holy Spirit to Nazareth.

(2) Luke weaves the accounts of the conception and birth of John the Baptist and Jesus together so that we see God's purposes in greater relief. Thus it was after Elizabeth had been pregnant six months that Mary was visited by the messenger from heaven whose name was Gabriel. Naturally the young virgin of Nazareth was taken aback by the angel's visit, but he comforted her and gave her the message from YHWH that she would become pregnant without knowing a man.

Do not be afraid, Mary, for you have found favor with God. And behold, you will conceive in your womb and bear a son, and you shall call his name Jesus. He will be great, and will be called the Son of the Most High; and the Lord God will give to him the throne of his father David, and he will reign over the house of Jacob for ever; and of his kingdom there will be no end (Luke 1:30-33).

Mary knew enough about human sexuality to ask how she could conceive when she did not as yet have a husband. Gabriel replied:

The Holy Spirit will come upon you, and the power of the Most High will overshadow you; therefore the child to be born will be called holy, the Son of God (1:35).

Here we have "God," "the Most High," and "the Lord God" referring to YHWH as "the Father." Then we have the Incarnation of "the Son of the Most High," who is "the Son of God"; this becoming man is because of the unique presence and action of "the Holy Spirit," who is "the power of the Most High." Though the preexistence of the Son is not specifically stated, the difference in the conception of John by Elizabeth and of Jesus by Mary points to this preexistence. John is conceived by normal means in an unexpected way through "the power of the Holy Spirit" working through the laws of nature. In contrast, Jesus is conceived "by the Holy Spirit" alone, for his (eternal) Father is God. Thus Elizabeth described the pregnant Mary as "the mother of my Lord" (1:43).

It is important to note that the Nicene Creed declares that "the only-begotten Son of God was incarnate by the Holy Spirit and the Virgin Mary." The Apostles' Creed declares that Jesus Christ, the only Son of the Father Almighty "was conceived by the Holy Spirit." The modern translation of these Creeds (as used, for example, by Roman Catholics and Episcopalians at the Eucharist) contains the added words "power of." Thus, Mary is said to have conceived "by the power of the Holy Spirit" not "by the Holy Spirit" (as in the original Greek/Latin). Such an erroneous translation is intended to remove the *uniqueness* of the conception by Mary, the virgin.

THE BAPTISM OF JESUS

Only when John the Baptist was engaged in his public ministry of calling the Jews to repentance did Jesus leave Nazareth to identify with John, with his own people the Jews, and to begin his ministry of proclaiming the arrival of the kingdom of YHWH. Each of the Synoptic Gospels provides an account of the baptism of Jesus (Matt. 3:13-17; Mark 1:9-11; Luke 3:21-22), and the Gospel of John assumes it took place (1:24-34).

Since Mark's account is generally regarded as the earliest, we shall examine it.

> In those days Jesus came from Nazareth of Galilee and was baptized by John in the Jordan. And when he came up out of the water, immediately he saw the heavens opened and the Spirit descending upon him like a dove; and a voice came from heaven, "Thou art my beloved Son; with thee I am well pleased" (Mark 1:9-11).

Jesus was given a vision of the heaven of heavens, the dwelling place of YHWH opened. From there he saw the Holy Spirit descending upon him as though a dove in flight. This was an objective vision through which genuine, divine communication occurred. Jesus experienced the arrival of the Holy Spirit to anoint/clothe him and to fill him; further, he heard the voice of YHWH, the Father, from heaven.

"Thou art my Son" is not the conferring of a messianic title. Rather, it is the confirming of a filial consciousness which Jesus already had. "Beloved" can either be taken with "Son" ("my beloved Son") or stand alone ("my Son, the beloved"). The Father is well pleased with his (incarnate) Son because he has dedicated himself to the vocation of the Servant of YHWH by his full identification with his people in John's ministry. What is said by the Father to the Son is, as we would expect, made up of phrases from the Old Testament—Psalm 2:7 and Isaiah 42:1.

In terms of the revelation of the Trinity, the Father is present as the One who addresses his Son; the beloved Son is present as the One who has the vision, receives the Holy Spirit, and hears the voice of the Father; and the Holy Spirit is present as the One who is sent by the Father from the heaven of heavens to his Son who is the Servant-Messiah.

Immediately following the baptism, Jesus, the Son, was driven by the Spirit to be tested by the Father through the temptations brought by Satan. Forty days later, in communion with the Father and led by the Spirit, the Servant Son returned to Galilee to proclaim the kingdom of God in word and deed (Mark 1:12-14). He went into the synagogue at Nazareth, where he had lived, and, as the Son of God, declared that the Spirit of YHWH, his Father, was upon him (Luke 4:16-21).

Later in Mark's Gospel there is the account of the amazing Transfiguration of Jesus (9:2-8; cf. Matt. 17:1-8; Luke 9:28-36), where again the Father speaks from heaven to the disciples telling them that Jesus is "my beloved Son" to whom they are to listen! Probably we are to understand this event, wherein the true glory of Jesus is revealed, as an anticipation or prolepsis of his future resurrection and the Parousia. The fact that the Holy Spirit is not mentioned here should not surprise us—he is the invisible One anointing and filling Jesus the Servant-Son and causing his raiment to glow with divine glory. (A comparison of Luke 9:34-35 and Luke 1:35 suggests the presence of the Spirit at the Transfiguration.)

Six days before the Transfiguration, Jesus had asked his disciples who they thought he really was. Simon Peter had confessed, "You are the Christ, the Son of the living God." In reply Jesus said, "Blessed are you, Simon Bar-Jona! For flesh and blood has not revealed this to you, but my Father who is in heaven" (Matt. 16:16-17). Again, while the Spirit is not mentioned, his presence and activity is surely understood as being the means of the revelation from the Father in heaven.

THE CRUCIFIXION OF JESUS

To read the accounts of the Passion and Crucifixion of Jesus in the Synoptic Gospels is to be aware of the filial consciousness of Jesus. The Father was always there and very real to him. According to Mark, in the Garden of Gethsemane, Jesus uttered the memorable words, "Abba, Father, all things are possible to thee; remove this cup from me; yet not what I will, but what thou wilt" (Mark 14:36). Then, as Jesus breathed his last on the Cross, the Roman centurion exclaimed, "Truly this man was a (the) Son of God" (15:39). Luke reports that Jesus cried with a loud voice from the Cross saying, "Father, into thy hands I commit my spirit!" (23:46)

In John's Gospel, the last recorded words of Jesus (who is always conscious that he is the unique Son of the Father) were, "I thirst," and then, after sipping the wine, he said, "It is finished" (19:30). Following these final words, we read that Jesus "bowed his head and gave up his spirit" [lit."he handed over the spirit"]. Then a little later we are told that there came forth from his side "blood and water" (19:34). In his comment upon these events Sir Edwyn Hoskyns wrote:

> If it be assumed that the author intends his readers to suppose that the Beloved Disciple and Mary, the Mother of Jesus, remain standing beneath the cross, the words *He bowed his head* suggest that He bowed His head towards them, and the words, *He handed over the Spirit* are also directed to the faithful believers who stand below. This is no fantastic exegesis, since verses 28-30 record the solemn fulfillment of vii. 37-39 [where Jesus spoke of the Spirit in terms of rivers of living water].

Hoskyns proceeds to explain what he has in mind.

> The thirst of the believers is assuaged by the rivers of living water which flow from the belly of the Lord, the author having already noted that this referred to the giving of the Spirit. The outpouring of the Spirit here recorded must be understood in connection with the outpouring of water and blood (v. 34). The similar association of Spirit and Water and Blood in 1 John v. 8 (*There are three who bear witness, the Spirit, and the water and the blood: and the three agree in one*) seems to make this interpretation not only possible, but necessary.[1]

Raymond E. Brown summarized this way of reading John 19 in these words: "the symbolism here is proleptic and serves to clarify that, while only the risen Jesus gives the Spirit, that gift flows from the whole process of glorification in the 'hour' of the passion, death, resurrection and ascension"[2]

So we find that in the Crucifixion of the incarnate Son of the Father there is (in John's presentation) the handing over of the Spirit who has anointed and filled Jesus the Servant-Son. In the darkness of the Crucifixion, which for John's Gospel is the first stage of the glorification of Jesus, there is the Revelation of the Father, of his Son, who is being glorified, and the Holy Spirit who is the gift of the Father and the Son to the disciples, represented by Mary and John.

In Hebrews the author compares the sacrifice of animals under the old covenant with the unique sacrifice of the incarnate Son inaugurating the new covenant:

> For if the sprinkling of defiled persons with the blood of goats and bulls and with the ashes of a heifer sanctifies for the purification of the flesh, how much more shall the blood of Christ, who through the eternal Spirit offered himself without blemish to God, purify your conscience from dead works to serve the living God (Heb. 9:13-14).

Christ, who is the Son, offers the sacrifice; the sacrifice of the Son is received by the Father in and through the Holy Spirit. Thus redemption is the work of the Holy Trinity.

THE RESURRECTION OF JESUS

The Gospel proclaimed by the apostles was the good news that God the Father had raised his incarnate Son, Jesus Christ, from the dead in and by the Holy Spirit. However, as exalted into heaven and away from earth Jesus was not, as it were, absorbed into the realm of Spirit — losing his own independent existence in exaltation. In the Book of Acts the resurrection of Jesus is usually said to be by the Father — "God raised Jesus from the dead" (2:24, 32). This, of course, leaves open the possibility that the Father acted in and by his Spirit.

Paul begins his letter to Rome by referring to the Gospel of God concerning his Son, who was declared or designated Son of God "in power according to the Spirit of holiness by his resurrection from the dead" (Rom. 1:4). Later in the same letter he wrote to the Christians: "If the Spirit of him [God the Father] who raised Jesus from the dead dwells in you, he who raised Christ Jesus from the dead will give life to your mortal bodies also through his Spirit which dwells in you" (8:11). However, Paul does not often attribute the actual bodily resurrection of Jesus to the Spirit and his reason was probably so as not to give the impression that Jesus in being raised in a transformed body was absorbed into the Spirit. As we saw in the previous chapter, though there is a vital and close relation of the Spirit and the Lord Jesus, they are not to be identified.

Certainly the Lord Jesus is presented in the narratives of his resurrection appearances as speaking of his Father and of the Holy Spirit. This is especially true of John 20. Jesus told Mary: "I am ascending to my Father and your Father, to my God and your God" (v. 17). He commissioned his disciples as he said: "As the Father has sent me, even so I send you"; and then he breathed upon them and said: "Receive the Holy Spirit" (vv. 21-22).

At the end of Matthew the resurrected Lord Jesus is with the eleven apostles on a mountain and they worship him — but apparently with some doubts. He then is reported as saying to them these remarkable words.

> All authority in heaven and on earth has been given to me. Go therefore and make disciples of all nations, baptizing them in the name of the Father and of the Son and of the Holy Spirit, teaching them to observe all that I have commanded you; and lo, I am with you always, to the close of the age (28:18-20).

Jesus presents himself as the exalted Son of Man who has received from the Father the universal and eternal dominion promised to him in Daniel 7:14. Because he actually has such authority he commands his apostles to go forth and make disciples in all the world, promising that he will always be with them.

Many commentators suppose that the trinitarian formula was not original at this point in Matthew's Gospel since there is no evidence anywhere else in the New Testament of such a formula. They point out that baptisms were performed "in the name of the Lord Jesus" (Acts 2:38; 8:16) in the early days of the church. So they suggest that the formula used by the church toward the end of the first century of performing baptism in the threefold Name was placed on the lips of the resurrected Lord Jesus by the evangelist. However, another way of looking at the evidence is to say that "in the name of the Lord Jesus" is Luke's summary of the longer "in the name of the Father and of the Son and of the Holy Spirit."

What is noteworthy, however, is this. Whether or not Jesus

actually said what he is recorded as having said, such a formula is actually present in the Gospels. At least it shows that when Matthew was written (A.D. 80–90?) Christianity was self-consciously trinitarian. The formula for baptism is very precise with its four definite articles — in THE Name of THE Father and THE Son and THE Holy Spirit. There is one and only one Name — YHWH. And YHWH is the one and only Father with his one and only Son and his one and only Holy Spirit. "The" tells us that each One is truly unique as well as being perfectly related to the other Two. Certainly it is not said that (in later patristic terms) there are Three Persons and One Substance. However, the two occurrences of "and" joining the three Persons, each of whom has the definite article, is in biblical terminology a very positive way of speaking of the Holy Trinity — and this formula has been used since the earliest times for baptism and in liturgy.

The Gospel of Luke, which is continued in Acts, presents Jesus as telling his disciples that they were witnesses of his death and resurrection and then saying, "I send the promise of my Father upon you; but stay in the city, until you are clothed with power from on high" (24:49). The reference is of course to the events described in Acts 2, to which we turn in the next section.

THE DESCENT OF THE HOLY SPIRIT

In Luke's account of the Ascension (Acts 1:6-11) the last words of Jesus to his disciples were: "You shall receive power when the Holy Spirit is come upon you; and you shall be my witnesses in Jerusalem and in all Judea and Samaria and to the end of the earth" (v. 8). So the disciples waited in Jerusalem for the promise to be fulfilled. And it was — at the Feast of Pentecost, ten days after the Ascension.

The Trinitarian character of this event — a great saving and revealing act of YHWH — is obvious to the careful reader of Acts 2. The arrival of the Holy Spirit in ways and with characteristics already known in the descriptions of the theophanies of YHWH under the old covenant (see chaps. 4 and 5) is central for all that follows. The disciples are anointed and filled with the Spirit.

There is the praise of God in a variety of languages. Peter's citing of the prophecy of Joel to explain the amazing turn of events identifies the Spirit and his relation to heaven and to Yahweh-Elohim. God, himself, has sent his Spirit to dwell with his people under the new covenant, the new epoch, and the new order. And his arrival and presence really make a difference!

But why has God sent his Spirit at this time? Peter has a very clear answer. It is because God has raised up Jesus from the dead and exalted him into heaven and there declared him to be both Lord and Christ. The Spirit descends because Jesus ascended as the victorious Messiah. In fact, the Lord Jesus, who is himself the recipient of the Spirit, joins with the Father in sending the Spirit (2:33). When sinners repent and believe the Gospel of God concerning Jesus the Lord then they receive the gift of the Holy Spirit, who is to them the Spirit of the exalted Lord Jesus.

There is a close relation between the Holy Spirit and the Father — the Spirit is sent by the Father from heaven. Also there is a close relation between the Spirit and the Lord Jesus Christ — the Spirit is sent both for the sake of Jesus and by Jesus so that he may dwell and work in those who belong to Jesus on earth and are continuing his mission. And, of course, there is a close relation between the Father and the Lord Jesus Christ, who is "exalted at the right hand of God" (2:33) sharing the divine throne and name. Obviously Acts 2 does not present a developed Trinitarian picture; the Holy Trinity is encountered in an implicit and functional way rather than an explicit and ontological way.

There is also the account of the giving of the Spirit in John's Gospel — sometimes called "John's Pentecost" — and to which we made reference in chapter 9. This account is decidedly Trinitarian in character. Jesus, the Son, said to the disciples, "As the Father has sent me, even so I [his Son] send you." Then breathing out upon them the Life-Force within him — that is, his personal Spirit — he said, "Receive the Holy Spirit" (John 20:21-22).

A VISION OF THE NEW JERUSALEM

It is God's purpose to create a new order of existence in a new age — "new heaven and a new earth." At the end of the Revelation of John there is a vision of the life of the age to come. The grand, theological finale of the book is in the description of "the holy city, new Jerusalem, coming down out of heaven from God, prepared as a bride adorned for her husband" and of the glorious declaration from the Throne, "Behold, the dwelling of God is with men. He will dwell with them and they shall be his people" (21:1-3). To know God is to know the Holy Trinity.

> Then he [the Spirit through one of the seven angels] showed me the river of the water of life, bright as crystal, flowing from the throne of God and of the Lamb, through the middle of the street of the city; also, on either side of the river, the tree of life with its twelve kinds of fruit, yielding its fruit each month; and the leaves of the tree were for the healing of the nations. There shall no more be anything accursed, but the throne of God and of the Lamb shall be in it, and his servants shall worship him; they shall see his face, and his name shall be on their foreheads. And night shall be no more; they need no light of lamp or sun, for the Lord God will be their light, and they shall reign for ever and ever (22:1-5).

Here in rich symbolic language drawn from the Old Testament and the tradition of the Gospel there is a portrayal of both the Holy Trinity and of the beatific vision. There is one throne—the throne of both God (the Father) and the Lamb (the crucified, exalted Son). Earlier in chapter 21 it had been made clear that the Father and the Son are so close that both are "the One who sits upon the throne" (21:5). At the throne and flowing from the throne is the Holy Spirit—presented here (as in John 7:38-39) as a river of living water. Already in 21:6, the Lamb had promised that "to the thirsty I will give water without price from the fountain of the water of life." The Spirit fills the city which is the church of the saints. And (in, through, and by the Holy Spirit) the dwellers in the New Jerusalem enjoy the beatific vision—"they shall see his face" (cf. Matt. 5:8; 1 John 3:2).

In this passage (and in the whole section 21:1–22:5) the scriptural revelation of the Holy Trinity reaches its zenith. The vision presented to the reader heralds for the saints a holy, glorious, progressive discovery—a growing in vital knowledge in the life of the age to come of the Three who are One and the One who is Three, YHWH-Elohim.

IN CONCLUSION

The "Trinity" is an abstract noun which has one and one meaning only for theology — it designates the concrete reality of the Father, the Son, and the Holy Spirit. In chapter 2 we noted how they came to be called "Three Persons" (Latin, *persona*). Here it will be useful to see how St. Augustine dealt with this word which he received within the tradition of the church.

Writing in his treatise, *De Trinitate*, Augustine faced the problems with using the word *persona*.

> When then someone asks: what are these Three [i.e., the Father, the Son and the Holy Spirit]? Three what? We are hard put to find a specific or a generic noun that will cover these Three [*haec tria*] but none comes to mind, for the transcendence of the divinity exceeds the resources of our normal vocabulary. When dealing with God, thought is more accurate than discourse, and the reality is more accurate than thought. . . . Where there is no difference in essence there is need of a specific name common to the Three, but we do not find one. Person is a generic term since it can be applied to man, even though there is such a distance from man to God.[3]

Augustine's difficulty was that he could not find a word to apply to each of the Three and to the Three alone — one without any possible reference to creatures. He accepted and used the word "Person," but he was not entirely happy to do so.

What seemed as a disadvantage to Augustine was later taken as an advantage by Thomas Aquinas because of his doctrine of analogy. In his *Summa Theologica* he expounds a notion of Person which can be applied analogically to men, to angels, and to God. As such it allows us to start from the datum of experience so as to reach in faith an understanding of the Holy Trinity as Three Persons and One God.[4] All serious exposition of the doctrine of the Trinity since the time of Thomas has had to take account of his exposition of *persona* and his doctrine of analogy.[5]

In modern English (as in other European languages) the meaning of "person" has moved a long way from its meaning in scholastic philosophy and theology. The current, usual meaning of the word is inextricably bound up with notions of personality and the input of psychology in a culture where individualism is dominant. Therefore, theologians have either to stop using the word "Persons" of the Three or they have to explain what precisely is the technical meaning. I can see no alternative but to adopt the second option and explain what it means — as I did briefly in chapter 2. In doing so, I believe that the doctrine of analogy is of great service for it allows us in the modern debate over appropriate language for God to defend with vigor the designation of the Three as Persons as also the naming and addressing of Them as the Father, the Son, and the Holy Spirit.

In some modern theology (as we noted in chap. 3) God is described as a/the Spirit and as one Person. Here the word "person" is being used in a modern rather than in the classical sense. The Dutch theologian, Hendrikus Berkhof, adopted this approach and vocabulary in his book, *The Doctrine of the Holy Spirit* (1965) but later modified it in his *The Christian Faith* (1975). Referring to God's presence and activity in Jesus and the Holy Spirit, he wrote:

> In all this God is Person, acting in a personal way, seeking a personal encounter. The triune God does not embrace Three Persons; he himself is a Person, meeting us in the Son and in his Spirit. Jesus Christ is not a Person beside the Person of God; in him the Person of God becomes the shape of a human person. And the Spirit is not a Person beside the Persons of God and of Christ. In creation he is the acting Person of God, in re-creation he is the acting Person of Christ, who is no other than the acting Person of God. Therefore we must reject all presentation of the Holy Spirit as an impersonal force. The Spirit is Person because he is God acting as a Person. He is a Person in relation to us, not in relation to God; for he is the personal God himself in relation to us.[6]

I have quoted this because it is the kind of thing which has often been said in one way or another when people attempt to state the doctrine of the Trinity. It sounds like and probably in fact is a form of Modalism—a doctrine which constantly appears in the church through history. In fact, it is an extreme statement of the Barthian position that God is One Person, who has Three Modes of Being. Despite its attractiveness in apparently simplifying the portrayal of the Holy Trinity, it is a long way from the orthodoxy of the Ecumenical Councils and Protestant Confessions of faith.

It is one thing to claim, as I have done, that we need to retain the language of three *personae* and *hypostaseis;* it is another to insist that we understand the meaning of person as applied to the Father and the Son and the Holy Spirit as identical in each case—that each in the same way is a person as if they are three members of a class. Is each One a divine person distinctively as the Father and as the Son and as the Holy Spirit? Much traditional theology has answered "no" claiming that person is used in an identical way of each of the Three. In challenging such a position Alisdair Heron writes:

It runs counter to the profoundest motive for the framing of a fully trinitarian theology in the fourth century [between the Council of Nicea of 325 and that of Constantinople in 381], where the application to the Spirit of the logic of argument already developed in reference to the Son itself depended upon the recognition that the pattern of God's work of salvation is complete in triunity, not in binity, that the movement issuing from the Father through the Son reaches us in the Spirit, that in the Spirit we are renewed in the image of the Son and drawn through him to the Father. Interlocking complementarity rather than simple threefold repetition determines and characterizes the pattern. Hence the need felt by the fathers to develop pneumatological concepts that would not simply *parallel* the Spirit to the Son, but also make essential *distinctions* between them—hence such terms as "procession." The same motive can be traced in Augustine's attempts to devise models for the Trinity which would not present it simply as "one plus one plus one" but as an organic three-dimensional unity.[7]

In the next chapter we shall examine this "interlocking complementarity" rather than simple "threefold repetition." And Augustine *On the Holy Trinity*, Books 9 to 16, has all the material necessary for those who wish to examine the models developed by the Bishop of Hippo to portray the Holy Trinity as an organic three-dimensional unity.

FOR FURTHER READING

Augustine. *On the Holy Trinity*. In Vol. 3 of A Select Library of Nicene and Post-Nicene Fathers. Grand Rapids: Eerdmans, 1956.

Berkhof, Hendrikus. *The Doctrine of the Holy Spirit*. London: Epworth, 1965.

Brown, Raymond E. *The Gospel according to John*. 2 vols., New York: Doubleday, 1966, 1970.

_____. *The Birth of the Messiah*. New York: Doubleday, 1977.

Heron, Alisdair. *The Holy Spirit*. London: Marshall, Morgan and Scott, 1983.

Hoskyns, Edwyn. *The Fourth Gospel*. London: Faber and Faber, 1947.

Ramsey, Michael. *The Glory of God and the Transfiguration of Jesus*. London: Longmans, Green & Co., 1949.

Rocca, Gregory P. "Aquinas on God Talk." *Theological Studies*, 54 (1993): 641–61.

Schaberg, J. *The Father, the Son and the Holy Spirit: The Triadic Phrase in Matthew 28:19b*. Chico, Calif.: Scholars, 1982.

Tavard, George H. *The Vision of the Trinity*. Washington, D.C.: Univ. Press of America, 1981.

11

FROM THE FATHER...
TO THE FATHER

Let us begin with the answering of a question. For Jewish monotheism, what is missing from the equation, "God minus the world $=$"? The answer is obviously God. God is always God whether or not there is a world. For pantheism the answer is "nothing at all" since God is the world and the world is God; and for panentheism the answer is "God without his/her Body" — not really God at all!

For Christianity, which confesses that Jesus Christ is the eternal Son of God in (everlasting) human nature, the completion of the equation, "The Holy Trinity minus the created universe $=$?" is not straightforward. The Second Person of the Trinity in becoming incarnate has made his very own, and his own unto all ages, created, human nature. Further, because of his union with mankind through the incarnation and by the very fact that he has a human nature, the Son has drawn into the most intimate communion with the Father in and by the Holy Spirit all those who believe on his name. Thus the completion of the equation cannot be answered as simply as it can in non-Trinitarian monotheism (Judaism, Islam, Unitarianism).

This puzzle and its related observations lead us on to consider how the Holy Trinity is portrayed in the Scriptures in relation to the cosmos and to mankind. There is a movement out from God in creation, salvation, and revelation into the world, and a movement back toward and into God in worship and service. In this "descent" and "ascent" the Holy Trinity is present, active, and revealed, and this conception of the living God is called by theologians the economic Trinity (economy being God's ordered relation to the world).

DESCENT – CREATION

The Old Testament makes it clear that YHWH is the Creator of the heavens and the earth (Gen. 1–3; Isa. 42:5). He creates and sustains the cosmos by his creative word/wisdom and his powerful breath or Spirit: "By the word of YHWH the heavens were made; and all their host by the breath of his mouth" (Ps. 33:6).

Three New Testament writers build upon this teaching concerning the word and wisdom of YHWH found in both the canonical and deuterocanonical books within the Septuagint as they develop their Christology. Jesus is the personal Word and Wisdom of God.

First of all, in the prologue of John's Gospel there are these statements:

In the beginning was the Word, and the Word was with God, and the Word was God. He was in the beginning with God; all things were made through him, and without him was not anything made that was made (1:1-3).

The whole of creation is included in one broad sweep as it is said that the Father created *through* (not "by") the Word, who is the Son.

In the second place, in Paul's letter to the church in Colossae there is this teaching:

For in him [the Lord Jesus Christ, the beloved Son] all things were created, in heaven and on earth, visible and invisible, whether thrones or dominions or principalities or authorities; all things were created through him and for him. He is before all things, and in him all things hold together (Col. 1:16-17).

By the prepositions *in* and *through* Paul communicates the agency and participation of the Son in the creation of heaven and earth. In another place, Paul presents the activity of Christ in the sustaining and maintaining of the creation: "There is . . . one Lord, Jesus Christ, through whom are all things and through whom we exist" (1 Cor. 8:6). Further, God's plan is "for the fullness of time to unite all things in him [Christ], things in heaven and things on earth" (Eph. 1:10). Here the movement is toward God, what shall be when Christ's redeeming work is totally completed. Finally, the writer of Hebrews, making use of the description of Wisdom in the Septuagint, wrote:

> In these last days he [God] has spoken to us by a Son, whom he appointed the heir of all things, through whom also he created the world. He reflects the glory of God and bears the very stamp of his nature, upholding the universe by his word of power (1:2-3).

Here Christ is presented as active with the Father in both the creating (*through* him) and the upholding of the universe.

In none of these texts is there a mention of the Holy Spirit. However, it is surely right to assume that his presence and activity were taken for granted. For the first Christians the biblical (O.T.) teaching concerning the Spirit's activity in creation was revealed by God and could not be set aside. Thus the Father through the Son [the Word] and by the Holy Spirit [the breath of his mouth] is the Creator and Sustainer of the universe.

DESCENT – SALVATION

Under the old covenant YHWH descended into his creation in a variety of ways — for example, in theophanies, sending angels, and placing his word in the mouths of prophets and sages. The new covenant was established to replace the old (1) by the descent and incarnation of the Word, who is the Son of the Father, and (2) by the descent of the Holy Spirit, sent by the Father and by his Son. Salvation which presupposes the created order and thus occurs within creation is from the Father, through the Son, and by the Spirit.

The Lucan narratives of the conception and birth of Jesus

assume and proclaim that God sent his own Son to become man; to achieve this miracle of Incarnation he sent his own Spirit to Mary so that she could and would conceive Jesus. The message is clear—YHWH is active as Creator again, creating a new epoch, order, and creation through his Son, who is Immanuel, and by his Spirit, the Life Giver.

At the beginning of Acts, Luke presents the descent of the Holy Spirit upon the assembled apostles and disciples. Now the new creation is beginning to take practical shape. The Son has descended and ascended and he has poured out his Spirit, who is the Spirit of the Father, upon his own disciples. Through this anointing and indwelling Spirit, the Lord Jesus will always be with his disciples on earth until the end of the age; and salvation from God will be proclaimed in his name throughout the world.

Paul's teaching

Speaking of the descent of the Son, Paul wrote: "When the time had fully come, God sent forth his Son, born of woman, born under the law, to redeem those who were under the law" (Gal. 4:4-5). Here is Incarnation to achieve redemption. The Lord Jesus Christ who was "rich" (in heavenly glory) for the sake of man and his salvation became "poor" (in earthly humiliation) so that, through his poverty, poor sinners might become rich (1 Cor. 8:9). The descent of the Son from the heaven of heavens into the world of sin and shame followed by his glorious exaltation back to the heaven of heavens is powerfully dramatized by Paul in Philippians 2:5-11. Here the Son sets aside his eternal privileges and position with the Father and descends into the evil world for the salvation of mankind. To achieve this he becomes a servant and dies on a cross.

Paul's writings assume that the Holy Spirit has descended and is present as the Spirit of Christ in the churches and within individual lives. He is present because many are confessing, "Jesus is Lord," and this is only possible by the presence of the Holy Spirit (1 Cor. 12:3). Evidence of spiritual gifts given by the exalted Lord through the Spirit abound in the congregations (1 Cor. 12). Believers know that God has sent the Holy Spirit for they experience the Spirit of the Father and the Son in their hearts as they cry out, "Abba, Father" (Gal. 4:6). In his own ministry as he proclaimed "Christ and him crucified," Paul knew that his speech was "in demonstration of the Spirit and power" and not in the wisdom of men (1 Cor. 2:1-5).

For the apostle to the Gentiles the work of salvation was the work of the Father, his Son, and his Spirit. As he explained to Titus, his son in the Faith: "When the goodness and loving kindness of God [the Father] our Savior appeared, he saved us, not because of deeds done by us in righteousness, but in virtue of his own mercy, by the washing of regeneration and renewal in the Holy Spirit, which he poured out upon us richly through Jesus Christ our Savior" (Titus 3:4-6).

At the beginning of his letters, Paul usually wrote, "Grace to you and peace from God our Father and the Lord Jesus Christ" (e.g., Rom. 1:7). This is the downward movement from God the Father and from (through) his Son. The presence and work of the Holy Spirit is not stated but is assumed — by the presence and activity of the Holy Spirit grace and peace become realities in the souls of believers.

In explaining the redemption and salvation of the Holy Trinity, Paul developed the theme of justification and made great use of it in his letters to Rome and Galatia. Here is an extract from his presentation of justification to the Romans.

> Since we are justified by faith, we have peace with God [the Father] through our Lord Jesus Christ. Through him we have obtained access to this grace in which we stand, and we rejoice in our hope of sharing the glory of God. More than that, we rejoice in our sufferings . . . because God's love has been poured into our hearts through the Holy Spirit which has been given to us (5:1-5).

Justification is being placed in a right relation with God the Father on account of the saving work and merit of Jesus Christ. Justification is therefore the gift from the Father through the Son and by the Spirit, and it is a gift which is received by faith. Those who are declared righteous for Christ's sake have open access by grace to the Father to commune with him through Jesus Christ and by the Holy Spirit. Further, the effect of being declared righteous and placed in this right relation with the Holy Trinity is that believers live joyfully and righteously; and this they do through the presence of the Holy Spirit in their hearts and through the love which he brings — the same love for and by which the Father sent his Son and Spirit to the church in the world.

Caught up in prayerful adoration of the Holy Trinity, Paul wrote these words at the beginning of Ephesians.

> Blessed be the God and Father of our Lord Jesus Christ, who has blessed us in Christ with every spiritual blessing in the heavenly places, even as he chose us in him before the foundation of the world, that we should be holy and blameless before him. He destined us in love to be his sons through Jesus Christ, according to the purpose of his will, to the praise of his glorious grace which he freely bestowed on us in the Beloved [Son]. In him we have redemption through his blood, the forgiveness of our trespasses, according to the riches of his grace which he lavished upon us (Eph. 1:3-8).

He continued by blessing God because "you . . . were sealed with the promised Holy Spirit, which is the guarantee of our inheritance until we acquire possession of it" (vv. 13-14).

The gracious, saving work of God in space and time is traced back here, as Paul engaged in holy contemplation, to the purposes of the Father before the creation of the world. Yet the movement for the salvation of man is the same as elsewhere in Paul's writings — the Father (in his transcendent, eternal glory) through the Son (by the shedding of his blood) and in by the Holy Spirit (the living guarantee of the fullness of the life of the age to come).

John's teaching

In earlier chapters, we have paid careful attention to what is said in the Gospel of John concerning the Father, the Son, and the Holy Spirit (Paraklete). Here what we need to notice is the theme of the Father sending his Son into the world and the Father with his Son sending the Holy Spirit into the world.

The prologue declares that the only Son comes into the world from the Father and that grace and truth (salvation and revelation) come through him. As Incarnate God, he is "the

Lamb of God who takes away the sin of the world" (1:29). And in the much quoted words of John 3:16-17: "For God [the Father] so loved the world that he gave his only Son, that whoever believes in him should not perish but have eternal life. For God sent the Son into the world, not to condemn the world, but that the world might be saved through him."

The sending and giving of the Spirit by the Father and the glorified Son to the disciples is given much emphasis in John 14–16, as we noted in chapter 9. The Paraklete comes from the Father in the name of the Son: he brings the virtues of the Son to the disciples and continues the mission of the Son in the hostile world. Yet already in John 3:1-8 it was made clear that the same Spirit, who alone causes spiritual birth into the kingdom of God, is the Holy Spirit who is "from above," that is, from the Father. There is salvation only for those who believe in the Son and are "born of the Spirit" and thus "born from above."

In 1 John it is made clear that the fellowship of Christians is not only with each other "but is with the Father and the Son"; further, this is because they have "an anointing from the Holy One" which abides in them.

> By this we know that we abide in him [God] and he in us, because he has given us of his own Spirit. And we have seen and testify that the Father has sent his Son as the Savior of the world. Whoever confesses that Jesus is the Son of God, God abides in him, and he in God. So we know and believe the love God has for us (4:13-16).

God the Father sent his Son into the world and gives his Spirit to those who believe in his Son in order that they may abide in God.

Other teaching

The movement from the Father through the Son and by the Spirit is well expressed in the opening words of 1 Peter: "To the exiles of the Dispersion . . . chosen and destined by God the Father and sanctified by the Spirit for obedience to Jesus Christ and for sprinkling with his blood: May grace and peace be multiplied to you" (1:1-2). Here the emphasis is not upon the Father sending the Son (which is assumed), but upon the electing love of the Father as the basis for the application of the atoning blood of Jesus, his Son, and the sanctification wrought by the Holy Spirit in believers.

After making it clear that God the Father had sent his Son, Jesus Christ, into the world and that this Son is superior to angels and Moses, the writer of the letter to the Hebrews portrayed Christ as the new High Priest offering the unique sacrifice to establish the new covenant:

> But when Christ appeared as a high priest of the good things that have come, then through the greater and more perfect tent (not made with hands, that is, not of this creation) he entered once for all into the Holy Place, taking not the blood of goats and calves but his own blood, thus securing an eternal redemption. For if the sprinkling of defiled persons with the blood of goats and bulls and with the ashes of a heifer sanctifies for the purification of the flesh, how much more shall the blood of Christ, who through the eternal Spirit offered himself without blemish to God [the Father], purify your conscience from dead works to serve the living God [the Father] (9:11-14).

Here in what we have called the "descent" the Son becomes the Priest and Victim in order to fulfill and bring to an end the sacrifices offered under the Mosaic covenant. Thereby he opened up "a new and living way" (10:20) to the Father. Thus already the "ascent" is included in this description of the "descent" — the Son pours out his blood that man might serve the living God with a clear conscience.

In sending his visions to the seven churches John wrote: "Grace to you and peace from him who is and who was and who is to come, and from the seven spirits who are before his throne, and from Jesus Christ the faithful witness . . . and the ruler of kings on earth. To him who loves us and has freed us from our sins by his blood and made us a kingdom, priests to his God and Father, to him be glory and dominion for ever and ever" (Rev. 1:4-6). Here the Trinity in heaven is presented (in the symbolic language of the seer) as facing the faithful on earth to bless and to keep them.

ASCENT—SALVATION

The four Gospels were not written merely to provide information concerning Jesus and satisfy curiosity as to his identity. They were written with an evangelistic purpose—to declare the Gospel of the Father concerning his Son, Jesus Christ, so that Jew and Gentile would believe in Jesus as Lord and Christ and receive God's salvation. The purpose of the Gospels is to cause men to turn from sin and idolatry to trust, serve, and worship the Father through his Son and by his Spirit. So while they certainly assume and powerfully declare the "descent," practically speaking they were written to make the "ascent" possible by providing the content of the good news of Jesus, in and by whom alone we know and come to the Father. In fact, we could say that everything in the New Testament was written in order to make possible the "ascent" from earth into the "new heaven and earth" and from this evil age into the glorious age of the kingdom of God.

To be saved by God into his everlasting kingdom of grace, it is necessary to be united in the Spirit to Jesus Christ and be presented or brought to the Father by this divine agency. Such an "ascent" out of sin into friendship with God is stated with clarity and power in the letter to Ephesus, where the apostle is discussing the unity of Jew and Gentile in Christ and before God.

> Now in Christ Jesus you who once were far off have been brought near [to God] in the blood of Christ. For he is our peace, who has made us [Jew and Gentile] both one, and has broken down the dividing wall of hostility . . . that he might create in himself one new man in place of the two, so making peace, and might reconcile us both to God in one body through the cross, thereby bringing the hostility to an end. And he came and preached peace to you who were far off and peace to those who were near; for through him we both have access in one Spirit to the Father (Eph. 2:13-17).

The last words are very important: "Through Christ we have access in one Spirit to the Father." Here is the basis of both salvation and worship. Then he continues:

So then you are no longer strangers and sojourners, but you are fellow citizens with the saints and members of the household of God, built upon the foundation of the apostles and prophets, Christ Jesus himself being the cornerstone, in whom the whole structure is joined together and grows into a holy temple in the Lord, in whom you also are built into it for a dwelling place of God in the Spirit (2:19-22).

Here is a powerful picture of a living temple centered on Christ, indwelt by the Holy Spirit and made not of stones of granite but of apostles, prophets, and all true believers, both Jews and Gentiles. The temple rises from earth toward heaven, which is its goal. This divine household is built upon the saving work of Jesus Christ, energized and indwelt by the Holy Spirit, who is the Spirit of Christ, and is oriented toward the Father.

Hebrews contrasts that to which the Israelites were brought by the old Exodus through the Red Sea with that to which Christians are brought through the new Exodus of the cross and resurrection of Jesus.

For you have not come to what may be touched, a blazing fire, and darkness, and gloom, and a tempest, and the sound of a trumpet, and a voice whose words made the hearers entreat that no further messages be spoken to them. For they could not endure the order that was given, "If even a beast touches the mountain, it shall be stoned." Indeed so terrifying was the sight that Moses said, "I tremble with fear" (Heb. 12:18-21).

The writer is recalling what is recorded in Exodus 19 and Deuteronomy 9. He continues:

But you have come to Mount Zion and to the city of the living God, the heavenly Jerusalem, and to innumerable angels in festal gathering, and to the assembly of the first-born who are enrolled in heaven, and to a judge who is God of all, and to the spirits of just men made perfect, and to Jesus, the mediator of a new covenant, and to the sprinkled blood that speaks more graciously than the blood of Abel (vv. 22-24).

The "ascent" into the new creation is clearly only possible because of the sacrifice of Jesus Christ, who is the Mediator of the new covenant. "For Christ has entered . . . into heaven itself, now to appear in the presence of God on our behalf" (Heb. 9:24).

Knowing what the Father through the Son and in the Spirit has done in establishing the new covenant, Christians ought to respond wholeheartedly. Because they know that the way to God is now wide open unto those who believe, they ought to respond in worship and service. Thus the writer of Hebrews declares:

Therefore, brethren, since we have confidence to enter the sanctuary by the blood of Jesus, by the new and living way which he opened for us through the curtain, that is, through his flesh, and since we have a great priest over the house of God, let us draw near with a true heart in full assurance of faith, with our hearts sprinkled clean from an evil conscience and our bodies washed with pure water (10:19-22).

And in terms of practice he wrote:

Let us hold fast the confession of our hope without wavering, for he [the Father] who promised is faithful; and let us consider how to stir up one another to love and good works, not neglecting to meet together, as is the habit of some, but encouraging one another, and all the more as you see the Day drawing near (vv. 23-25).

As they wait for the Parousia of Christ, the Day of the Lord, Christians are to ascend to the Father in spirit by offering him the sacrifice of good works and the corporate activity of spiritual worship. This theme naturally leads us on specifically to the "ascent" in prayer.

ASCENT – PRAYER

Salvation has three tenses in the New Testament. By the unique, sacrificial, atoning death of Jesus Christ salvation is procured once for all and forever. We are saved by the expiatory and propitiatory death of the Lord Jesus. Once a person believes in Jesus and confesses that he is Lord, then he enters into salvation—he is being saved from sin and into the life of the Holy Trinity. Salvation is for him "already" experienced, but it is "not yet" fully realized. He knows that he is still a sinner in a mortal, sinful body. However, he will certainly enjoy the fullness of salvation when, after the Parousia of the Lord Jesus Christ, in his resurrection body and with all the saints he beholds the glory of God the Father in the face of Jesus Christ in the power of the Holy Spirit.

The New Testament has a lot to say about the privileges and duties of those who are being saved from this evil age into the fullness of salvation in the life of the age to come. Within these privileges and duties we find worship and prayer. In such holy activities, the church on earth is united in the Holy Spirit with the Lord Jesus Christ, Son of the Father, and High Priest in heaven: her worship ascends to the Father within the worship and prayer offered unceasingly by Jesus to the Father. Is not Christ at the right hand of the Father, interceding for us? And is not the Holy Spirit interceding from within our hearts? (Rom. 8:26, 34) And will not this continue until the end of the age when Christ shall come again to judge the living and the dead?

Speaking as a Christian to Christian believers, Paul told the church in Philippi: "We are the true circumcision, who worship God in spirit, [or "worship by the Spirit of God"] and glory in Christ Jesus, and put no confidence in the flesh" (Phil. 3:3). Here is Paul's simple theology. Because of Jesus Christ (who he is and what he has done and is doing), worship ascends in the Holy Spirit to the Father.

Worship (prayer) is not only thanksgiving, praise, and worship, it can also be petition and intercession. Thus Paul made this request of the church in Rome—a church he had not yet visited: "I appeal to you, brethren, by our Lord Jesus Christ and by the love of the Spirit, to strive together with me in your prayers to God on my behalf, that I may be delivered from the unbelievers in Judea, and that my service for Jerusalem may be acceptable to the saints, so that by God's [the Father's] will I may come to you with joy and be refreshed in your company. The God of peace be with you all. Amen" (Rom. 15:30-33).

In writing to the church in Colossae, Paul expressed the "ascent" in simplicity: "Whatever you do, in word or deed, do everything in the name of the Lord Jesus, giving thanks to God the Father through him" (Col. 3:17). And Paul told the church in Rome: "I appeal to you therefore, brethren, by the mercies of God, to present your bodies as a living sacrifice, holy and acceptable to God [the Father], which is your spiritual worship" (Rom. 12:1).

First Peter is clear that, as those who are chosen by the Father, redeemed by the precious blood of Christ, and being sanctified by the Holy Spirit (1:1-2, 19), Christians are placed in such a privileged relation to God that they have a joyous duty both to proclaim the Gospel and to offer spiritual sacrifice in worship and service.

> You are a chosen race, a royal priesthood, a holy nation, God's [the Father's] own people, that you may declare the wonderful deeds of him who called you out of darkness into his marvelous light. Once you were no people but now you are God's people; once you had not received mercy but now you have received mercy (1 Peter 2:9-10).

And recalling Psalm 118:22 and Isaiah 28:16, which refer to Christ as the chief cornerstone of God's new temple, Peter wrote:

> Come to him, to that living stone, rejected by men but in God's [the Father's] sight chosen and precious; and like living stones be yourselves built into a spiritual house to be a holy priesthood, to offer spiritual sacrifices acceptable to God [the Father] through Jesus Christ (2:4-5).

The assembled local church, as the holy priesthood, offers its worship, prayer, and service in the Holy Spirit to the Father through Christ the High Priest.

In his very short letter Jude told his fellow Christians, whom he addressed as "those who are called, beloved in God the Father and kept for Jesus Christ" (v. 1) to "build yourselves up on your most holy faith; pray in the Holy Spirit ... wait for the mercy of our Lord Jesus Christ unto eternal life" (vv. 20-21). His letter ended with a doxology which points to the "ascent" of the faithful to the Father: "Now to him who is able to keep you from falling and to present you without blemish before the presence of his glory with rejoicing, to the only God, our Savior through Jesus Christ our Lord, be glory, majesty, dominion, and authority, before all time and now and for ever. Amen" (vv. 24-25).

In fact, there are many doxologies in the New Testament, most of which (as we would expect) are addressed to the Father. This is true of the powerful doxologies provided by Paul in Romans 11:33-36 and 16:25-27, as well as that of Peter in 1 Peter 1:3-5 and those of John in his Revelation (e.g., 4:11). Yet there are also doxologies to Jesus Christ—had he not said, "that all may honor the Son, even as they honor the Father"? (John 5:23) Here are two:

> Grow in the grace and knowledge of our Lord and Savior Jesus Christ. To him be the glory both now and to the day of eternity (2 Peter 3:18).

> To him who loves us and has freed us from our sins by his blood and made us a kingdom, priests to his God and father, to him be glory and dominion for ever and ever. Amen (Rev. 1:5-6).

Then there is the brief Aramaic prayer, *Maranatha* (1 Cor. 16:22) meaning "the Lord is coming" or "our Lord come," which points to the highest honors and true worship being offered to Jesus Christ as YHWH. Mention also ought to be made of the Old Testament expression "calling upon the name of the Lord" (Rom. 10:12-17; 1 Cor. 1:2) as further evidence of prayer to Jesus Christ.

So the church, the bride of Christ, invokes her Lord, giving him the honor which is his due and moves in, with, and through him to render her worship to the eternal Father. In this movement of "ascent" the Spirit is wholly present, but invisible and often anonymous. In the New Testament there is no example of prayer being offered directly to the Holy Spirit. This practice came later after the dogma of the Trinity had been clarified and the divine personhood of the Holy Spirit clearly established as a truth of the Faith.

Direct addressing of the Holy Spirit in liturgy is, however, rare. When it is found, its presence is as significant as its rarity (e.g., the *Veni, Creator Spiritus* at ordinations). It is important to note that while the Father is made known to the church by the Son, and the Son is made known by the Holy Spirit, there is no fourth divine Person to make the Spirit known in the church. This is because he is the *locus* (as the Son is the *agent*) of both the "descent" and the "ascent" of God's economy.

IN CONCLUSION

If we look at what are called the two Gospel sacraments — baptism and the Lord's Supper — we see clearly in them the recognition and proclamation of the "descent" and the active participation in the "ascent." As the sacraments of salvation, they symbolize what the Gospel proclaims and teaches.

In submitting to baptism in the apostolic age, the repentant sinner was committing himself (through the active work of the invisible Holy Spirit) to the Lord Jesus Christ and to the Father of the Lord Jesus Christ. He was entering the "ascent" because he had received the message of the "descent" and been changed by it. The act of being dipped, immersed, washed, or sprinkled with water pointed to cleansing and forgiveness through the blood of Jesus Christ and identification with Christ in death, burial, and resurrection. Baptism placed him in a new relation to God and to fellow Christians and pointed him in one direction only — to the service and praise of the Father through the Son in and by the Spirit in this age and the age to come (see e.g., Gal. 3:26-27; Rom. 6:1-11; Col. 2:11-12; Titus 3:5-7). So even if it was the case that the first baptisms were "in the name of Jesus" (Acts 2:38) and only later "in the name of the Father and the Son and the Holy Spirit" (Matt. 28:19), they were Trinitarian from the beginning for they presumed, symbolized, and participated in the great movement, the *missio Dei*, from the Father and to the Father.

In coming to the table of the Lord and receiving sacramentally the body and blood of Jesus, Christians proclaimed the Lord Jesus Christ, who had died for them, who was now exalted in heaven, and who would come in glory to judge the world (1 Cor. 11:23-34). It was, therefore, entirely in accord with this central theme of the Lord's Supper that it soon came to be called "the Eucharist"—from *eucharisteo* meaning to give thanks. (An interesting statistic is that Paul mentions the subject of thanksgiving more often, line for line, in his letters than does any other Hellenistic author!) In the fellowship of the meal and in receiving Christ's body and blood sacramentally, Christians were united in and by the Spirit with Christ to the Father. They participated in the "ascent" as they partook by the presence of the Spirit of the future feast of the kingdom of God of the age to come—the Messianic banquet.

This structure is clearly found within the early liturgies of the church in both the East and West. Both daily prayer and the Sunday Eucharist were offered to the Father in and by the Holy Spirit through Jesus Christ. And worship was offered in this way because of the clear recognition and celebration of the fact that all things come "from the Father by and through the Son and in and with the Holy Spirit" to man.

Because of the need to defend the Faith and set forth the clear, ecclesial doctrine of the Trinity as defined by the ecumenical councils, the Liturgies were later fine-tuned to include the developed doctrine of the Holy Trinity. Thus, for example, the shorter Gloria became the praise of the immanent Trinity and the economic Trinity, "Glory be to the Father and to the Son and to the Holy Spirit . . ." instead of the earlier praise of the economic Trinity alone, "Glory be to the Father through the Son in the Holy Spirit. . . ." Here we see from the fourth century onward what has been called the ontological Trinity replacing the economic Trinity. Because heresies arose in the early church and keep on arising in the modern church, it seems that the church must always use metaphysical and ontological statements in order to ground the biblical, functional affirmations on a firm base.

The Second Council of Constantinople in 553 provided both a statement of the doctrine of the Trinity in biblical, functional terms (the economic Trinity) and in metaphysical terms (the ontological Trinity).

There is one only God and Father, from whom everything comes, and one only Lord Jesus Christ, through whom everything exists, and one only Holy Spirit, in whom everything subsists (cf. 1 Cor. 8:6; Rom. 11:36; Eph. 4:5-6).

If anyone does not confess the one nature or essence, the one force and power of the Father, the Son and Holy Spirit, the consubstantial Trinity and one divinity, which must be adored in three hypostases or persons, let him be anathema.

The Latin translation of the original Greek rendered *hypostaseis* as *subsistentiae*, subsistences.

In order to preserve the biblical theology of the economic Trinity (from the Father through the Son and in the Holy Spirit; to the Father through the Son and in the Holy Spirit), which is fundamental to the maintenance of authentic Christian faith and worship, the confessing of the orthodox dogma of the ontological Trinity is absolutely necessary. Yet teachers and preachers need to be clear as to the difference between, and the necessary union of, the economic and the immanent (or ontological) Trinity. This theme will be developed in the next chapter.

FOR FURTHER READING

Bradshaw, P.F. *The Search for the Origins of Christian Worship.* London: SPCK, 1992.

Martin, Ralph P. *The Worship of God.* Grand Rapids: Eerdmans, 1982.

Percival, Henry R., ed. *The Seven Ecumenical Councils.* Vol. 14 of the Nicene and Post Nicene Fathers. New York: Scribner's, 1900.

Toon, Peter. *Proclaiming the Gospel Through the Liturgy.* Largo, Fla.: Prayer Book Society of the Episcopal Church, 1993.

_____. *Which Rite Is Right?* Swedesboro, N.J.: Preservation, 1994.

Vagaggini, Cyprian. *Theological Dimensions of the Liturgy.* Collegeville, Minn.: Liturgical, 1976.

12

CONFESSING THE
TRINITY TODAY

In this final chapter, we shall reflect upon aspects of what it means in a practical sense to confess the Holy Trinity today, recalling as we do the words of wisdom from Augustine that were quoted in the Preface.

THE HOLY TRINITY IN SCRIPTURE

When we speak about the biblical doctrine of the Trinity, we need to be clear what we mean. The word "Trinity" is not found in the Bible. For millions of Christians over the centuries the biblical doctrine of the Trinity has meant providing proof texts from the Bible for the theological statements of the Nicene and Athanasian Creeds — or for the later confessions of faith and public statements of doctrine, based on the Creeds. At the same time, because to believe that somehow three is one and one is three is contrary to normal logical thinking, there have always been those in the Catholic and Protestant traditions who have swung toward Unitarianism, Modalism, or Deism.

However, it is only in modern times, since the Enlightenment and with the development of the historical-critical method and its application to the Bible, that serious questions have been raised within the mainline churches as to what portrayal of God is actually found in the New Testament, and to what extent the early church dogma of the Trinity in the Nicene Creed is the growth of the Gospel in the soil and atmosphere of Hellenism. There has been a swing from one extreme where the Bible is a quarry of proof texts to the other extreme where it is a book so complicated in its origins and its content that only scholars can possibly fathom its purpose and meaning.

In this book the conviction has been expressed that what the Bible provides is not a developed doctrine of the Holy Trinity and not even proof texts for developing such a doctrine. Rather the whole of the New Testament stands as a witness to a basic Trinitarian consciousness in the hearts of the writers and of the early Christian church. They knew the reality of the Father, the Son, and the Holy Spirit in their Christian experience, worship, and contemplation. Sometimes they expressed an implicit Trinitarianism and sometimes an explicit Binitarianism. Yet underlying these varying expressions there is a vision of YHWH as the Three, a conviction that the Father, his only Son, and his Holy Spirit are in some profound sense One.

So the church with the Old and New Testaments in its possession could only go theologically in one direction, even though the road was not straight and easy. That direction was to confess in the ecumenical Councils the full doctrine of the Holy Trinity. Having confessed the Holy Trinity, then the Bible was read from this doctrinal perspective and released ever deeper levels of meaning to believing hearts.

THE ONTOLOGICAL TRINITY IN PERSPECTIVE

If a person is introduced to the mystery of the Holy Trinity through a careful statement of what is called the ontological or immanent Trinity (God as God is toward and unto himself) then it is not surprising if he thinks that the doctrine of the Trinity is merely an intellectual puzzle. The first half of the *Quicunque Vult*, often called the Athanasian Creed, and part of the doctrinal heritage of the Western church, is primarily a brief and concise exposition of God in his substance (essence), of the Three Persons within the One Godhead. Here is part of it.

The Catholic Faith is this: that we worship one God in Trinity, and Trinity in Unity; neither confounding the Persons, nor dividing the Substance; for there is one Person of the Father, another of the Son and another of the Holy Ghost. But the Godhead of the Father, of the Son and of the Holy Ghost, is all one: the Glory equal, the Majesty co-eternal. Such the Father is, such is the Son and such is the Holy Ghost. The Father uncreate, the Son uncreate and the Holy Ghost uncreate. The Father incomprehensible, the Son incomprehensible and the Holy Ghost incomprehensible. The Father eternal, the Son eternal and the Holy Ghost eternal. And yet there are not three eternals but one eternal, as also there are not three incomprehensibles, nor three uncreated but one uncreated and one incomprehensible, so likewise the Father is Almighty, the Son Almighty and the Holy Ghost Almighty. And yet there are not three Almighties, but one Almighty. So the Father is God, the Son is God and the Holy Ghost is God. And yet there are not three Gods but one God. So likewise the Father is Lord, the Son is Lord and the Holy Ghost is Lord. And yet not three Lords, but one Lord. . . . So that in all things . . . the Unity in Trinity and the Trinity in unity is to be worshipped.[1]

To read this alone and in isolation from the study of the portrayal of the Holy Trinity in Scripture and the development of the doctrine of the Trinity in the Patristic period is certainly to run the danger of thinking that the doctrine of the Holy Trinity is merely a cerebral, intellectual extra to the Christian Faith. Historically, the Christian in the West was introduced first to the Apostles' Creed and its presentation of the economic Trinity and only later to the Athanasian Creed.

The *Quicunque Vult* was produced in the fifth century in Latin as an orthodox response to two major heresies which were plaguing the church in Gaul — Arianism and Modalism. As such it remains valuable for the church today since Arianism and Modalism in various forms are still with us, and they have to be recognized and rejected on the solid grounds provided by this creed and the testimony of sacred Scripture. Yet if we give the impression that the doctrine of the Holy Trinity is only and solely the doctrine of the immanent or ontological Trinity then we run the risk of its confession being irrelevant to Christian worship, life, and service. This doctrine of the Trinity appears to have no practical relevance to life in this world because it speaks of that which is outside space and time.

Unless we begin with God-as-God-is-toward-us and think first of all in terms of God in relation to us and we in relation to God, we shall miss the biblical emphasis upon the Holy Trinity. Christians are baptized into "the Name of the Father and of the Son and of the Holy Spirit," and they know the Father through the Son and in and by the Holy Spirit, even as they look to the Father through the Son and in and by the Holy Spirit. They are led to adore the Holy Trinity and contemplate the relations between the Three Persons only because the Father has graciously called them through the Son and in and by the Spirit. The natural way for the ontological Trinity to enter Christian experience is through contemplation.[2]

However, since some prevalent heresies and errors can only be shown to be such by speaking of what we know of God in his essence, that is, reflecting upon and speaking the truth concerning the ontological Trinity, it is necessary for teachers and preachers to have the intellectual facility to move from the economic to the ontological Trinity and back again in order rightly to defend the Faith. Practically speaking, this means that teachers and preachers must be wholly familiar with the exposition of the Holy Trinity in the Nicene and Athanasian Creeds, and know how this teaching was incorporated into the major Protestant confessions of faith in the sixteenth and seventeenth centuries.

The major point here is that preachers and teachers need so to communicate the Faith and so direct public worship that they really and truly give the impression that the Holy Trinity is God and God is the Holy Trinity. That is, when they speak of creation and salvation they speak of the Father through the Son and in/by the Spirit as Creator and Savior, and when they pray and worship they address the Father through the Son and in and by the Holy Spirit. In such a context and atmosphere their hearers and congregations will recognize that we only know God-as-God-is-in-himself because by grace we know God-as-God-is-toward-us. Then, from time to time and when occasion requires, the people will be prepared to appreciate the teaching of the Athanasian Creed — especially if they are encountering heresy.

Alisdair Heron, the Scottish Reformed theologian, has expressed the truth of this point very well.

> The heart of the matter is that the doctrine of the Trinity is not an abstract mathematical puzzle, not the articulation of the rhythm of life, and not the projection upon the Ultimate of the manifold triplicities that a little inspired imagination can easily suggest to us. It arises from the fundamental recognition that Jesus Christ is Immanuel, God with us, a recognition which is itself enabled by awareness of participation in the Spirit in that same mystery. The rhythm is that of faith and of worship, and the mystery at the center is the crucified and risen Christ, the sacrament and pledge of the reconciling and redeeming good favour of the Father extended even to us. Yet just because he is God with us, the awareness of faith opens into recognition of the triune being of God, for nothing less is required if the truth of the Gospel is not in the last resort to be set aside.[3]

Christians believe in the Holy Trinity because of the Incarnation and the gift of the Holy Spirit, who is the Spirit of Christ.

Heron continued by referring to the constant danger of Modalism (= Sabellianism):

> Sabellianism, open or concealed, implies that the trinitarian structure of redemption has nothing really to do with the nature of God, and loses hold on God in his own reality, like a climber on a rock face who can find no crevice to give him a grip. Only if there is genuine differentiation within God is there space and room for him so to reach out that he engages us with himself, going forth to become his own creature and at the same time enabling and empowering an authentic creaturely response. In this sense the doctrine of the Trinity cannot and must not be understood as the speculative projection of the

theological mind into realms too high for it, but as the doxological answer evoked in us by the divine condescension that in Christ comes down to meet us and in the Spirit bears us up from within.[4]

God's movement is from the Father through the Son and by the Holy Spirit unto his creatures who are called and enabled by grace to ascend in the Spirit and through the Son unto the Father. Only so will they become "partakers of the divine nature" (2 Peter 1:4), enjoy and glorify God forever and behold the glory of God in the face of Jesus Christ.

ON THE NEED FOR PRECISE LANGUAGE

Anyone who has studied the theological controversies concerning the precise relation of the Lord Jesus Christ to God the Father will know that precision in language is important. For example, there is, theologically speaking, a major difference in meaning between saying with the orthodox that Jesus is *homoousios* (consubstantial—of one and the same identical substance) with the Father and of saying with others that Jesus is *homoiousios* (of like substance). The iota made a difference in the Arian controversy in the fourth century!

There is a world of difference between the now common expression, "God: Father, Son, and Holy Spirit," and the more traditional, "In the Name of the Father and of the Son and of the Holy Spirit" or "God the Father, the Son, and the Holy Spirit." Here the point is that to be precise in English the definite article matters. In speaking of Yahweh-Elohim, Christians do not speak of any father but of the one, unique Father, from whom all fatherhood is derived; they do not speak of any son but of the one and only Son, begotten of the one, unique Father before all ages; and they do not speak of any spirit but of the one and only eternal Spirit, who proceeds from the one, unique Father. From the time before the Athanasian Creed was produced, Christians have been aware of the danger of falling into Modalism—of saying that God is One Person with three Names or three forms of manifestation. In writing and speaking in English we cannot be accused of being modalist if we speak of the glorious transcendence of the living God and we use carefully the definite article in naming the Blessed, Holy, and Undivided Trinity. YHWH is not "Father, Son, and Holy Spirit" but "the Father and the Son and the Holy Spirit."

Many times I have heard this benediction at the end of a service: "The blessing of God Almighty, Father, Son, and Holy Spirit be upon you and remain with you always." This sounds as though it is Almighty God who has three names! In contrast, as handed down in Western Christianity, the authentic benediction is, "The Blessing of Almighty God the Father and the Son and the Holy Spirit. . . ." Here, as in the Nicene Creed, "God" is "the Father" and a genuine Trinity of Persons gives the Blessing.

B.B. Warfield emphasized the presence of four definite articles in our Lord's baptismal command — "in *the* Name of *the* Father, and of *the* Son and of *the* Holy Spirit." He wrote:

In seeking to estimate the significance of this great declaration, we must bear in mind the high solemnity of the utterance, by which we are required to give its full value to every word of it. Its phrasing is in any event, however, remarkable. It does not say, "In the names [plural] of the Father and the Son and the Holy Ghost"; nor yet (what might be taken as the equivalent to that), "In the name of the Father and in the name of the Son and in the name of the Holy Ghost," as if we had to deal with three separate Beings. Nor, on the other hand, does it say, "In the name of the Father, Son and Holy Ghost," as if "the Father, Son and Holy Ghost" might be taken as merely three designations of a single Person. With stately impressiveness it asserts the unity of the Three by combining them all within the bounds of a single Name; and then throws up into emphasis the distinctness of each by introducing them in turn with the repeated article: "In the Name of the Father, and of the Son and of the Holy Ghost." These Three, the Father, and the Son, and the Holy Ghost, each stands in some clear sense over against the others in distinct personality: these Three, the Father, and the Son, and the Holy Ghost, all unite in some profound sense in the common participation of the one Name.[5]

The "one Name" is that of YHWH ("Jehovah" for Warfield).

Very few theologians write or speak today as did Warfield! At this time within modern American culture people do not generally place too great an emphasis upon either clarity of speech or precision in expression. While it can be argued that vagueness and imprecision of expression make little or no difference for the ordinary aspects of daily living, the same cannot be argued for specific areas of life. For example, a doctor has to state precisely what medical problem he has diagnosed and to be accurate for the sake of right treatment he usually has to use words which mean little or nothing at first to the patient. However, the patient has to learn the basics of the new vocabulary in order to know precisely what is his problem and how to make responsible decisions.

Words, phrases, and sentences about the Holy Trinity belong both to the realm of public speech (e.g., corporate worship) and also to the realm of doctrinal clarity (e.g., distinguishing truth from error). We need to be as careful and accurate as possible in addressing and speaking of the Trinity in both spheres, reserving the full weight of technical language for the latter. Certainly correct speech can be an empty shell but, on the other hand, it can be, should be, and must be the verbal adornment of the mystery of the living YHWH.

We can never be as those who lived before the great debates which helped to clarify the mind of the church and to produce the dogma of the Holy Trinity. We cannot pretend that the Councils of Nicea and Constantinople did not take place. We cannot deny the existence of the Apostles', the Nicene, and the Athanasian Creeds. We live in a world which has known and still knows many doctrinal errors concerning the identity of God and the identity of Jesus Christ. Yet we also live in a church which has developed a precise way of talking about God. Surely we ought to pay attention to that (not dead but) living tradition of precise expression in words and learn gratefully from it.

ON THE REJECTION OF
INCLUSIVE LANGUAGE

If the "Name" of YHWH is revealed by God to man; and if the "Name of the Father and the Son and the Holy Spirit" is also revealed by God to man, then there is no room for negotiation. The Name of the Holy Trinity of the Father and the Son and the Holy Spirit is a given.

However, if the name of YHWH is merely the projection into the metaphysical sphere by Moses of his view of God, and if "the name of the Father and the Son and the Holy Spirit" is the projection by Jesus and his disciples of images in their minds related to their patriarchal culture, then these "holy" Names are all negotiable. They may be changed at any time with or without general consent.

It is clear that many of the claims made by feminist theologians concerning the supposed androcentric, sexist, and patriarchalist basis of Israelite and Christian speech about God are false or in need of revision. However, even if all the feminist theologians were to disappear overnight and take with them all their ideology and claims, we would still have to face and hear again that which for over a century liberal theology has been proclaiming — that we name God out of our religious experience and thus project our naming of God into God (whoever God as ultimate Mystery be). We cannot avoid the question: Has God in self-revelation named God, and, do we have the right and capacity to name God ourselves? Christian orthodoxy answers decisively in terms of God's self-naming, and especially so with regard to the Holy Trinity.

A further question to arise for orthodoxy today is whether there is any relation between God's self-naming and the way Christians speak about the creatures whom the Holy Trinity has made in his image and after his likeness. If we are not free to use inclusive language about YHWH (e.g., not to baptize "in the name of Creator, Redeemer, and Sanctifier" or "in the name of Mother-Father, Child, and Spirit"), are we free to use inclusive language about God's creatures made in his image? This is a question which receives various answers from orthodox Christians. All I can indicate here is the relation I see between the Name of the Holy Trinity and the way we speak of men and women in Christian discourse.

There is holy order in the divine Name. It is the Father and the Son and the Holy Spirit. Of course, as we have seen, when the actual work of God for and in man is being described, then the order of the Persons may be different — e.g., "the grace of our Lord Jesus Christ, the love of God, and the fellowship of the Holy Spirit." However, concerning God in his own essence, we say that the Father is truly the first in order for he is the Father of the only Son; the Son is second in order for he is the Son of the unique Father; and the Holy Spirit is third in order for he is the Spirit who proceeds from the Father through the Son. This order does not mean inferiority of the Second and Third Persons, for they are all equal in that each Person is as fully God as are the other two Persons. (This is a truth clearly stated in the *Quicunque Vult* and the major Reformation confessions of faith.)

As the Creator, the Holy Trinity has communicated holy order into his creation including the creature who is made in his image and after his likeness. We read: "So God created man in his own image, in the image of God he created him; male and female he created them" (Gen. 1:27). There is holy order in the creation where the male man is first in order and the female man is second in order; but, at the same time there is a perfect equality in terms of essential being of the male and female man. In the New Testament Jesus Christ, the male Man who is the Word made flesh, is proclaimed as the true image of God.

To maintain holy order we need also to maintain the long-established custom of speaking of God's creatures made in his image as man or as mankind. We do not have to be saying "man and woman" and "he and she" all the time. The use of the word man in the traditional sense conveys the notion of order for he being first in order contains in himself she who is second in order. It is wholly appropriate that the word man can mean both the human race and the male species; and that the word woman can only mean female man and never the human race. This, in a trinitarian perspective, mirrors the truth that the Father is first and the Son is included in the Father, for he is begotten of the Father before all ages.

From this perspective responsible fatherhood can be proclaimed — and it is certainly needed in modern society. Yet at the same time, the approach can easily be intentionally or unintentionally misunderstood and also used by sinful men to justify evil attitudes and actions. What seems clear to me is that too many who profess an orthodox doctrine of God have swung on the pendulum of inclusivity too far away from traditional Christian discourse with regard to human beings. Paul K. Jewett's fine exposition of the doctrine of God, *God, Creation & Revelation* (1991), is one clear example. He denies any connection between the classic dogma of the Holy Trinity and the preservation of traditional ways of speech using the word "man."

When we feel the need to use the adjective "human" as a noun to avoid speaking of "man," when we consistently use the word "gender" instead of "sex" to refer to the chromosomal and physical reality of maleness or femaleness, and when we cannot write "he" without adding "she" in a sentence then perhaps we have gone too far on the pendulum of modernity. When we use the word "patriarchy" in a pejorative sense and have not examined the nature and character of fatherhood in Israel, when we suggest that the male images for God imply that God is sexually male or favors male human beings, and when we translate "the male man" in Psalm 1:1 as "they" or "the one" then perhaps we have been blown away from our anchors by the winds of modernity.

The doctrine of the Holy Trinity gives us the assurance and the humble confidence to speak of man in such a way as to celebrate the divine order in creation. To do this is not (see chap. 1) to say that God is male!

We must also add that the Christian understanding of personhood flows from the Christian doctrine of the Three Persons who are God. The decision by God to create man in his image was an *interpersonal* decision. Elohim (God in his plurality) said, "Let us make man in our image after our likeness"—the decision of the Three. Yet the Three acted as one: "Elohim created man in his own image, in the image of Elohim he created him" (where the plural noun takes the singular verbs). If God is simply a monad then he cannot be or know personality. To be personal otherness must be present together with oneness, the one must be in relation to others. Personhood is only a reality where there are relations, relatedness, and relationships. In the holy, eternal life of the Blessed Trinity personhood as relation is eternally present and human personhood exists because man is created by the Holy Trinity in the image of God and because (as we saw in chap. 8) the Son is the Image of God.

ON MODALISM AND PANTHEISM

On various occasions we have made reference to Modalism (Sabellianism) and to pantheism. Widmert, the Genevan, Calvinist theologian, offers a summarizing comment: "Modalism, on the level of popular piety, dissolves into gross Pantheism."[6] I take this as a very important observation, and I fear that it is very true of much North American religion.

In chapter 1, the presence of pantheism in European religion and culture and, very particularly, in American popular religion and culture was described. One point made there was that in modern democratic society, where evolution and development are taken for granted, the tendency is to think of God as in some way the equivalent of the cosmos, the Zeitgeist, or the mind and unity of the cosmos. Then, in reference to modern feminist theology, we noted that it is normally panentheistic in its description of God in order to allow for the naming of God as "Mother" (with the world as God's body). So pantheism is evident on all sides.

In much religion of both a conservative and liberal kind, the tendency is to refer to the Trinity in such a way as to imply by the grammar used and illustrations given that God is One Person with Three Names. It is often said that the triangle with its three sides, or the man who is simultaneously the son of his father, the husband of his wife, and the father of his son, illustrate how God is One in Three. And both "God: Father, Son, and Holy Spirit" from the conservatives and "God: Creator, Redeemer, and Sanctifier" from the liberals can reflect Modalism, just as the illustrations obviously do. Now if this way of thinking of God as one Person with several names is not set in the context of a clear belief in YHWH, who is the Creator of the world out of nothing (*ex nihilo*), then the belief expressed is probably not even Unitarianism; it is more likely pantheism.

Another way of stating this matter is to say that where the expression of religion is primarily experiential in a modern sense (i.e., in terms of self-worth, self-expression, self-development, "meeting my needs," and so on) and horizontal and immanentalist (God is primarily in the here and the now), and not primarily experiential in the classic sense (i.e., an encounter with the transcendent God of glory to whom we ascend through Christ and in the Holy Spirit) then the danger of modalistic pantheism is real—and real whether we be conservatives or liberals.

If there is truth in what has just been explained, then the duty of pastors and teachers in their congregations joyfully and clearly to proclaim the Holy Trinity in both his Transcendence and his Immanence (where his Immanence flows from his Transcendence) is always necessary. Only when God is known and adored first and foremost as the Majestic, Transcendent, Holy and Glorious Unity in Trinity, who creates the world and redeems his creatures in love, will experience be of such a kind as to rise heavenward and not to slip from Modalism into pantheism.

Let us not forget that to love God is to love in unity the Father and the Son and the Holy Spirit—to love their equality and their order. To love God is to love and not confound the operations, the eternal communications, and the mutual relations of the Father and the Son and the Holy Spirit. To love God is to love all that makes the Father, the Son, and the Holy Spirit to be One, and all that makes them Three.

A RECENT CONFESSION OF FAITH

In the midst of much uncertainty and little doctrinal clarity in the churches, it is good to find solid orthodoxy being professed. On the nineteenth centenary of the martyrdom of the apostles Peter and Paul in Rome (June 30, 1968), the Bishop of Rome, Pope Paul VI, closed the liturgical celebrations with a profession of faith. Here is the first part of it which states the received Western doctrine of the immanent Holy Trinity—God-as-God-is-in-himself.

> We believe in one God, the Father, the Son and the Holy Spirit, Creator of all things visible—such as this world in which our brief life runs its course—and of things invisible—such as the pure spirits which are also called angels—and Creator in each man of his spiritual and immortal soul.
>
> We believe that this unique God is as absolutely one in his infinitely, holy essence as in his other perfections: in

his almighty power, his infinite knowledge, his providence, his will and his love. He is "the One who is" as he
revealed to Moses (Ex. 3:14, Vulgate). He is "Love" as
the apostle John has taught us (1 Jn. 4:8); so that these
two names, Being and Love, express ineffably the same
divine Reality of him who has wished to make himself
known to us and who, "dwelling in light inaccessible"
(1 Tim. 6:16) is in himself above every name and every
created thing and every created intelligence. God alone
can give us true and full knowledge of this Reality by
revealing himself as the Father, the Son and the Holy
Spirit, in whose eternal life we are by grace called to
share, here on earth in the obscurity of faith and after
death in eternal light. The mutual bonds which from all
eternity constitute the Three Persons, each one of whom
is one and the same Divine Being, constitute the blessed,
inmost life of the most holy God, infinitely above all that
we can humanly understand. We give thanks, however,
to the divine goodness that very many believers can
testify with us before men of the unity of God, even
though they do not know the mystery of the Holy Trinity.

We believe then in God who eternally begets the Son;
we believe in the Son, the Word of God, who is eternally
begotten; we believe in the Holy Spirit, the uncreated
Person who proceeds from the Father and the Son as
their eternal Love. Thus in the three divine Persons, who
are co-eternal and co-equal among themselves, are found
in superabundant and consummated fashion, the life and
beatitude of God, who is perfectly one; and we must
always worship the unity in Trinity and the Trinity in the
unity.[7]

In the following paragraphs of the confession, the Incarnation of the only begotten Son is confessed in detail and the
Person and mission of the Holy Spirit is described. At this point
the creed has moved from God the Holy Trinity in eternity to
the revelation and work of the Holy Trinity in space and time. In
Christian confession of the Faith, knowledge of God-as-God-is-

in-himself is inextricably united to knowledge of God-as-God-is-toward-us.

So we return to where we began. The Holy Trinity is revealed for those with eyes to see in the creation and sustaining of the cosmos; in the election and redemption of Israel; in the birth, life, ministry, death, and resurrection of Jesus of Nazareth; in the formation of the church; in the gift of the Holy Spirit to the church; and in the experience of God in worship, fellowship, and service within the church. In fact, Holy Scripture bears witness in its inspiration and its content to the Holy Trinity: the books of the Bible present the glorious, majestic YHWH, the Father, and his only-begotten Son together with his Holy Spirit, active in the creation and redemption of the world. Thus God has been/is revealed in what he did/does and said/says for he is the living God. Because the Father makes himself known through his only Son and in his Holy Spirit, the church militant on earth (on behalf of the whole, visible creation) unites with the invisible world of holy angels and the church triumphant in heaven to adore and serve the Father through the Son (the great high priest) in the Holy Spirit. Led by the Holy Spirit to contemplate the glory of the Father in the face of Jesus Christ (2 Cor. 4:6), the church on earth is given insight into the ordered, eternal relations within the one Godhead of the Father, his only-begotten Son, and his Holy Spirit. Reverential knowledge of the immanent Holy Trinity comes through experiential knowing of the Father, through the Son and in the Holy Spirit.

With knowledge through revelation of the immanent Trinity, Christians know and experience the economic Trinity in grace and in prayer. In illustration of this, I end this book with one of the much used prayers of the Anglican tradition — the General Thanksgiving from the Daily Service in *The Book of Common Prayer* (1549, 1662, 1928, etc.).

Almighty God, Father of all mercies, we, thine unworthy servants, do give thee most humble and hearty thanks for all thy goodness and loving-kindness to us, and to all men. We bless thee for our creation, preservation, and all the blessings of this life; but above all, for thine inestimable love in the redemption of the world by our Lord

Jesus Christ; for the means of grace, and for the hope of glory [i.e., the presence and work of the Holy Spirit in the church]. And we beseech thee, give us that due sense of all thy mercies that our hearts may be unfeignedly thankful; and that we show forth thy praise, not only with our lips, but in our lives, by giving up ourselves to thy service, and by walking before thee in holiness and righteousness all our days; through Jesus Christ our Lord, to whom, with thee [O Father] and the Holy Ghost, be all honor and glory, world without end. *Amen.*

"Glory be to the Father and to the Son and to the Holy Spirit, as it was in the beginning, is now, and ever shall be, even unto ages of ages." *Amen.*

FOR FURTHER READING

Heron, Alisdair. *The Holy Spirit.* London: Marshall, Morgan and Scott, 1983.

Hughes, Philip E. *The True Image: The Origin and Destiny of Man in Christ.* Grand Rapids: Eerdmans, 1989.

Kelly, J.N.D. *The Athanasian Creed.* London: A & C Black, 1965.

Tavard, George H. *The Vision of God.* Washington, D.C.: Univ. Press of America, 1981.

Toon, Peter. *The Art of Meditating on Scripture.* Grand Rapids: Zondervan, 1993.

_____. *Yesterday, Today and Forever: Jesus Christ and the Holy Trinity in the Teaching of the Seven Ecumenical Councils.* Swedesboro, N.J.: Preservation, 1995.

Warfield, B.B. "The Biblical Doctrine of the Trinity." In *Biblical and Theological Studies.* Philadelphia: Presbyterian and Reformed, 1968.

NOTES

Preface

1. Augustine, *On the Holy Trinity,* vol. 3 of *A Select Library of Nicene and Post Nicene Fathers* (Grand Rapids: Eerdmans, 1956), 1.3.5.

Chapter 1

1. C.S. Lewis, *Miracles* (London: Collins, 1965), 101.

2. Ibid., 99.

3. Alexis de Tocqueville, *Democracy in America* (New York: Doubleday, 1969), 241.

4. Ibid., 242.

5. Robert Pattison, *The Triumph of Vulgarity* (New York: Oxford Univ. Press, 1991).

6. Robert W. Jenson, "The Father, He . . . ," in *Speaking the Christian God: The Holy Trinity and the Challenge of Feminism,* ed. Alvin F. Kimel, Jr. (Grand Rapids: Eerdmans, 1992), 96.

7. Mary Daly, *Beyond God the Father* (Boston: Beacon, 1973), 19.

8. Herbert Lockyer, *All the Divine Names and Titles in the Bible: A Unique Classification of All Scripture Designations of the Three Persons of the Trinity* (Grand Rapids: Zondervan, 1975).

9. Alvin F. Kimel, Jr., ed., *Speaking the Christian God: The Holy Trinity and the Challenge of Feminism* (Grand Rapids: Eerdmans, 1992).

Chapter 2

1. Paul K. Jewett, *God, Creation & Revelation* (Grand Rapids: Eerdmans, 1991), 299.

2. Ibid., 297.

3. Eric Mascall, *Whatever Happened to the Human Mind?* (London: SPCK, 1980), 117–18.

Chapter 3

1. Arthur W. Wainwright, *The Trinity in the New Testament* (London: SPCK, 1962), 3.

2. Ibid., 2.

3. Ibid., 266.

4. G.W.H. Lampe, *God as Spirit: The Bampton Lectures, 1976* (Oxford: Clarendon, 1977), 228.

5. Ibid.

6. C.F.D. Moule, "The New Testament and the Doctrine of the Trinity," *The Expository Times* 78/1 (October 1976): 17.

7. Ibid.

8. Ibid., 18.

9. C.F.D. Moule, *The Holy Spirit* (Grand Rapids: Eerdmans, 1978), 101.

10. A similar position to that of Moule was taken by Hendrikus Berkhof in his Warfield lectures on "The Spirit." In *The Doctrine of the Holy Spirit* (Atlanta: John Knox, 1964) he argued that we now have just reason to say farewell to the "person-concept in pneumatology" because modern biblical scholarship has made it clear that "Spirit" simply denotes the work of the exalted Lord Jesus in the world.

11. Royce G. Gruenler, *The Trinity in the Gospel of John: A Thematic Commentary on the Fourth Gospel* (Grand Rapids: Eerdmans, 1986), 6.

12. Ibid., 8.

13. Cornelius Plantinga, Jr., "Social Trinity and Tritheism," in *Trinity, Incarnation and Atonement: Philosophical and Theological Essays*, ed. Ronald J. Feenstra & Cornelius Plantinga, Jr. (Notre Dame, Ind.: Univ. of Notre Dame Press, 1989), 27–28.

14. Anthony Kelly, *The Trinity of Love: A Theology of the Christian God* (Wilmington, Del.: Michael Glazier, 1989), 37.

15. Ibid., 39.

16. Ibid., 45–46.

17. Ibid., 47.

18. Clifford Geertz, "Religion as a Cultural System," in *Anthropological Approaches to the Study of Religion*, ed. Michael Banton, ASA Mono-

graphs 3 (New York: Routledge/Tavistock, 1969), quoted in Kelly, *Trinity of Love*, 49.

19. Sebastian Moore, *The Fire and the Rose Are One* (London: Darton, Longman and Todd, 1980), 83–84, quoted in Kelly, *Trinity of Love*, 53.

20. James D.G. Dunn, *Jesus and the Spirit* (London: SCM, 1975), 67, quoted in Kelly, *Trinity of Love*, 57.

21. Ralph P. Martin, *The Worship of God* (Grand Rapids: Eerdmans, 1980), 210.

Chapter 4

1. George F. Knight, *A Christian Theology of the Old Testament*, rev. ed. (Richmond Va.: John Knox, 1964), 74–75.

2. Augustine, *On the Holy Trinity*, 47, n. 3.

3. Ibid., 2.11.20.

4. Ibid., 2.12.22.

5. Hilary of Poitiers, *The Trinity*, vol. 25 of *The Fathers of the Church* (New York: Fathers of the Church, 1954), 23–30.

6. John Calvin, *The Institutes of the Christian Religion*, 1.13.10.

7. For a learned discussion of the origin and meaning of the words *'elohim* and *yahweh* see G. Johannes Botterweck and Helmer Ringgren, eds., *Theological Dictionary of the Old Testament*, vols. 1 and 5 (Grand Rapids: Eerdmans, 1986).

8. Augustine, *On the Holy Trinity*, 2.15.26.

Chapter 5

1. Aubrey Johnson, *The One and the Many in the Israelite Conception of God* (Cardiff: Univ. of Wales Press, 1961), 15.

2. Ibid., 17.

3. Walter Kasper, *The God of Jesus Christ* (New York: Crossroad, 1984), 239–40.

4. Irenaeus, *Against Heresies*, ed. Alexander Roberts and James Donaldson, vol. 1 of *The Ante Nicene Fathers* (Grand Rapids: Eerdmans, 1953), 4, preface, sec. 4.

5. Ibid., 4.20.1.

6. For the evidence see Wainwright, *Trinity in the New Testament*, 24–27.

7. Kasper, *God of Jesus Christ*, 242.

8. Bertrand de Margerie, S.J., *The Christian Trinity in History* (Still River, Mass.: St. Bede's, 1982), 4.

9. Derek Kidner, *The Proverbs: An Introduction and Commentary*

(London: Tyndale, 1972), 79.

10. Elisabeth Schüssler Fiorenza, *In Memory of Her: A Feminist Theological Reconstruction of Christian Origins* (New York: Crossroad, 1985), 132.

11. Knight, *Christian Theology of the Old Testament*, 85.

12. Benjamin B. Warfield, "The Biblical Doctrine of the Trinity," in *Biblical and Theological Studies* (Philadelphia: Presbyterian and Reformed, 1968), 30.

13. Knight, *Christian Theology of the Old Testament*, 87.

14. Kasper, *God of Jesus Christ*, 243.

Chapter 6

1. Larry W. Hurtado, *One God, One Lord: Early Christian Devotion and Ancient Jewish Monotheism* (Philadelphia: Fortress, 1988), 100.

2. Ibid., 114.

3. Ibid., 104.

4. James D.G. Dunn, *The Parting of the Ways between Christianity and Judaism, and their Significance for the Character of Christianity* (Philadelphia: Trinity, 1991), 204.

5. Hurtado, *One God, One Lord*, 107.

6. Michael Ramsey, *Holy Spirit: A Biblical Study* (London: SPCK, 1977), 119–20.

7. Warfield, "Doctrine of the Trinity," 30.

8. Ibid., 32.

9. Ibid., 33.

Chapter 7

1. Paul V. Mankowski, "Old Testament Iconology and the Nature of God," in *The Politics of Prayer*, ed. H.H. Hitchcock (San Francisco: Ignatius, 1992), 167.

2. John W. Miller, *Biblical Faith and Fathering* (New York: Paulist, 1989).

3. *The Apocrypha and Pseudepigrapha of the Old Testament*, 2 vols. (Oxford: Clarendon, 1913).

4. Robert Hamerton-Kelly, *God the Father: Theology and Patriarchy in the Teaching of Jesus* (Philadelphia: Fortress, 1979), 54.

5. Francis Martin, *The Feminist Question* (Grand Rapids: Eerdmans, 1994), 278.

6. Hamerton-Kelly, *God the Father*, 81.

7. In the supplementary volume of *The Interpreter's Dictionary of the*

Bible (1976), the article on "God, Nature of, in the OT," is written by Phyllis Trible. Here and in her book *God and the Rhetoric of Sexuality* (1978) she made claims concerning the femininity of God, which have been repeated many times by feminists since the late 1970s. One such claim is based on the use of the word *rehem* (womb) and its use in declaring the compassion of God. However, her philological and linguistic arguments have been shown to be false and thus her conclusions also to be false. See further Mankowski, "Old Testament Iconology and the Nature of God," 160–65.

8. Jürgen Moltmann, "Theological Proposals," in *Spirit of God, Spirit of Christ,* Faith and Order Paper, WCC., no. 103 (London: SPCK, 1981), 167.

9. De Margerie, *The Christian Trinity,* 148.

Chapter 8

1. Raymond E. Brown, *An Introduction to New Testament Christology* (New York: Paulist, 1994), 101.

2. George Tavard, *The Vision of the Trinity* (Washington, D.C.: Univ. Press of America, 1981), 10–11.

3. Tryggve N.D. Mettinger, *In Search of God: The Meaning and Message of the Everlasting Names* (Philadelphia: Fortress, 1988), 44.

4. Pliny *Epistle* 10.96.7.

5. Philip E. Hughes, *The True Image: The Origin and Destiny of Man in Christ* (Grand Rapids: Eerdmans, 1989), 26.

6. Ibid., 28.

7. J.N.D. Kelly, *Early Christian Creeds,* 5th ed. (San Francisco: Harper & Row, 1978), 297.

8. Ibid., 339–40.

Chapter 9

1. J.E. Davey, *The Jesus of St. John: Historical and Christological Studies in the Fourth Gospel* (London: Lutterworth, 1958), 75.

2. Gary Burge, *The Anointed Community: The Holy Spirit in the Johannine Tradition* (Grand Rapids: Eerdmans, 1987), 147.

3. See the full discussion by Burge, *The Anointed Community,* 114ff.

4. Eduard Schweizer, *Spirit of God: Bible Key Words* (London: A & C Black, 1960), 83.

5. J.D.G. Dunn, *Christology in the Making* (Philadelphia: Westminster, 1980), 149.

6. Augustine, *On the Holy Trinity,* 5.6.12.

7. De Margerie, *The Christian Trinity*, 118.

Chapter 10

1. Sir Edwyn Hoskyns, *The Fourth Gospel* (London: Faber and Faber, 1947), 532.

2. Raymond E. Brown, *The Gospel According to John* (New York: Doubleday, 1966, 1970), 2:951.

3. Augustine, *On the Holy Trinity*, 7.4.7.

4. Thomas Aquinas *Summa Theologica* 1.29.

5. For which see Gregory P. Rocca, "Aquinas on God-Talk," *Theological Studies* 54 (1993): 641–61.

6. Berkhof, *Doctrine of the Holy Spirit*, 116.

7. Alisdair Heron, *The Holy Spirit* (London: Marshall, Morgan and Scott, 1983), 175.

Chapter 12

1. J.N.D. Kelly, *The Athanasian Creed* (London: A & C Black, 1964), 17–18.

2. See further Tavard, *Vision of the Trinity*, chap. 4; and Peter Toon, *The Art of Meditating upon Scripture* (Grand Rapids: Zondervan, 1993).

3. Heron, *Holy Spirit*, 172–73.

4. Ibid., 173.

5. Warfield, "Doctrine of the Trinity," 42.

6. G.P. Widmert, *Gloire au Pere, au Fils, au Saint-Esprit* (Neuchâtel: Brémond, 1963), 30.

7. The creed is found in Latin in *Acta Apostolicae Sedis*, 60 (Rome: The Vatican, 1968), 433ff.

SELECT NAME AND SUBJECT INDEX

Creed (Nicene)   *10, 27, 38–41, 67, 79, 148, 153, 171, 193, 199, 231, 234, 237–38*
Cullman, Oscar   *173*

D

Daly, Mary   *24, 247*
Danielou, Jean   *93*
Davey, J.E.   *193, 251*
Deism   *231*
De Margerie, Bertrand   *49, 101, 111, 129, 149–50, 193, 249, 251–52*
Democracy   *18–19*
Deus Absconditus   *110*
Deus Revelatus   *110*
Diaspora   *109*
Distich (medieval)   *79*
Dunn, J.D.G.   *113, 118, 121, 129, 150, 173, 188, 194, 249–51*

E

East (Christian)   *41ff*
Ego eimi   *162–63*
Eichrodt, Walther   *93*
Eikon (Jesus as)   *166ff*
Ekpempis   *41*
Elijah   *76*
Elohim (God)   *82, 86–88, 98, 100, 156, 164, 241*
El Shaddai   *96*
Enlightenment   *21, 23, 46, 231*
Enoch   *76*
Epicureanism   *71*
Erickson, Millard J.   *47–48*
Essentia   *42*
Experience (religious)   *23*
Experience (of the Spirit)   *122–24*
Experience (trinitarian)   *63, 66*

F

Father (God as a)   *133ff*
Father (God the)   *9–11, 15–16, 20, 27, 29, 31–32, 34–41, 43–45,*

SCRIPTURE INDEX

Old Testament

New Testament

Apocrypha